AF606898

THE WORLD IS MINE & I'M THINKING ABOUT YOU

The Art of Jesse Draxler

The World Is Mine & I'm Thinking About You
The Art of Jesse Draxler

Printed in China.

ISBN: 978-1-7361469-1-0

Published by Sacred Bones Books
Layout by Mercy Correll, Sacred Bones Design

First Edition

1 2 3 4 5 6 7 8 9 10

All requests and correspondence can be addressed to:

Sacred Bones Books
144 N. 7th Street #413
Brooklyn, NY 11249

SBB-020

AMR

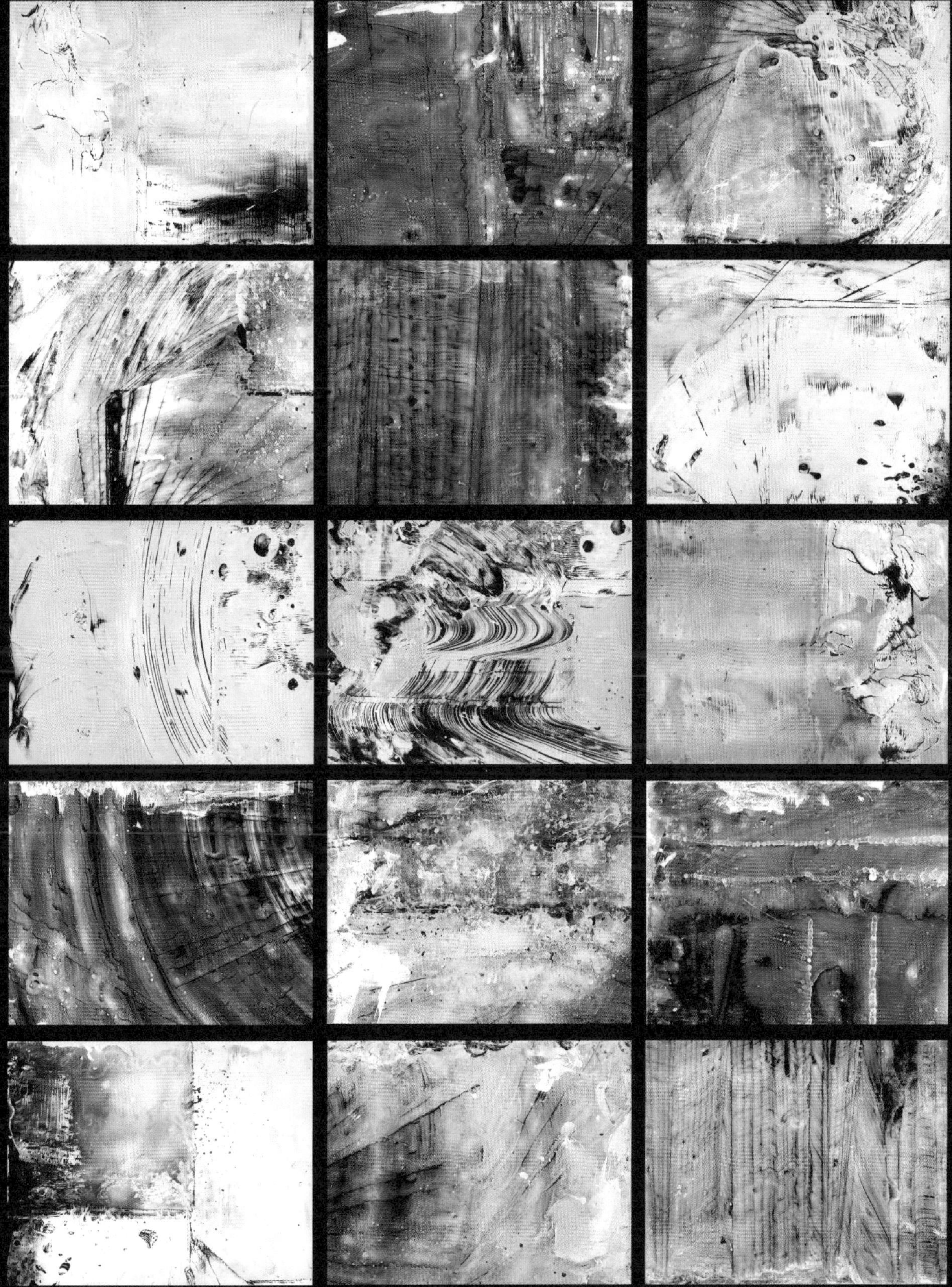

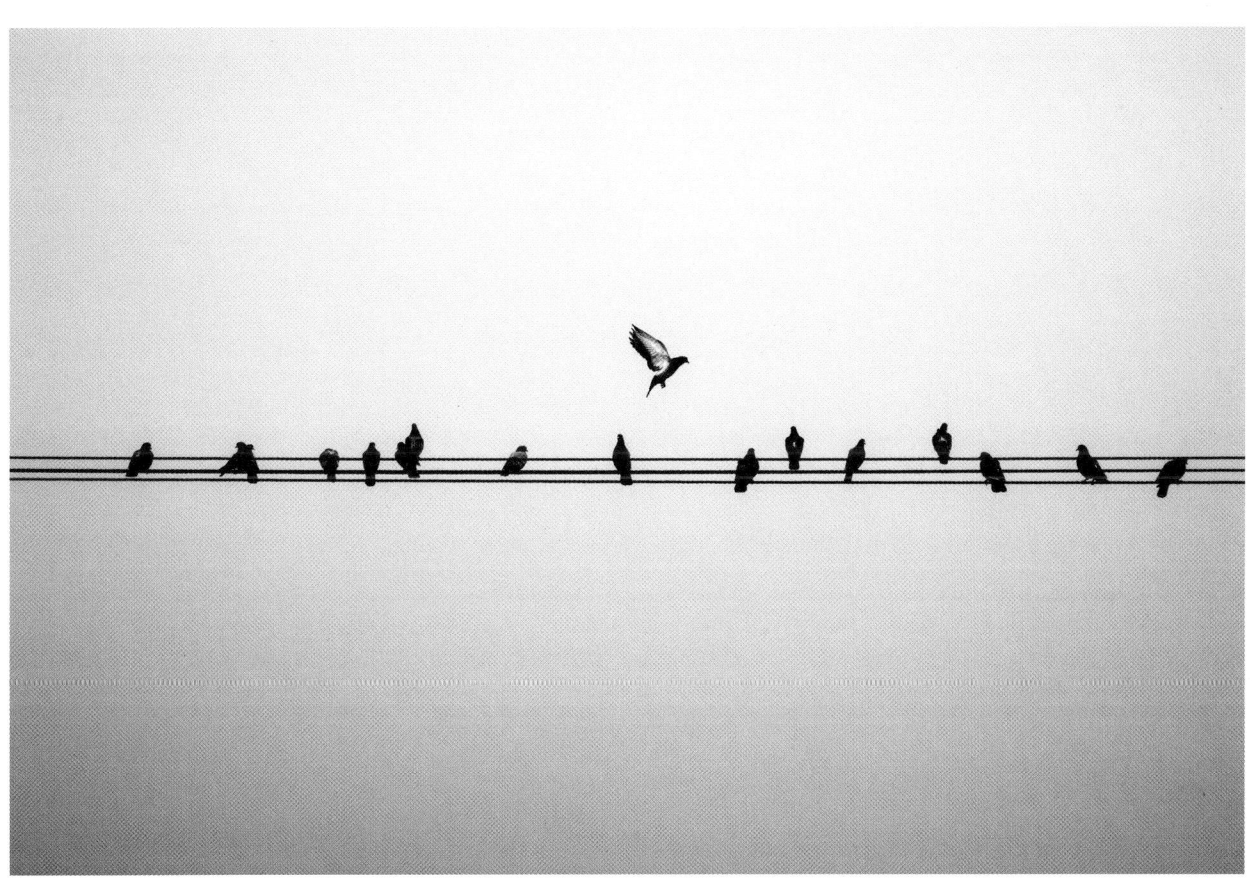

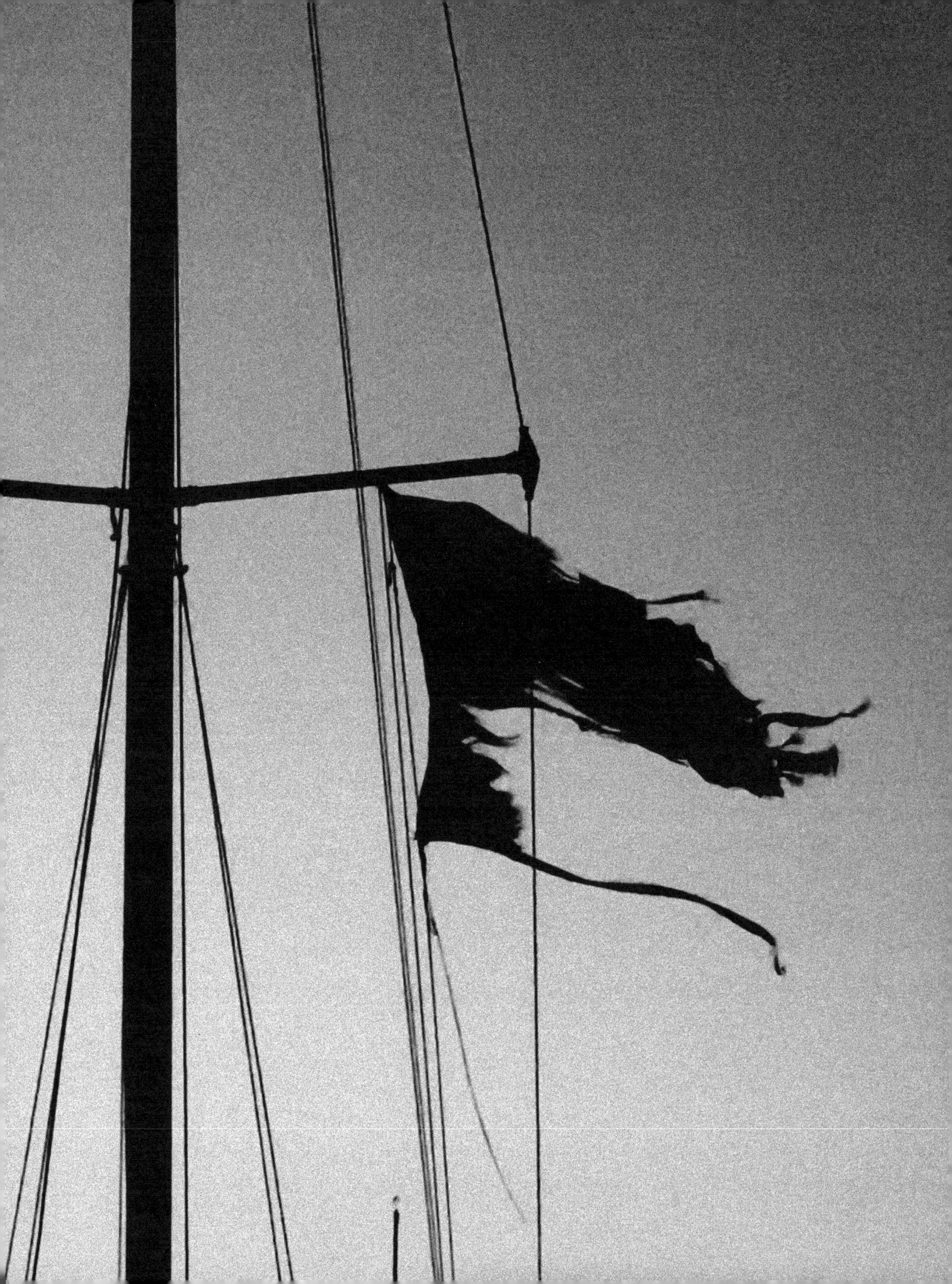

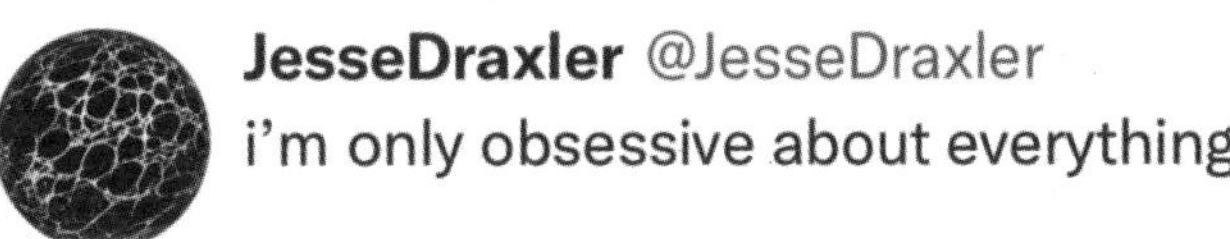
JesseDraxler @JesseDraxler
i'm only obsessive about everything

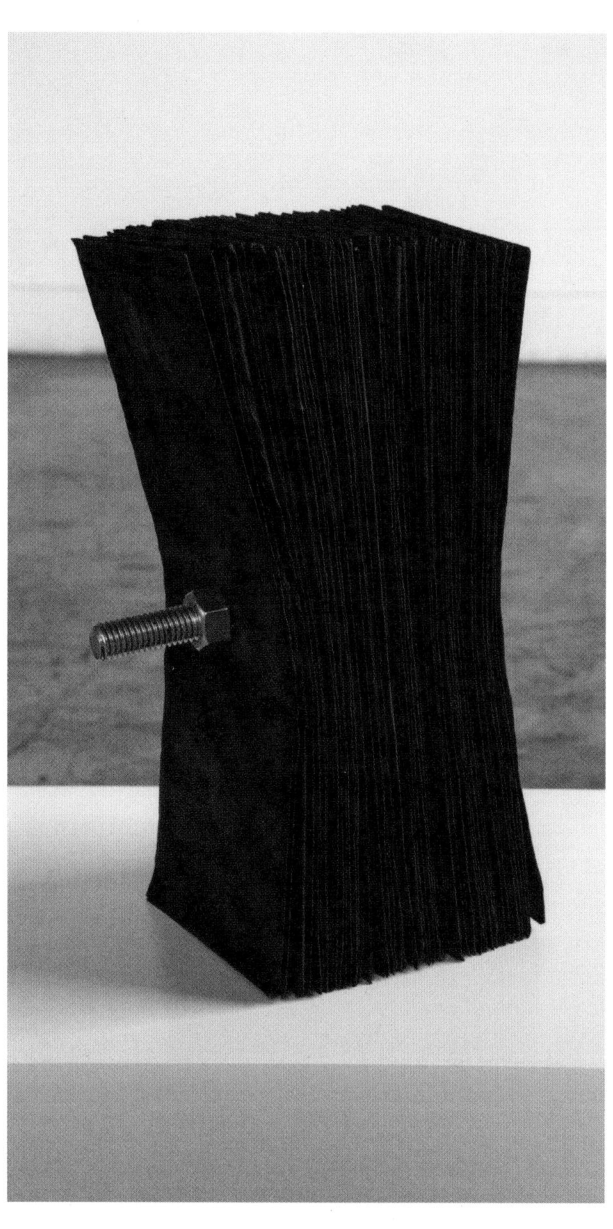

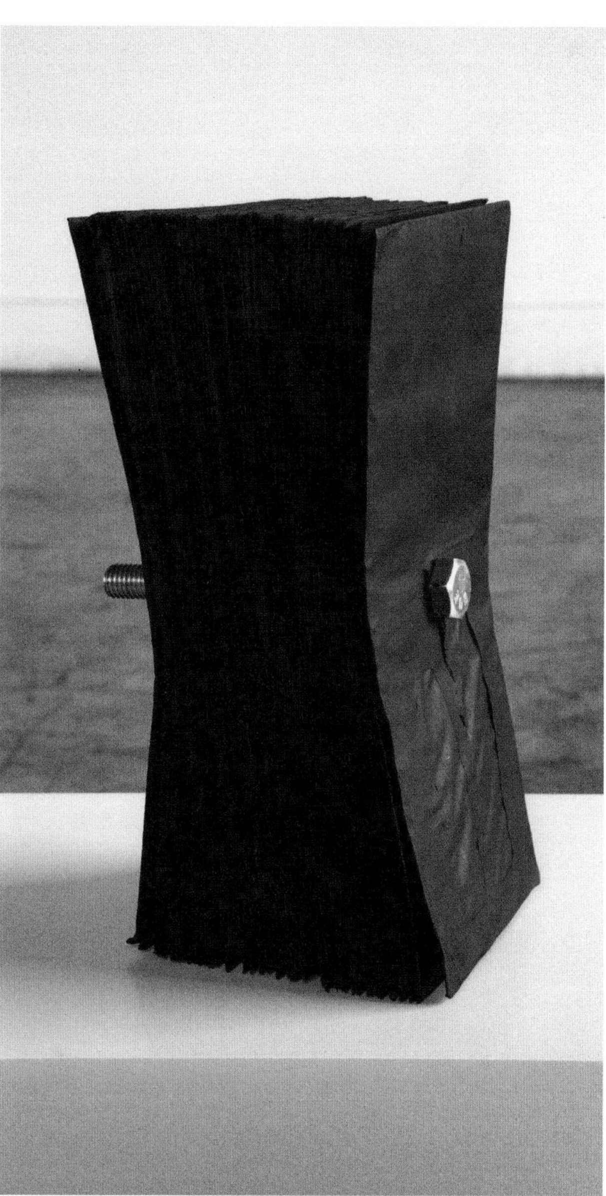

Black Mail

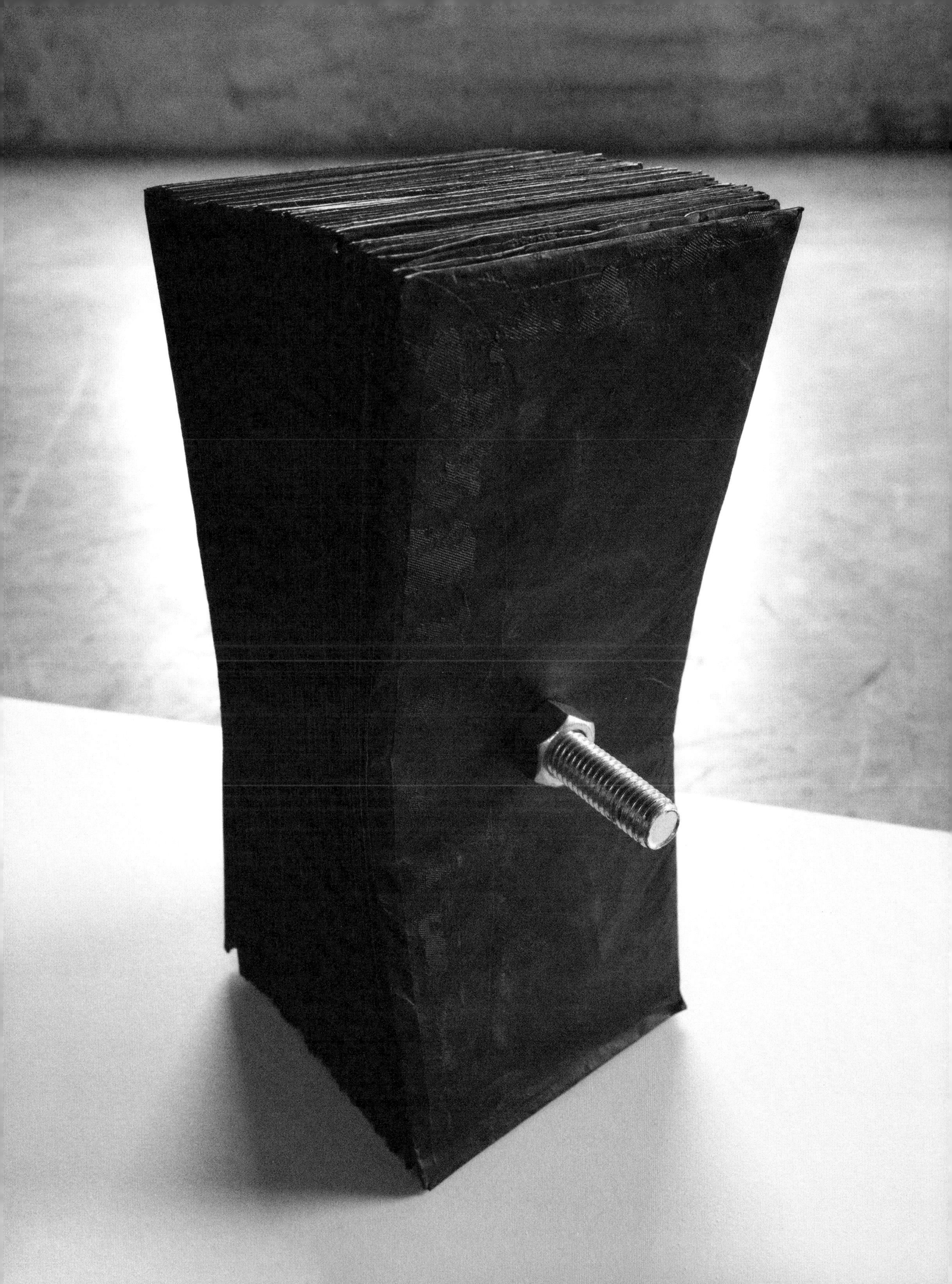

He thinks it might work for your cart if you get bigger tires. Don't bother with brakes... you probably won't live long enough to need them

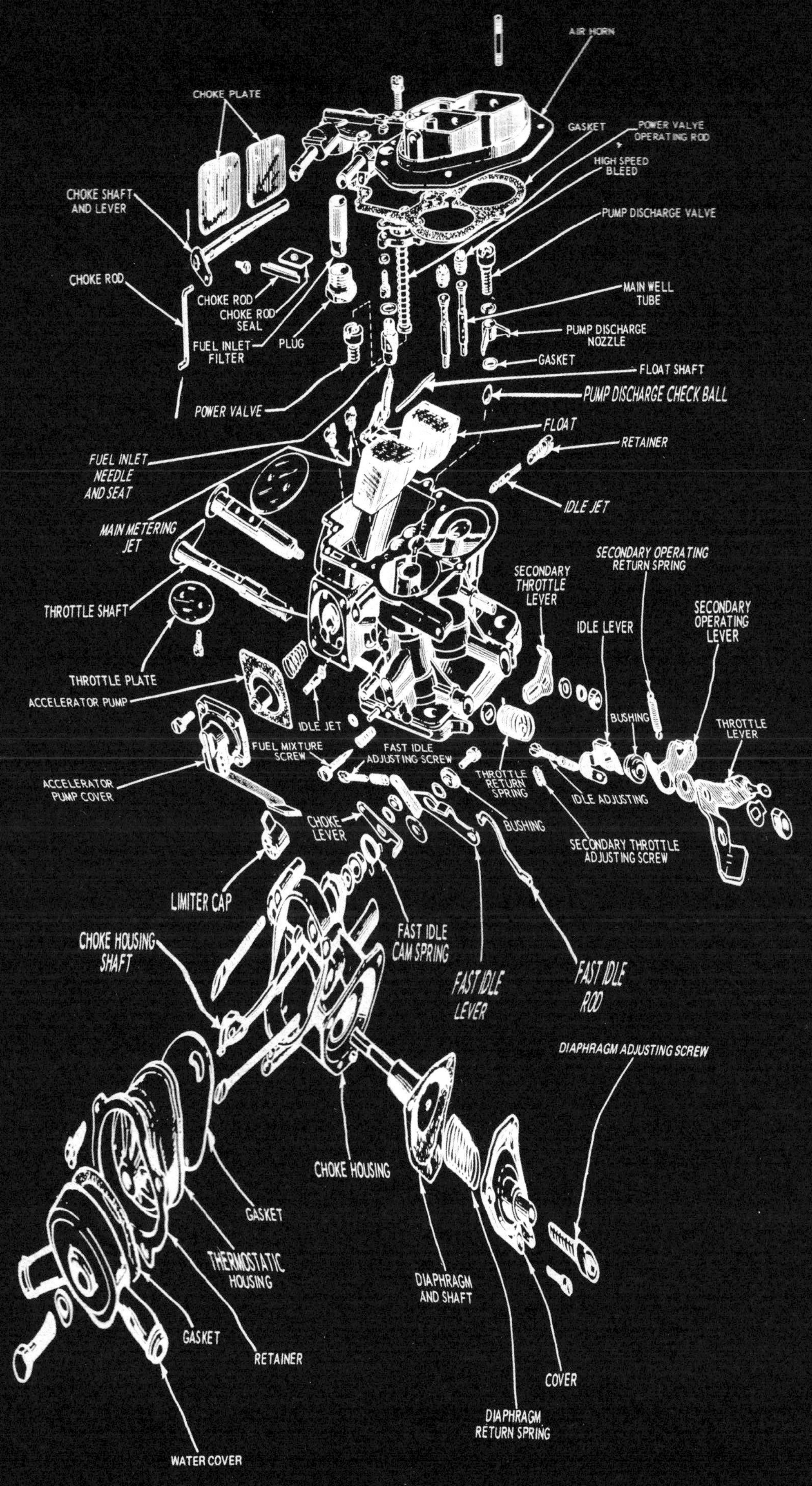
AIR HORN
CHOKE PLATE
GASKET
POWER VALVE OPERATING ROD
HIGH SPEED BLEED
PUMP DISCHARGE VALVE
CHOKE SHAFT AND LEVER
CHOKE ROD
CHOKE ROD
CHOKE ROD SEAL
MAIN WELL TUBE
PUMP DISCHARGE NOZZLE
FUEL INLET FILTER
PLUG
GASKET
FLOAT SHAFT
PUMP DISCHARGE CHECK BALL
POWER VALVE
FLOAT
RETAINER
FUEL INLET NEEDLE AND SEAT
IDLE JET
MAIN METERING JET
SECONDARY OPERATING RETURN SPRING
SECONDARY THROTTLE LEVER
THROTTLE SHAFT
SECONDARY OPERATING LEVER
IDLE LEVER
THROTTLE PLATE
ACCELERATOR PUMP
BUSHING
THROTTLE LEVER
IDLE JET
FUEL MIXTURE SCREW
FAST IDLE ADJUSTING SCREW
ACCELERATOR PUMP COVER
THROTTLE RETURN SPRING
IDLE ADJUSTING
CHOKE LEVER
BUSHING
SECONDARY THROTTLE ADJUSTING SCREW
LIMITER CAP
CHOKE HOUSING SHAFT
FAST IDLE CAM SPRING
FAST IDLE LEVER
FAST IDLE ROD
DIAPHRAGM ADJUSTING SCREW
CHOKE HOUSING
GASKET
THERMOSTATIC HOUSING
DIAPHRAGM AND SHAFT
GASKET
RETAINER
COVER
DIAPHRAGM RETURN SPRING
WATER COVER

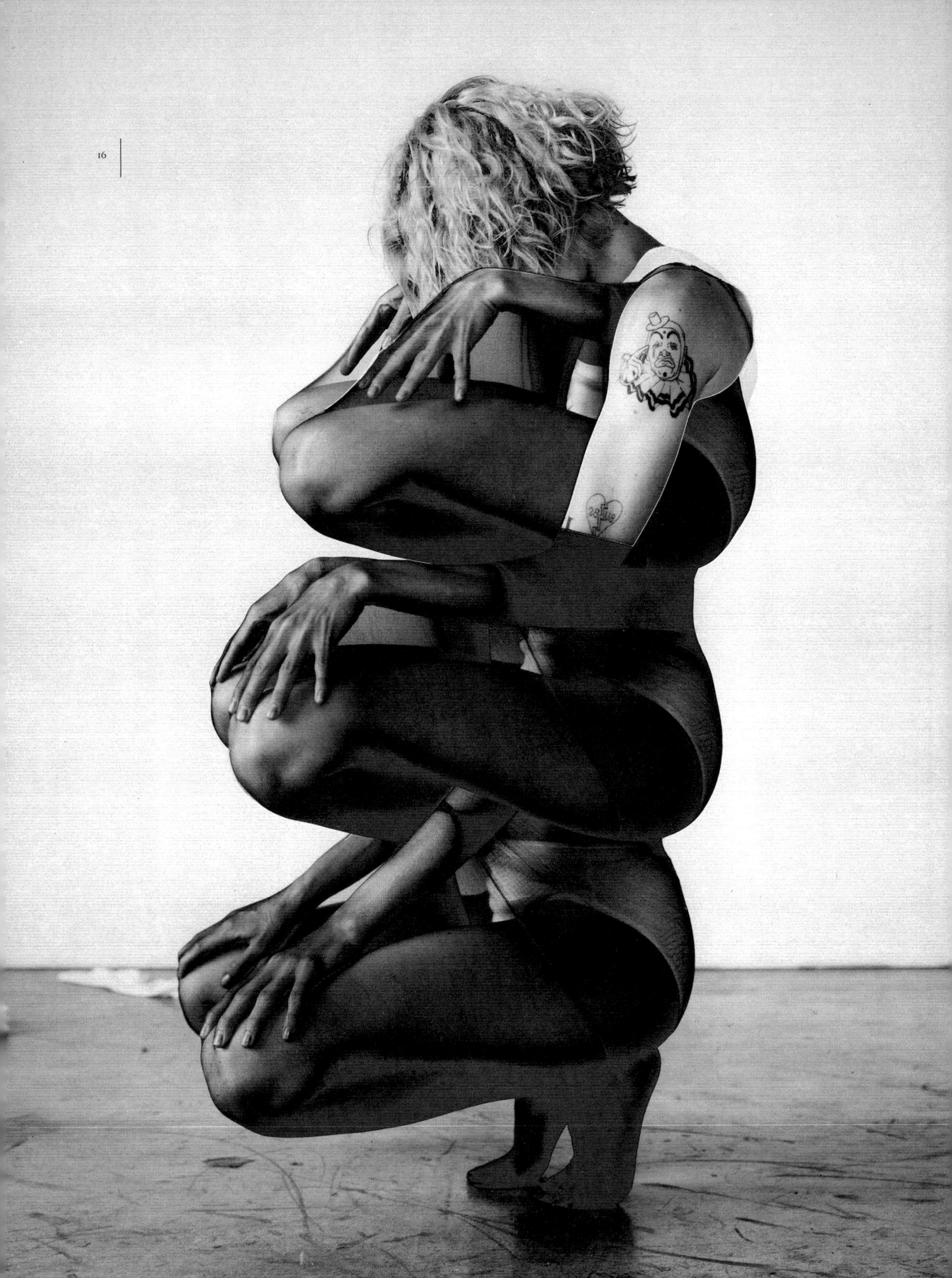

burning OBJKT

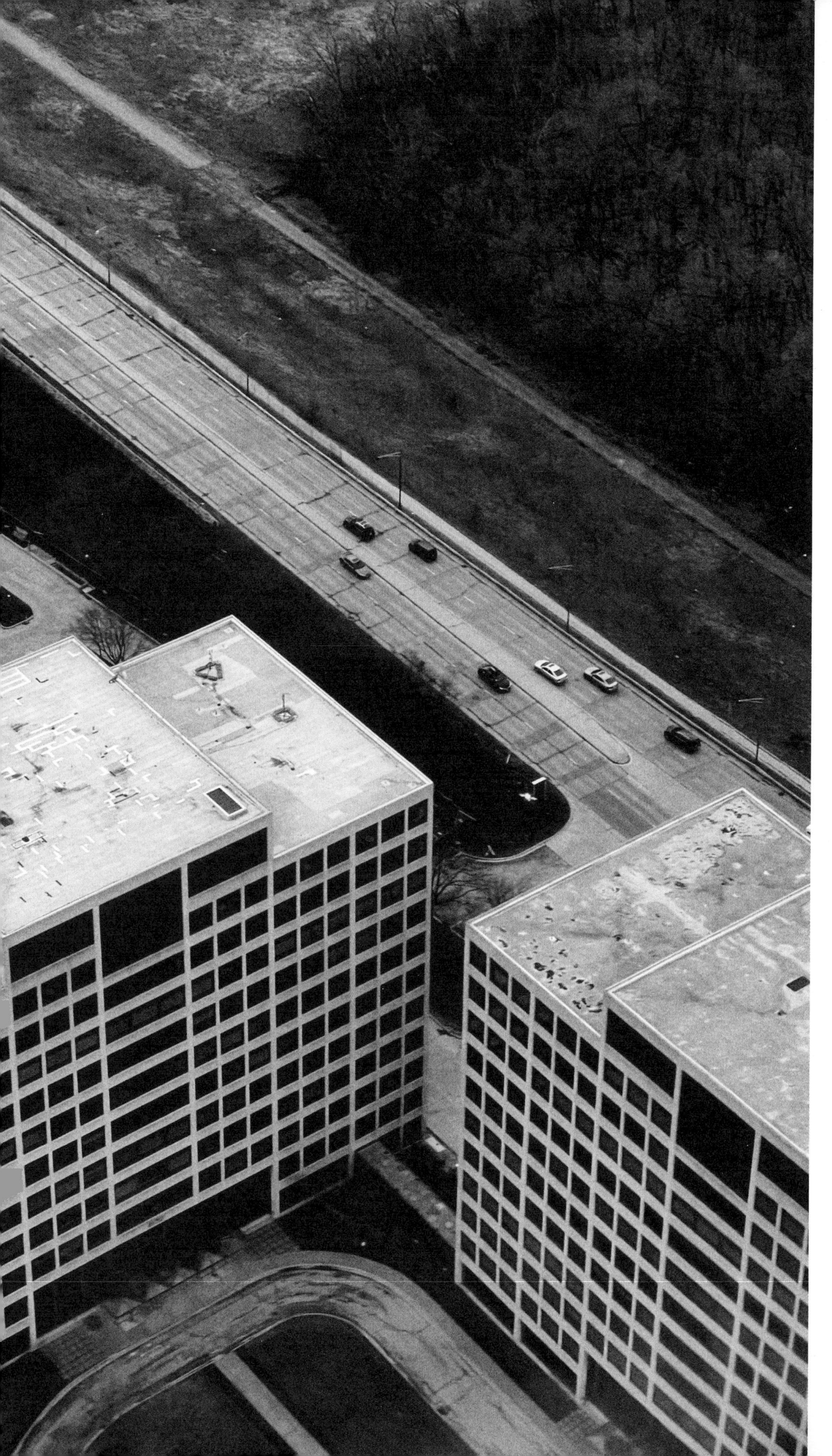

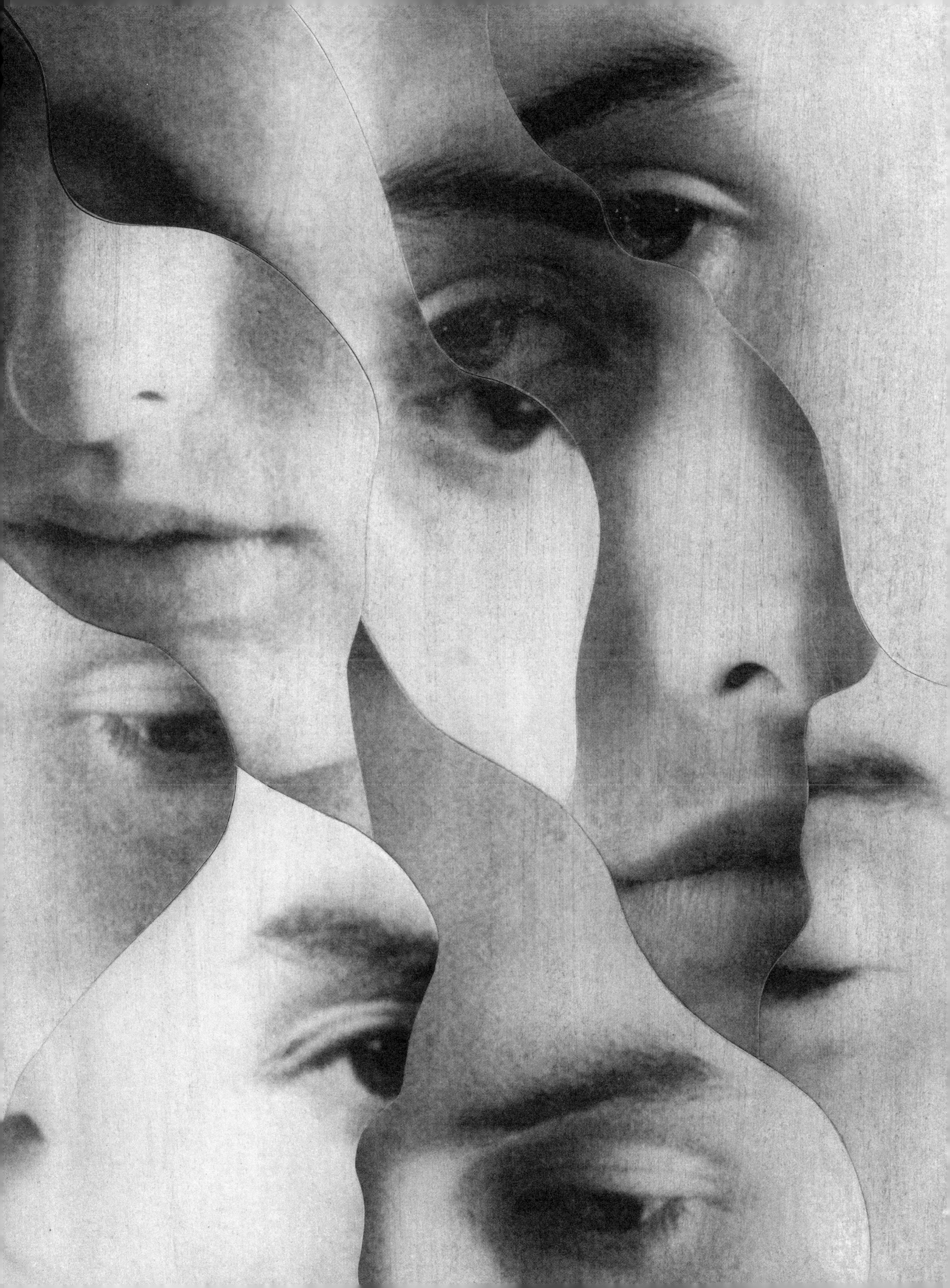

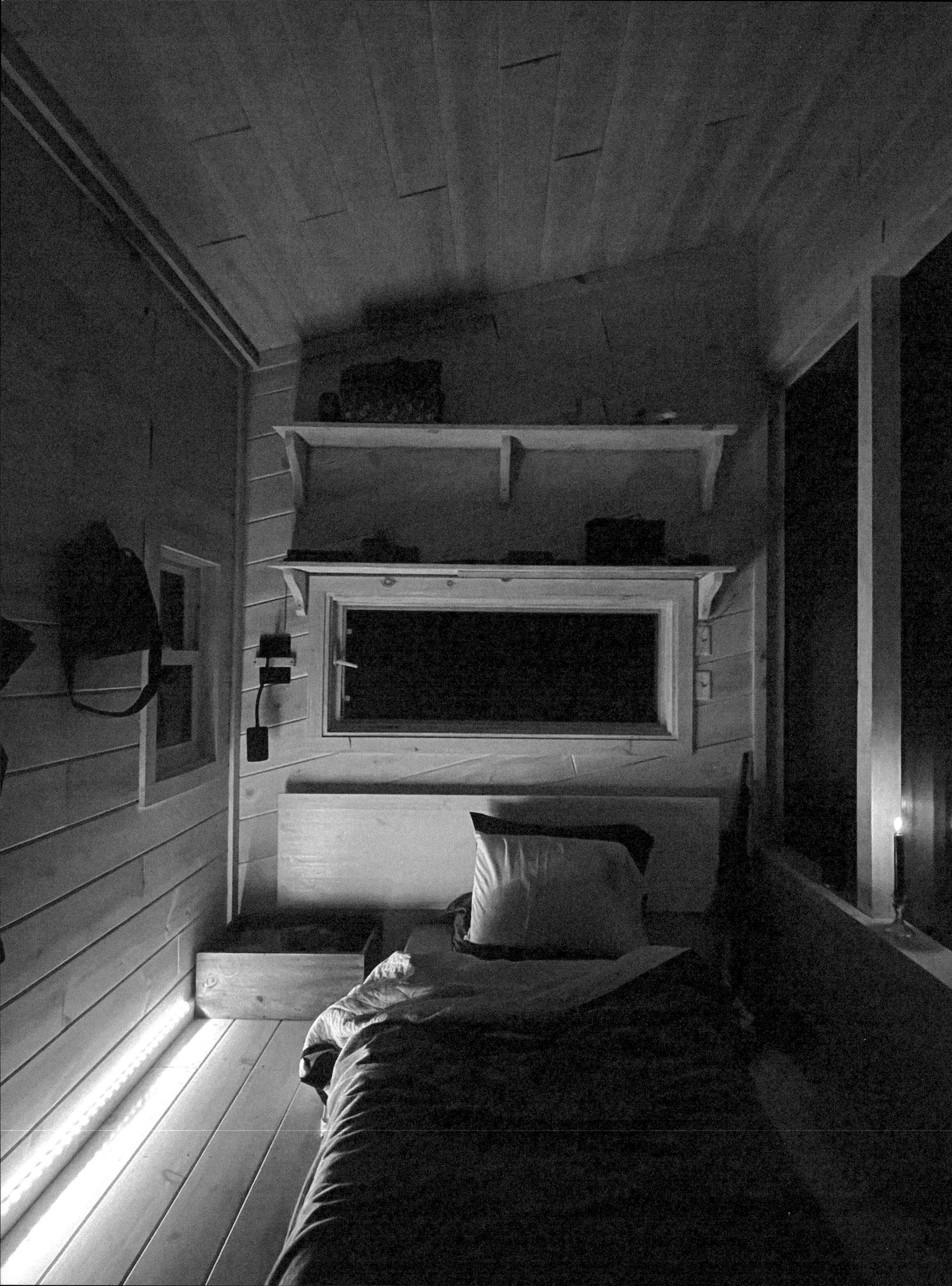

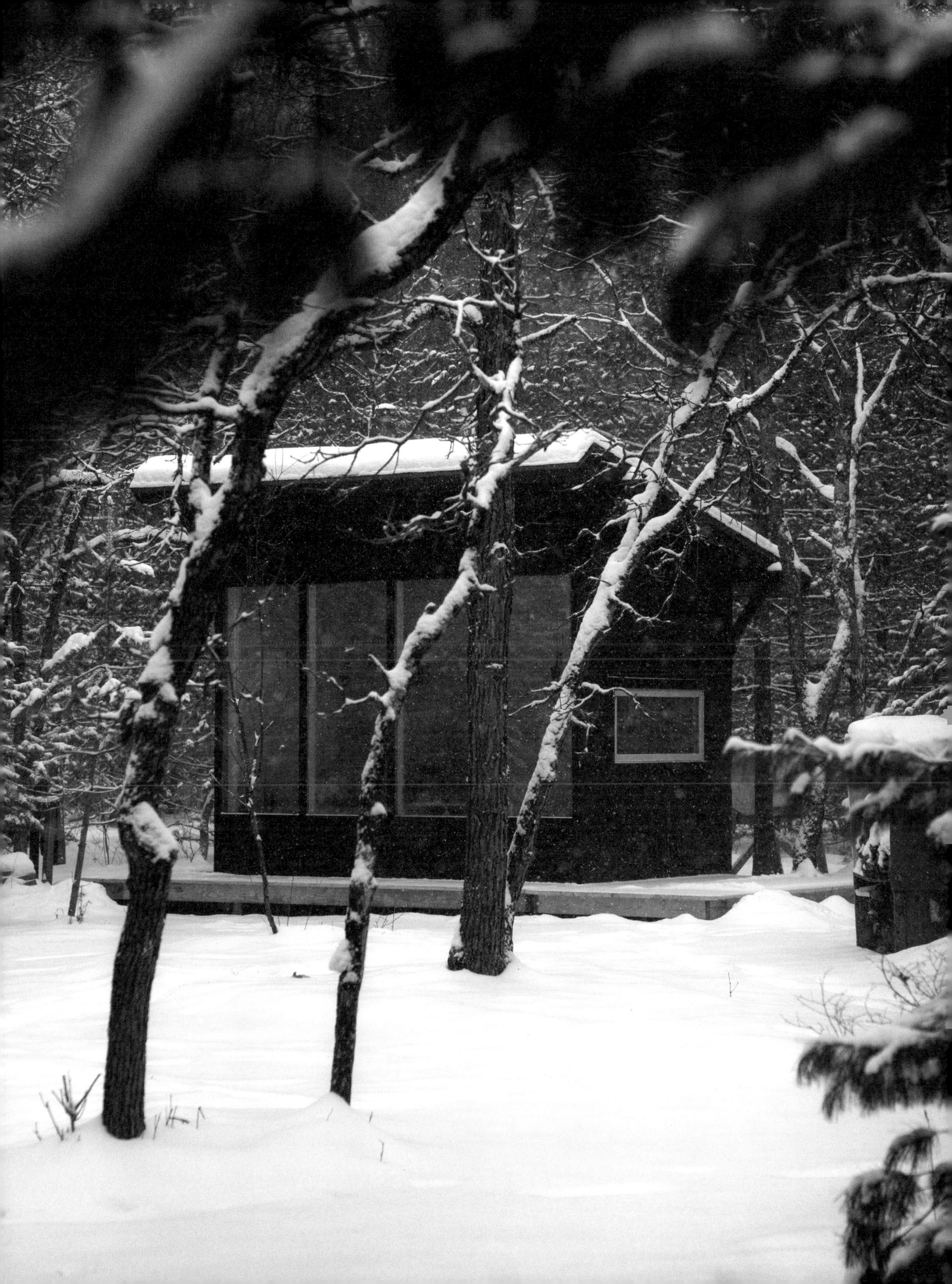

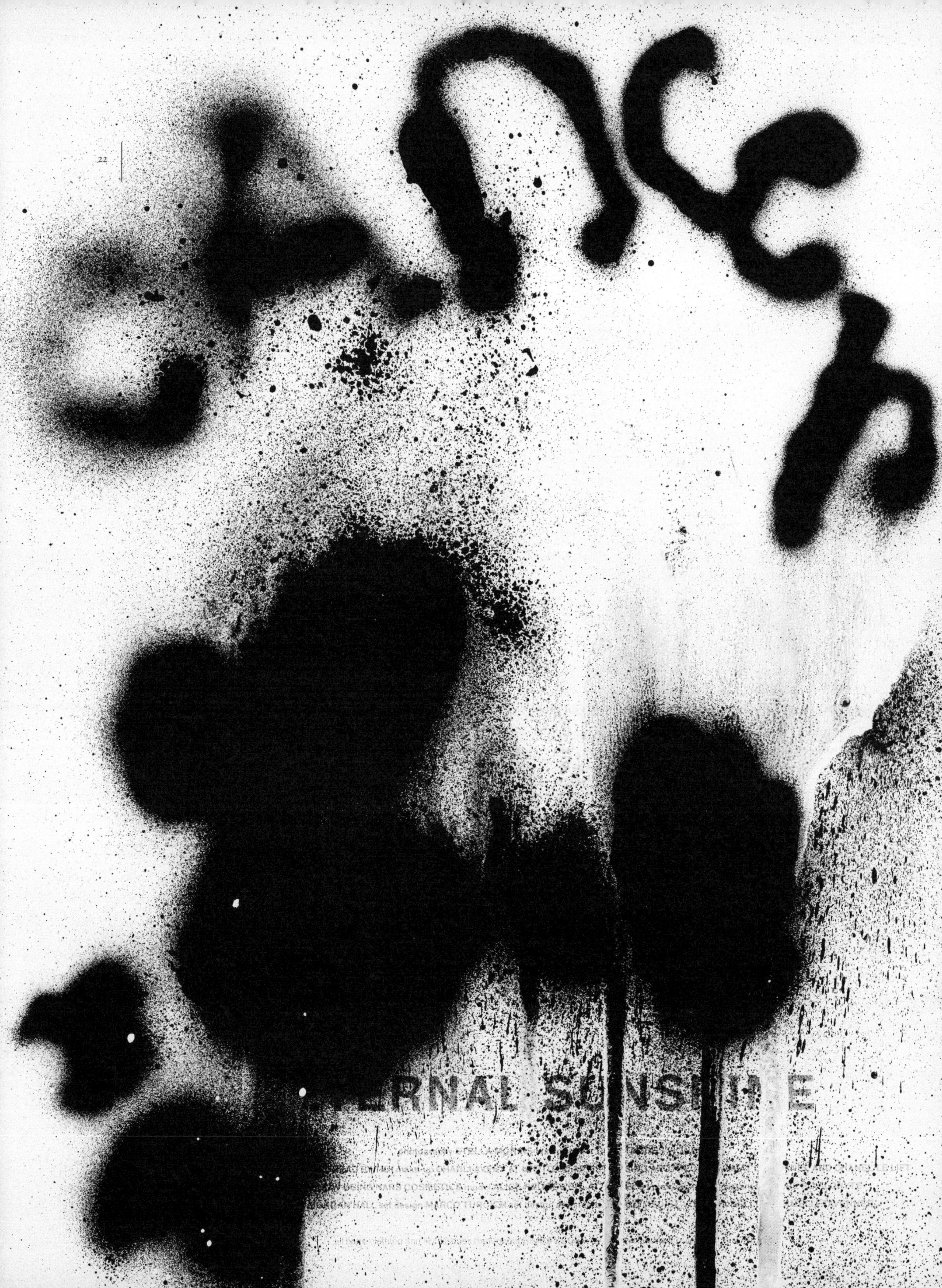

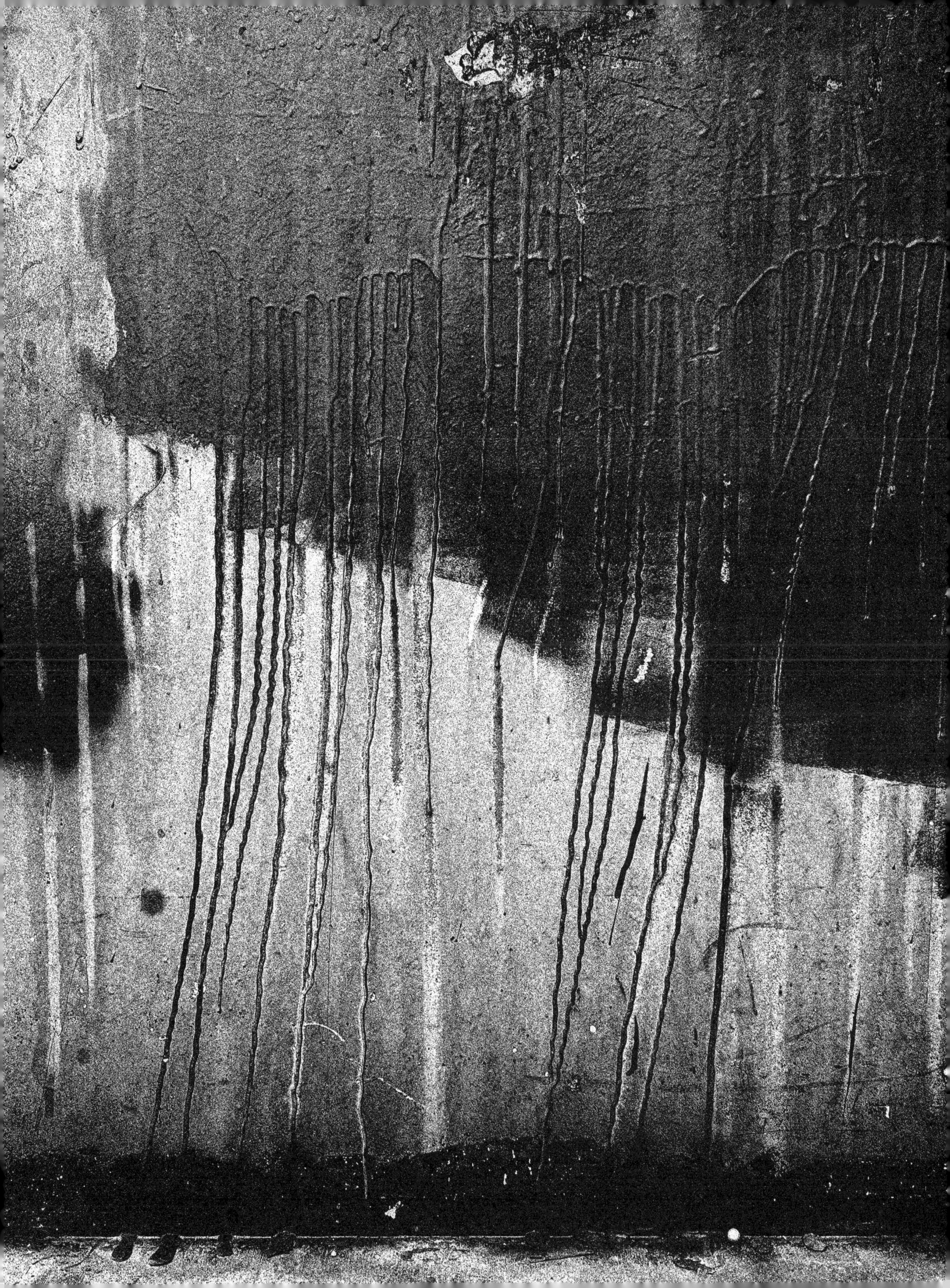

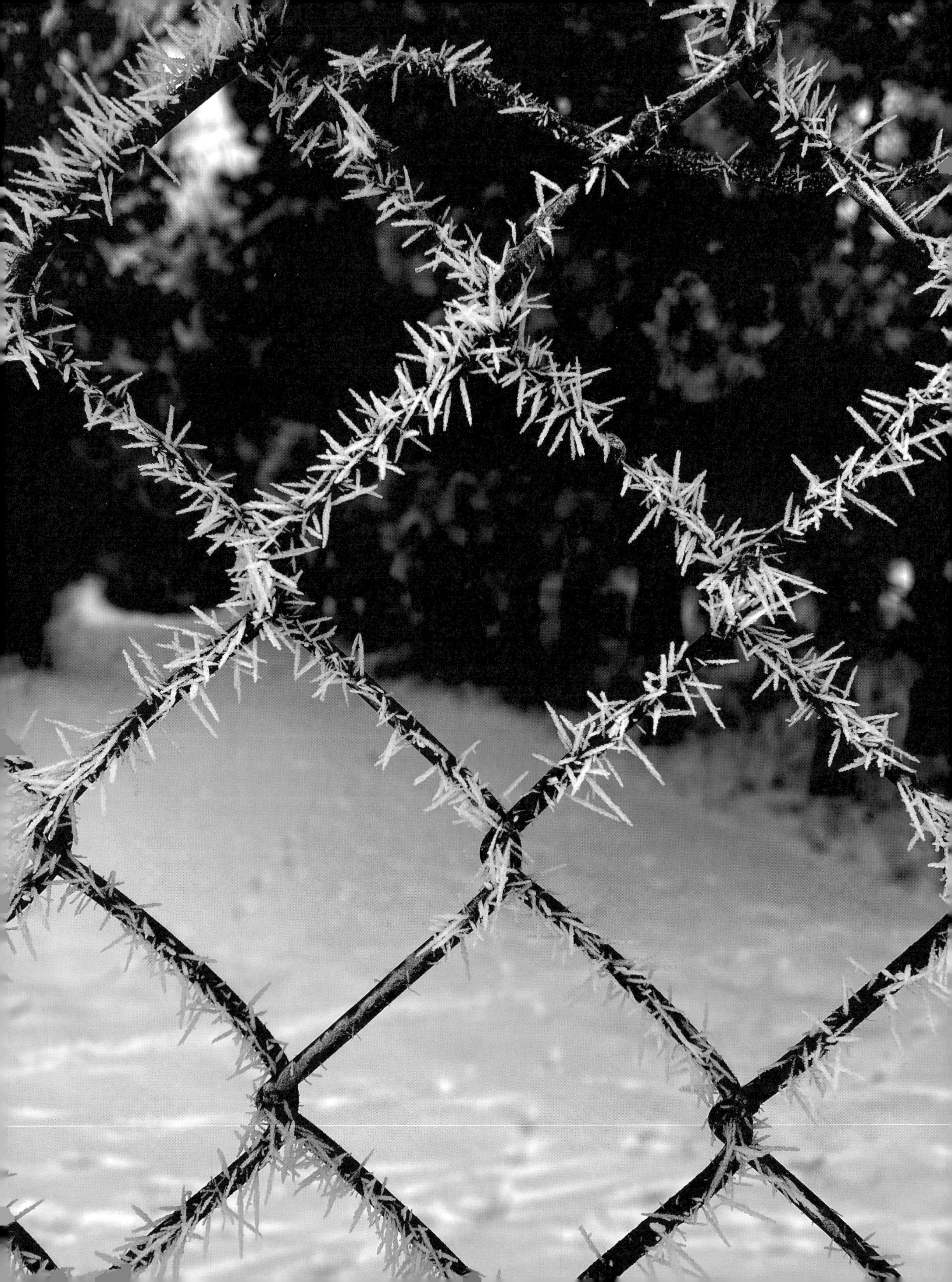

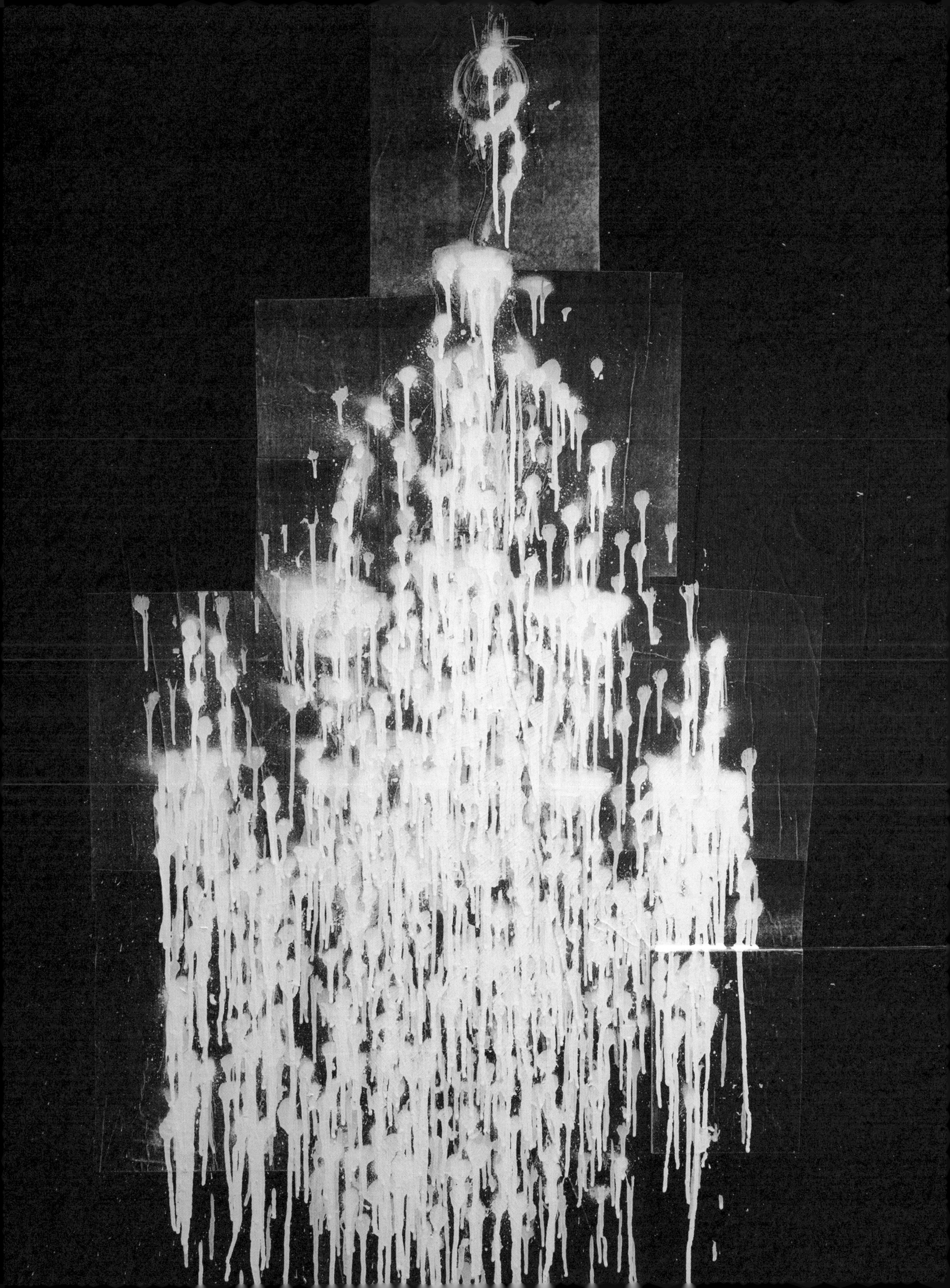

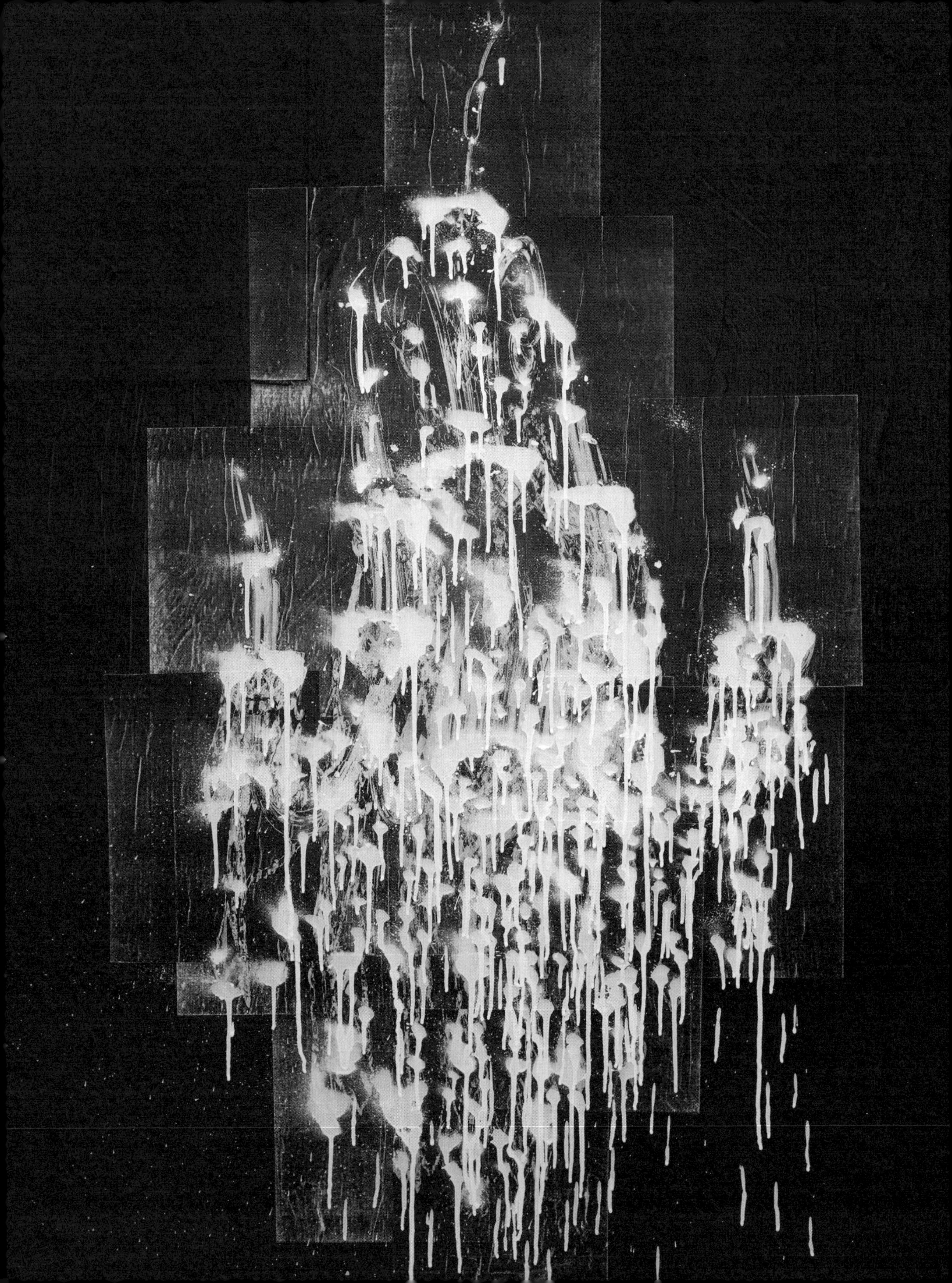

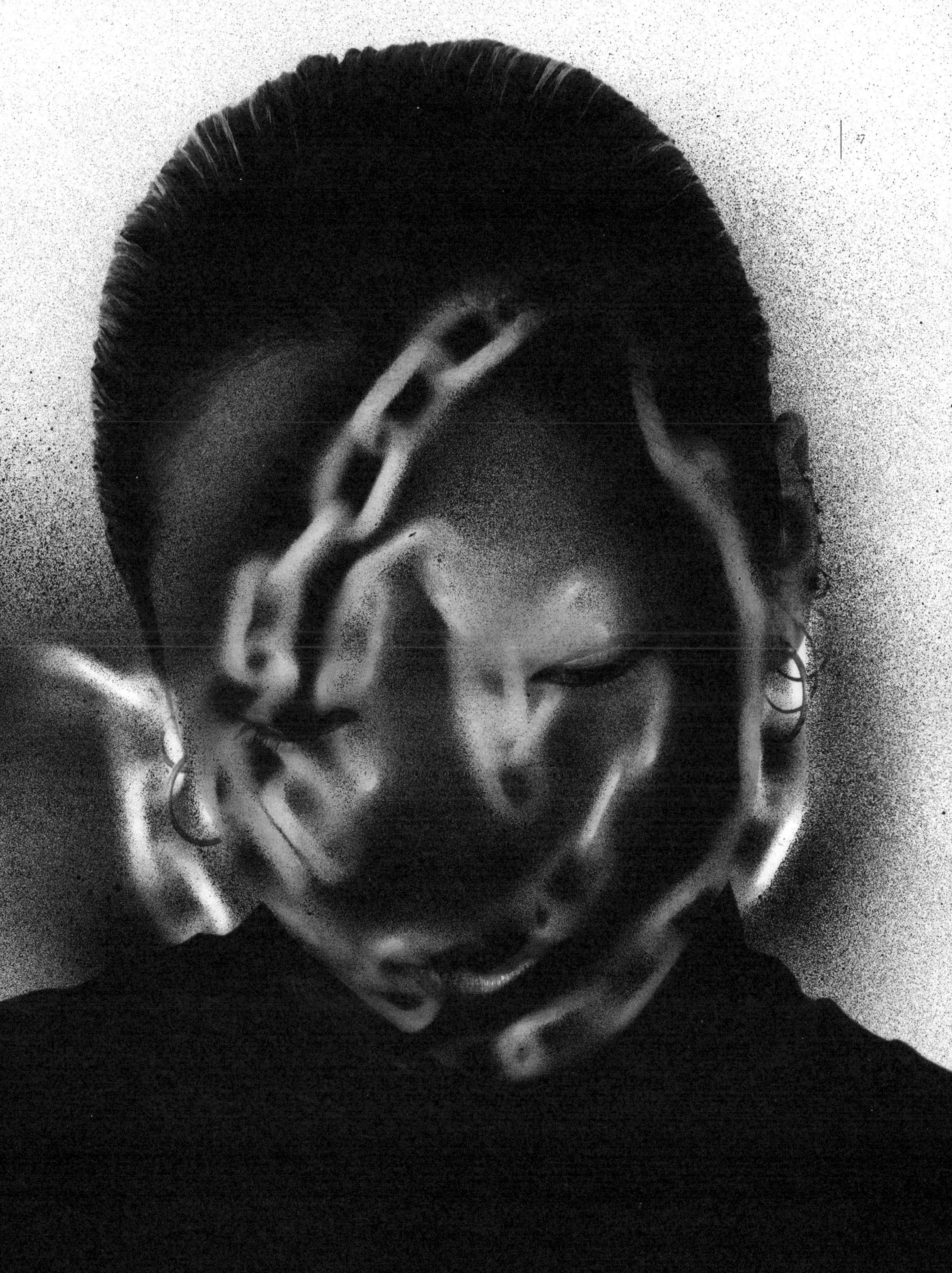

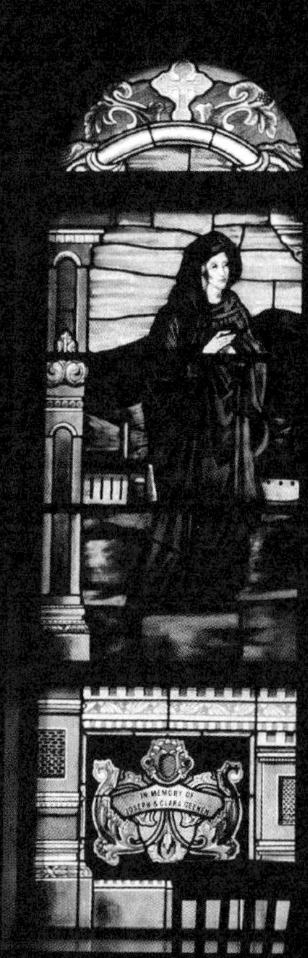

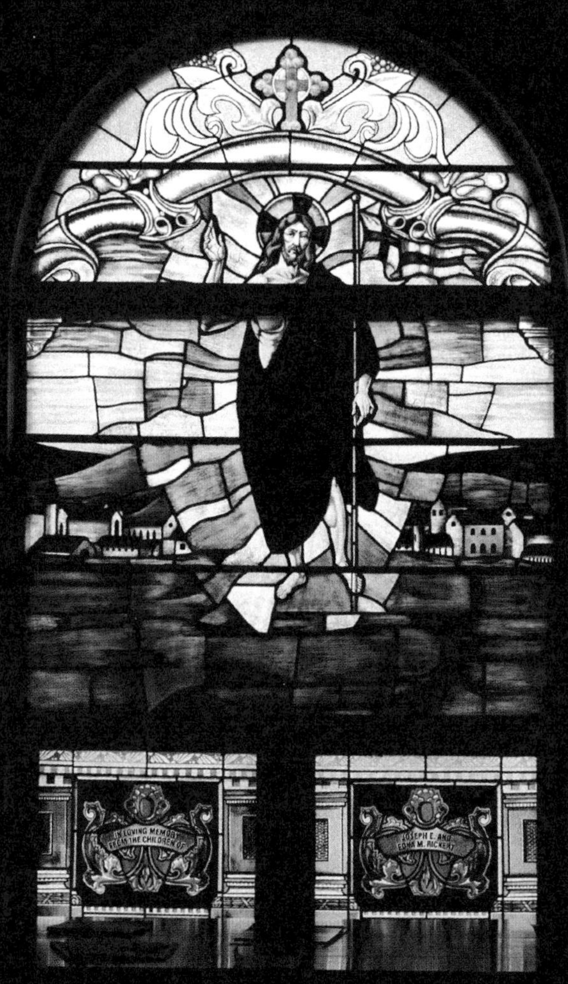
EXIT

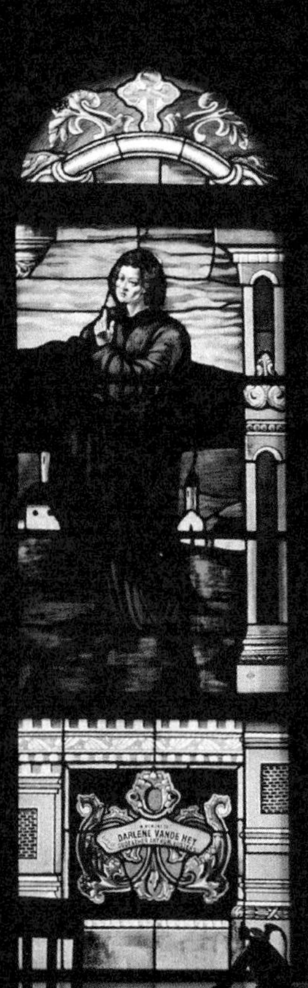

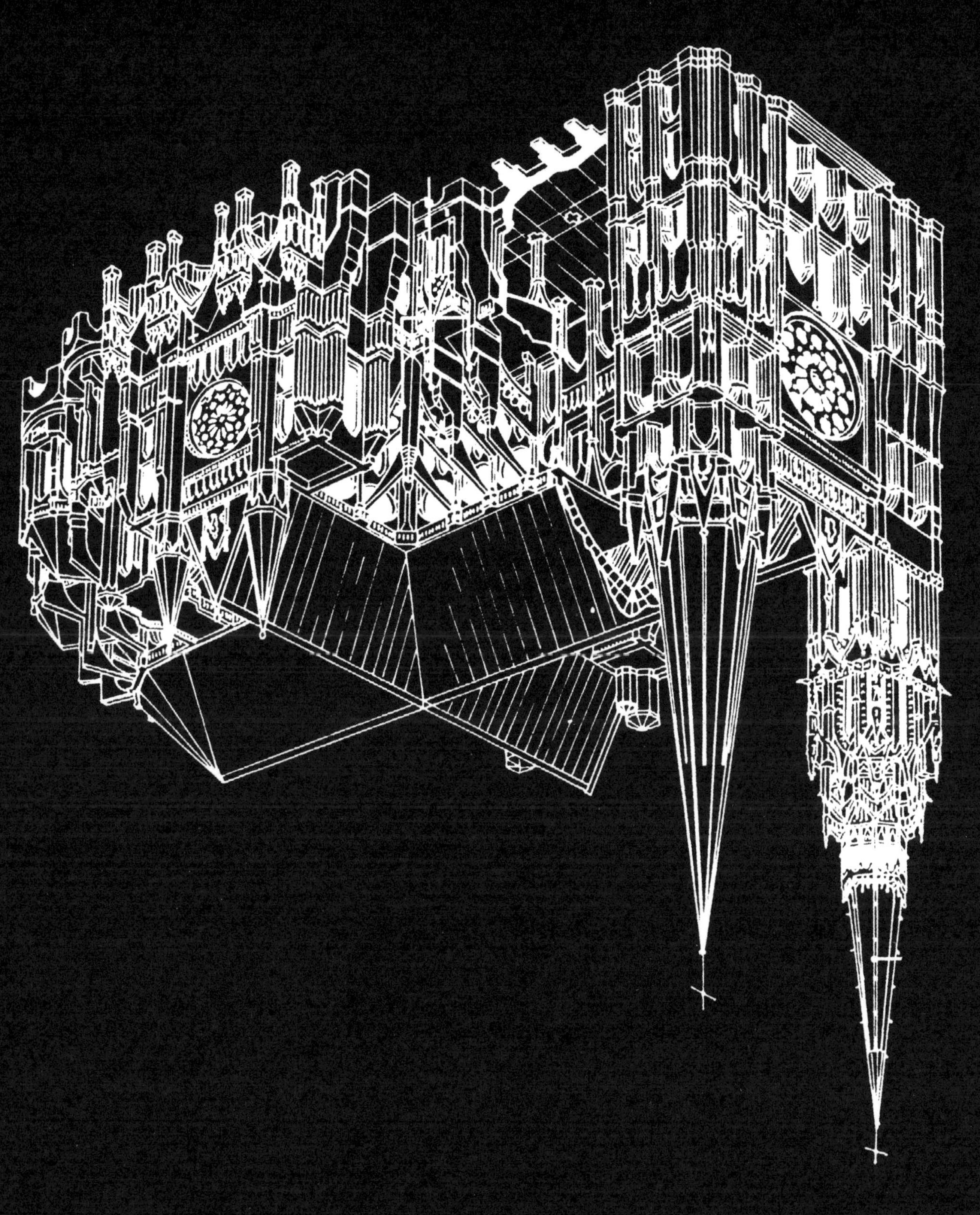

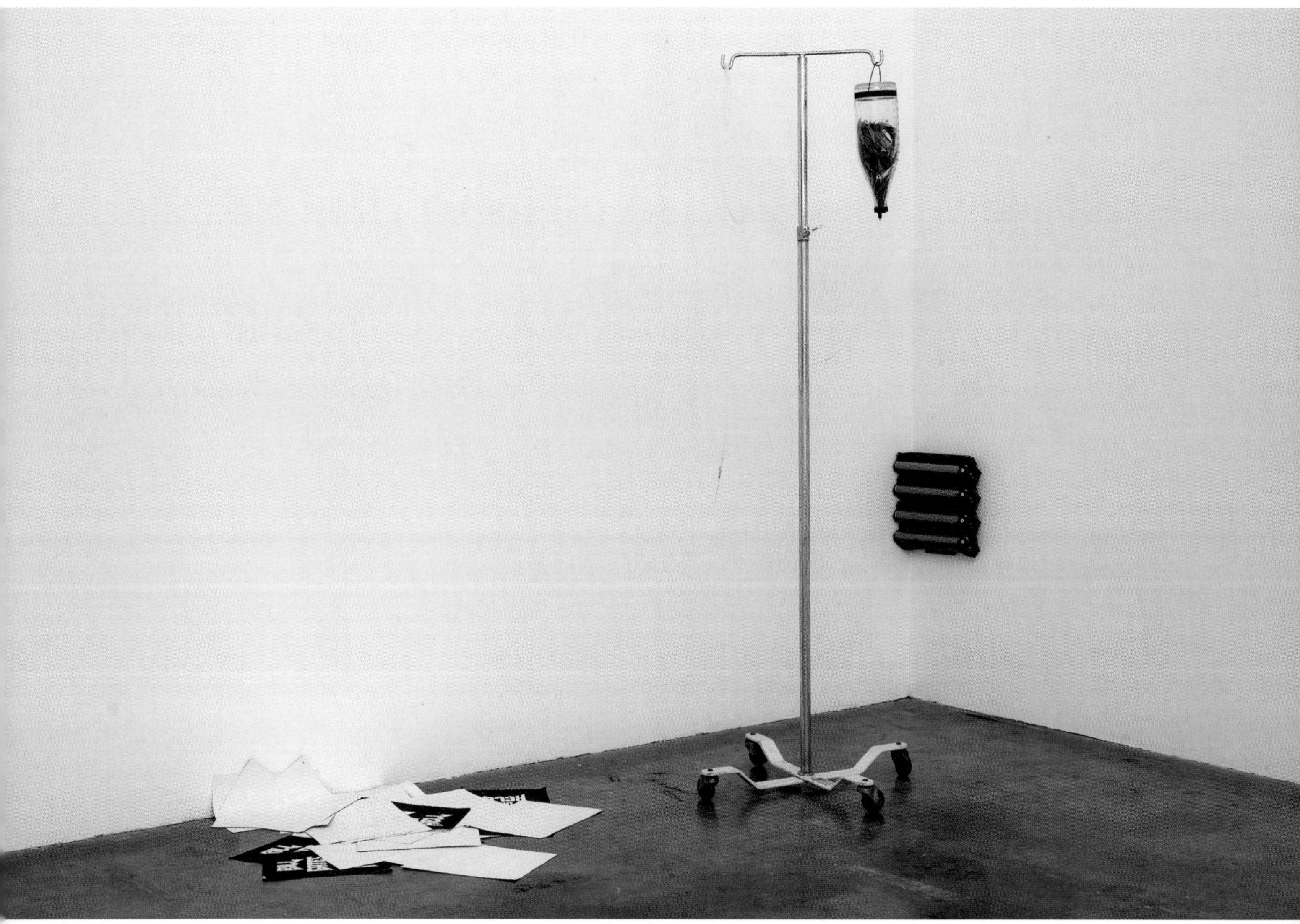

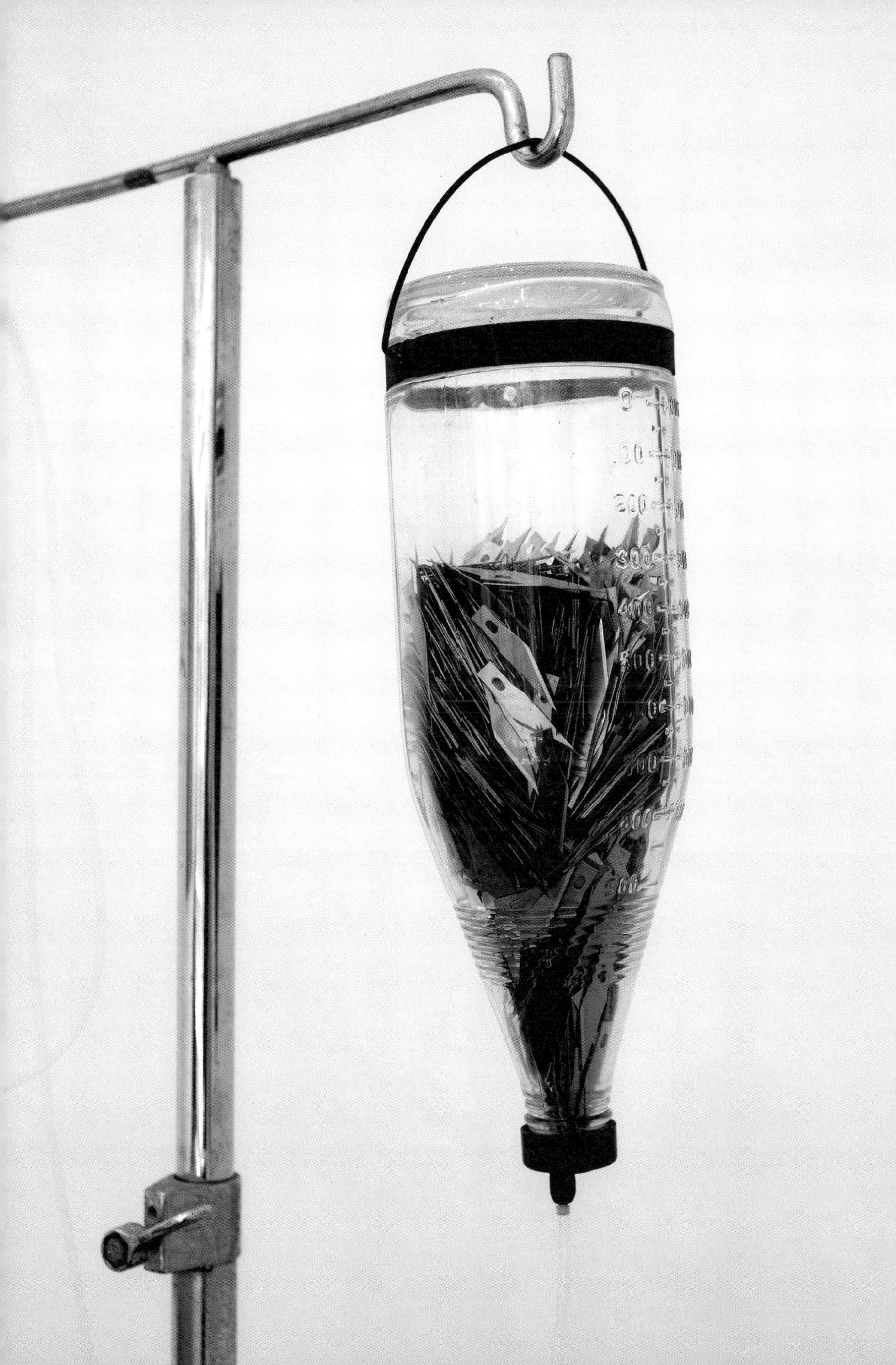

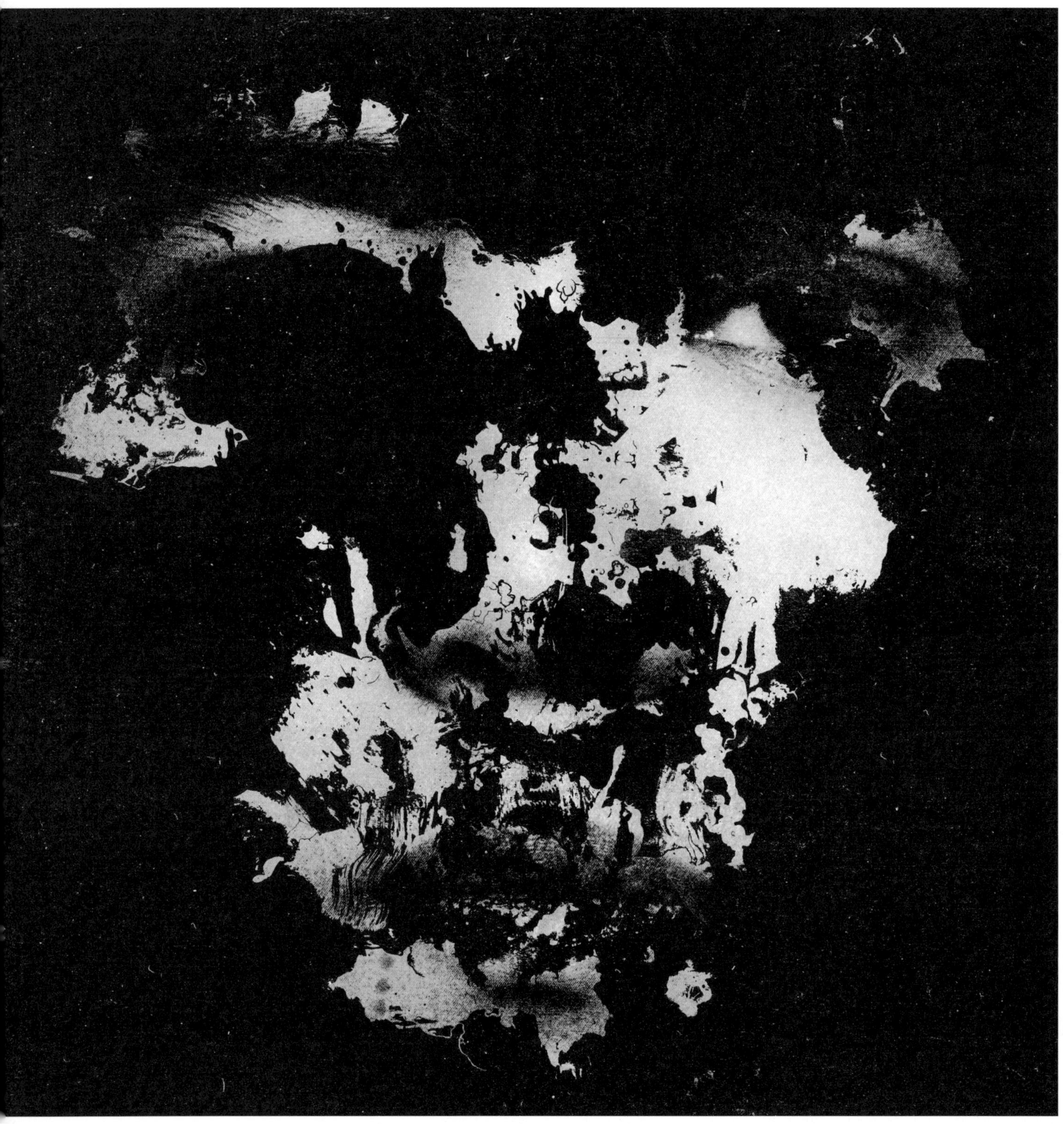

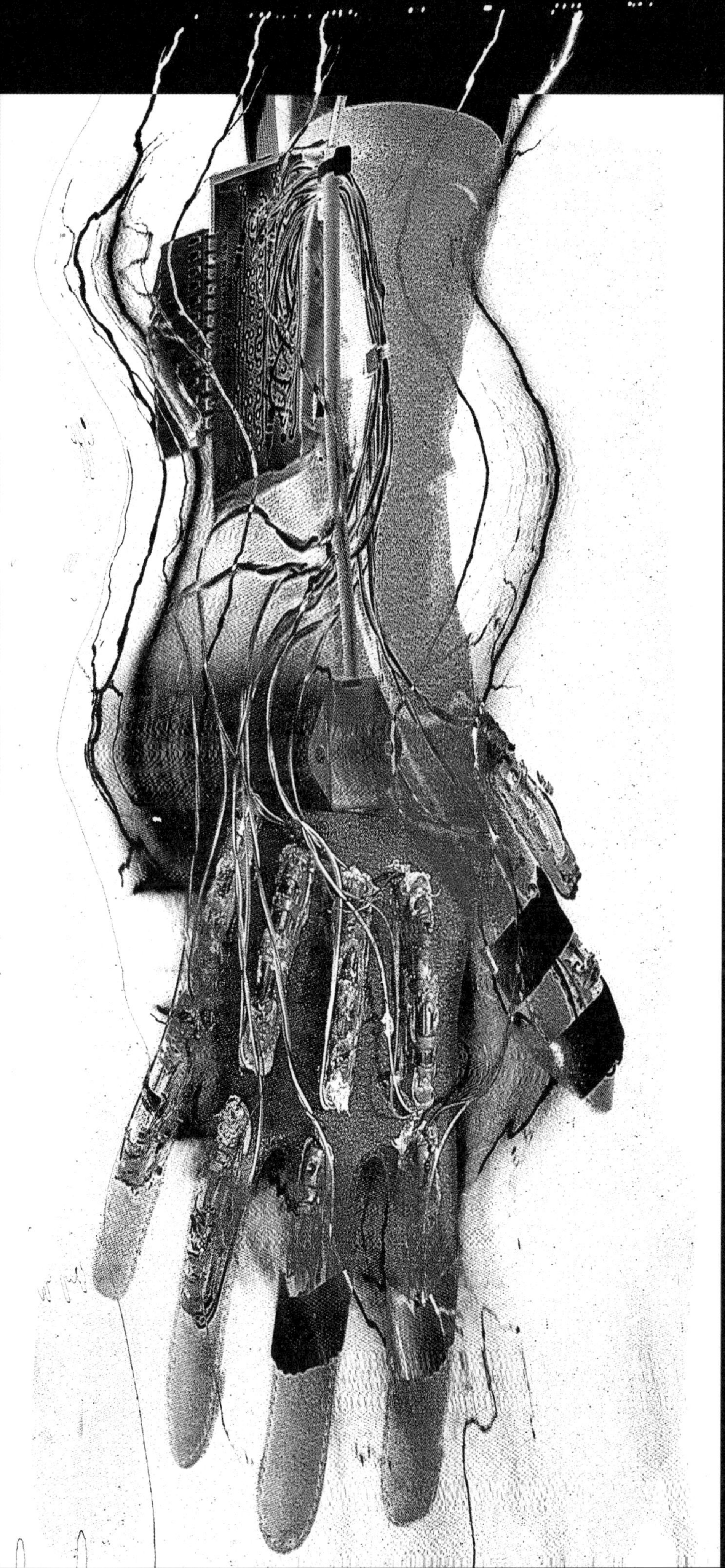

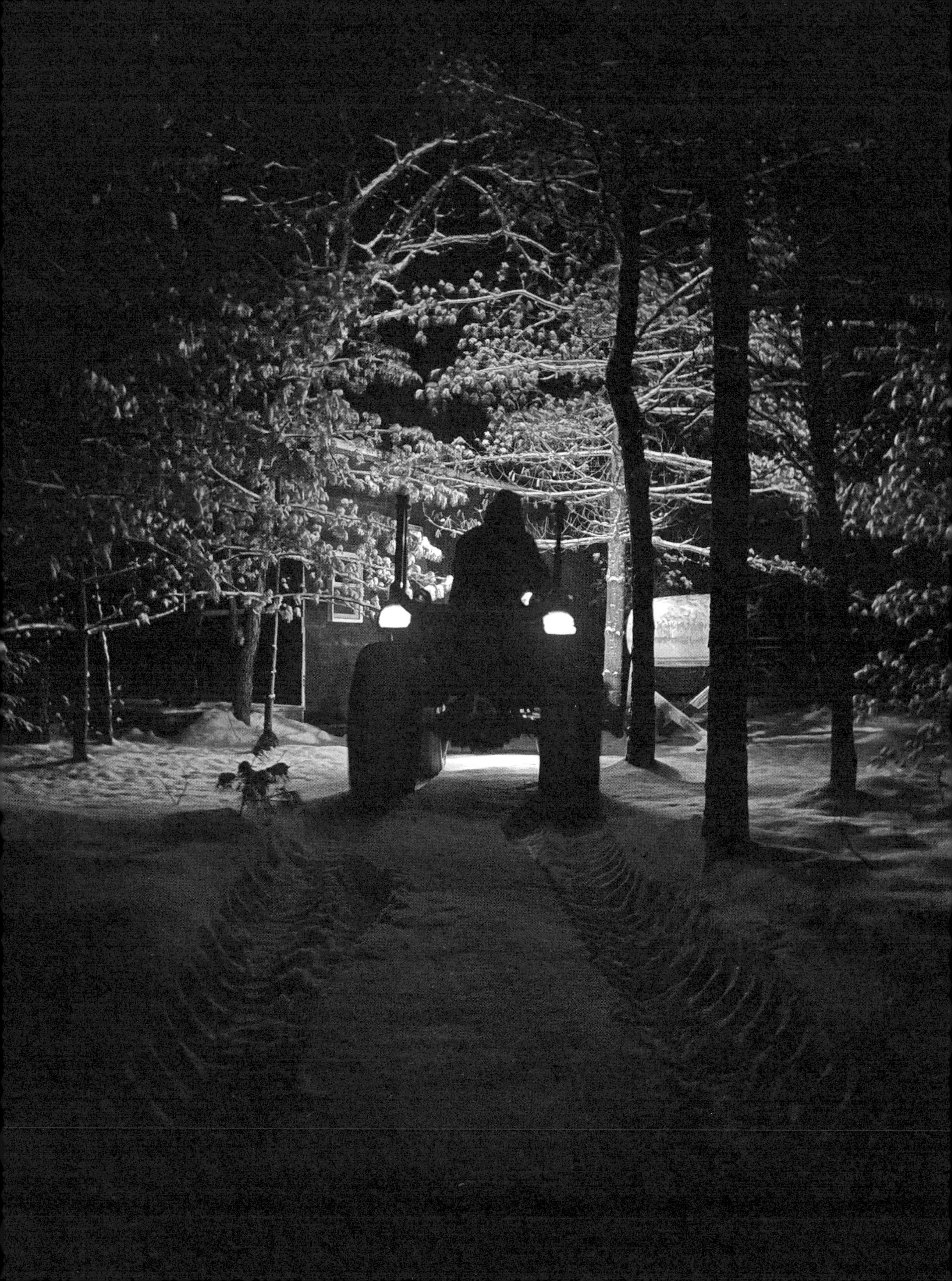

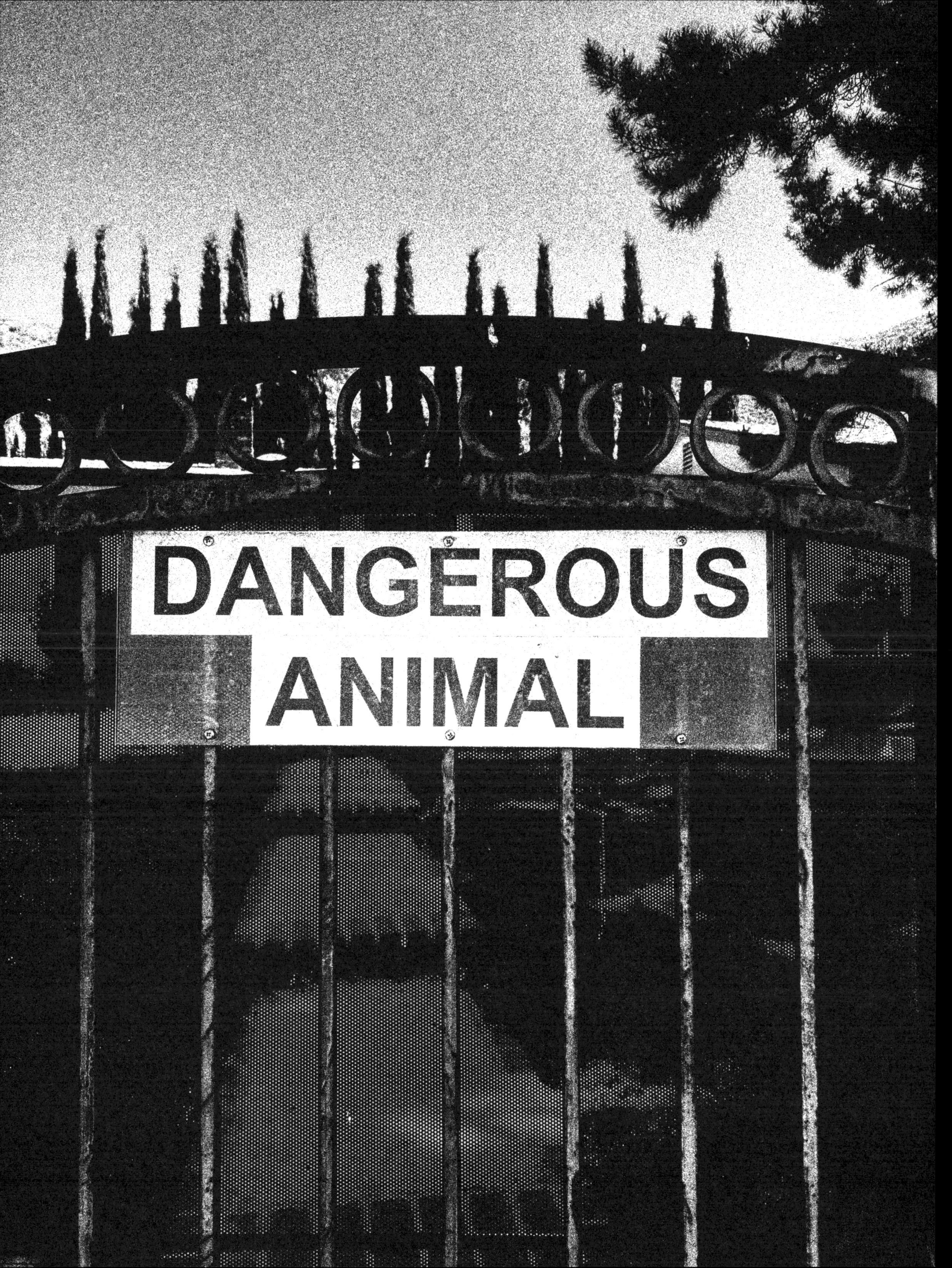

DANGEROUS
ANIMAL

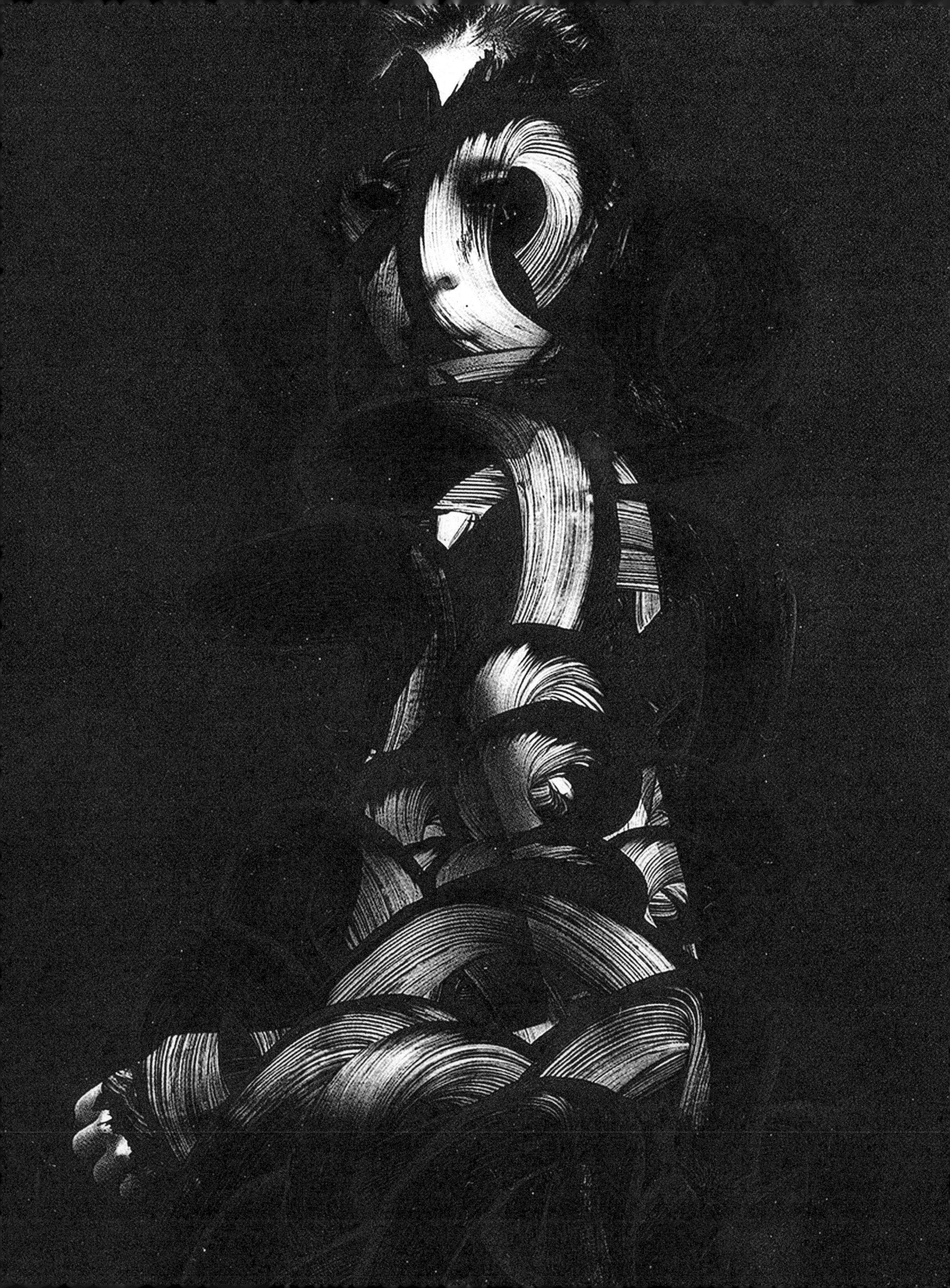

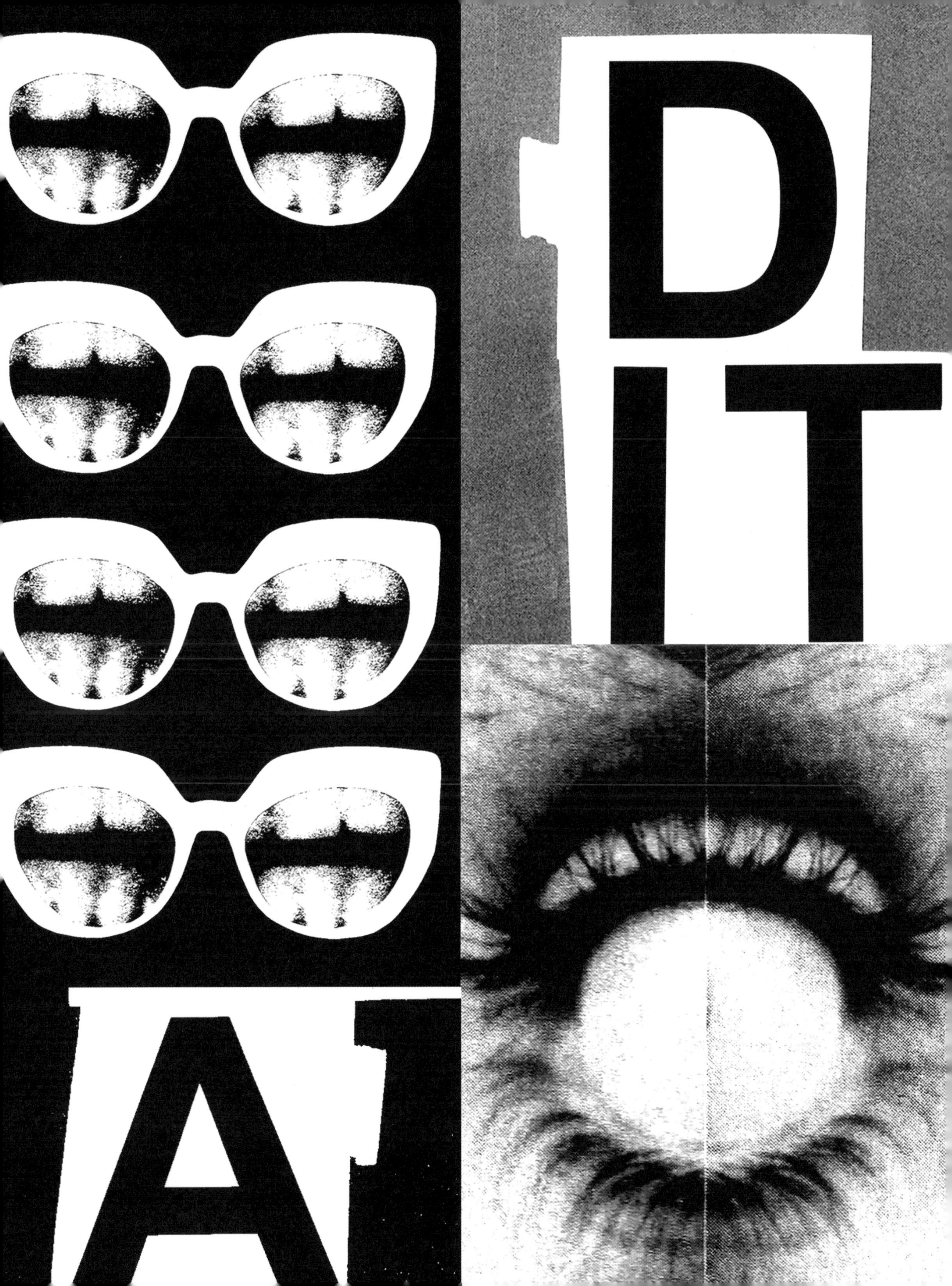

A

D

IT

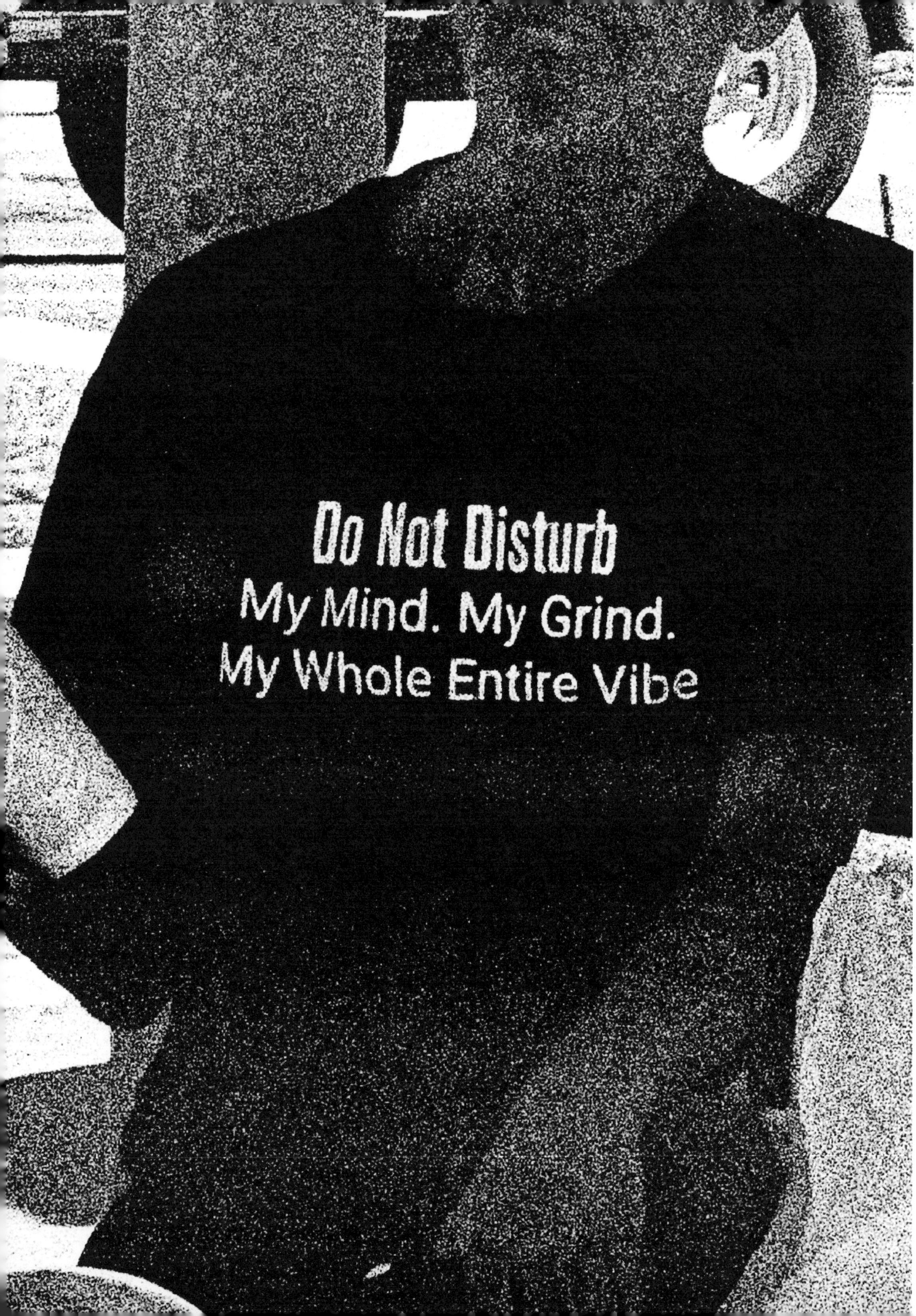

Do Not Disturb
My Mind. My Grind.
My Whole Entire Vibe

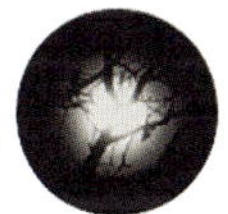

JesseDraxler @JesseDraxler
do you care if our species lasts forever?

NO	**50.5%**
NO	49.5%

I Got Everything I Asked For & I Hate It
May All Your Dreams Be Nightmares
Embrace Violence
I'm Only Scared Of You And Me
Your Ghost Reminding Me To Moisturize
Damage Leaking Out
The World Is Mine And I'm Thinking About You
Death Is A Theft Of Resources To Power
Death Is The Anesthesia That Saves Us From The Pain Of Infinity
We Can Never Be Happy In The Conceptual Mind
The Future Is Not The Solution To The Present
No Body Knows Me In The Streets
Bleeding Through The Band Aid
Crime SZN
Eating Citrus

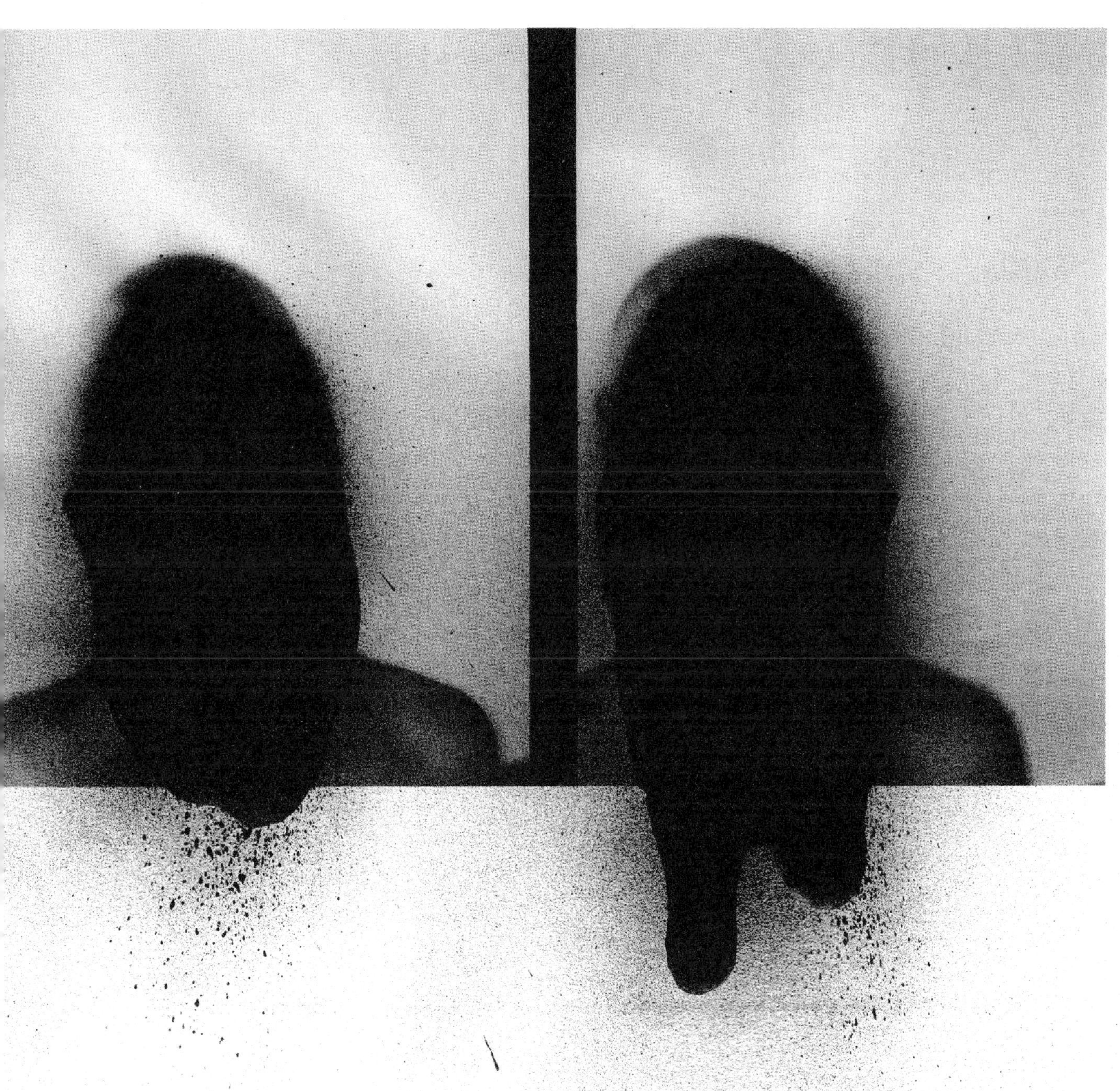

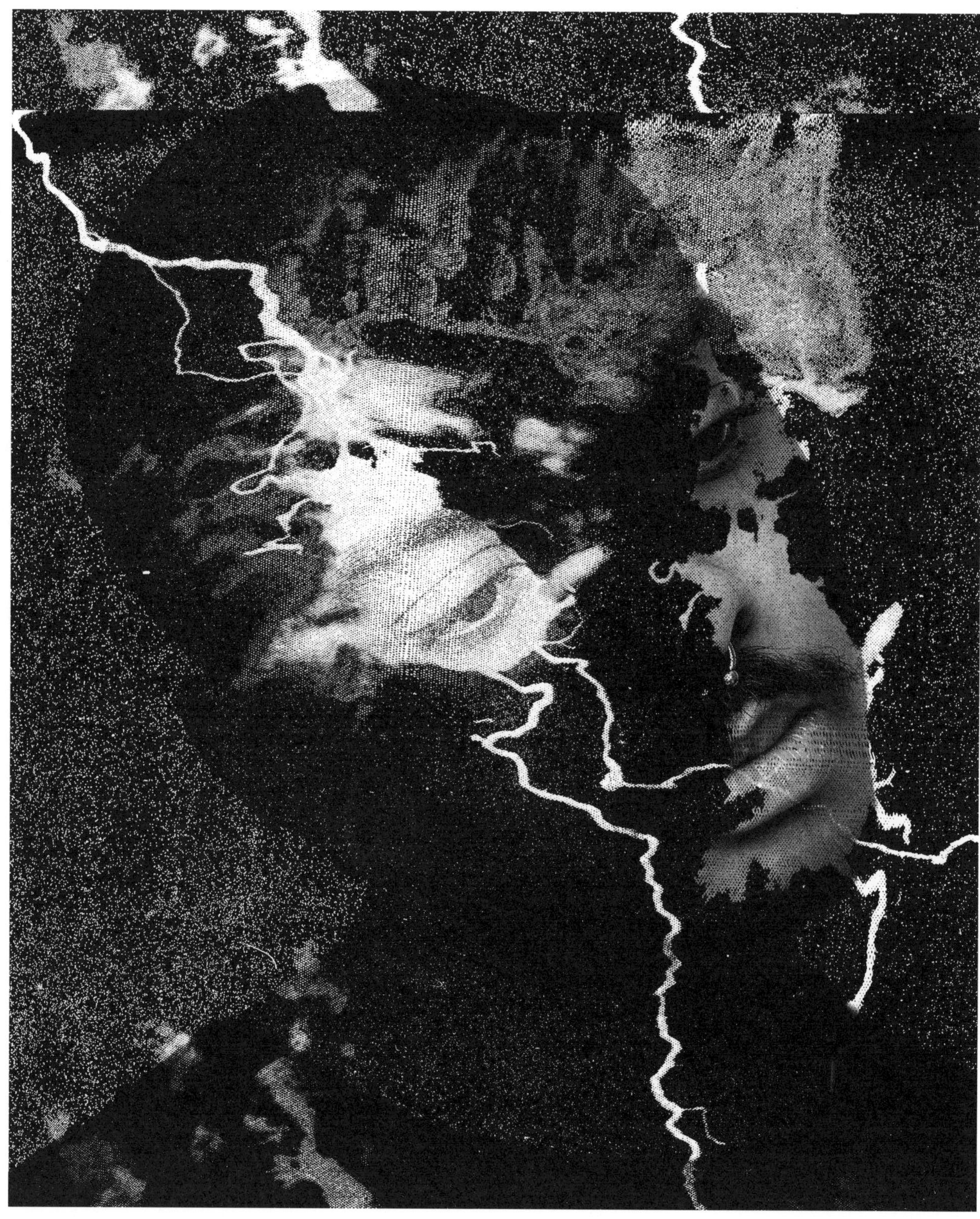

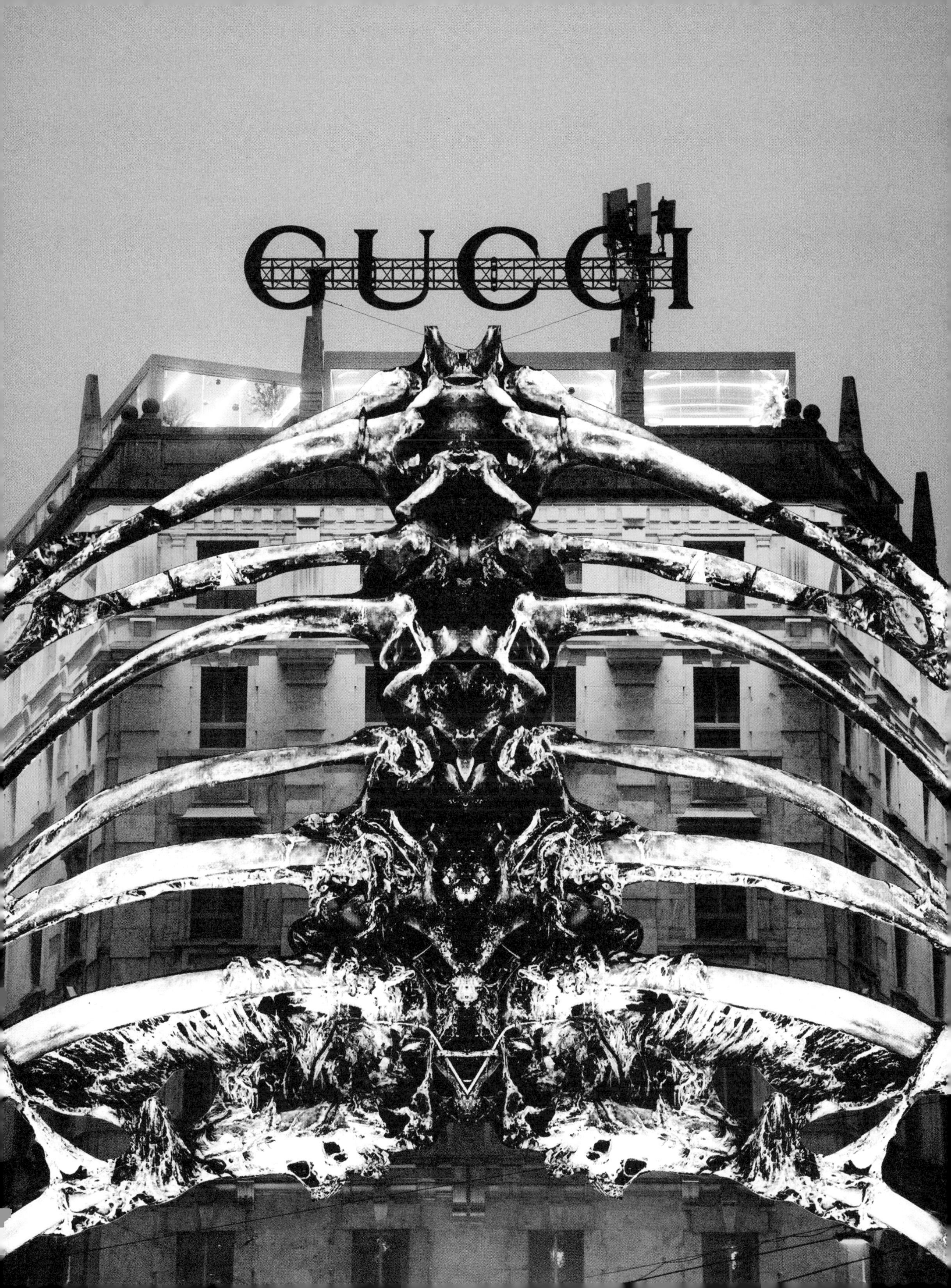
GUCCI

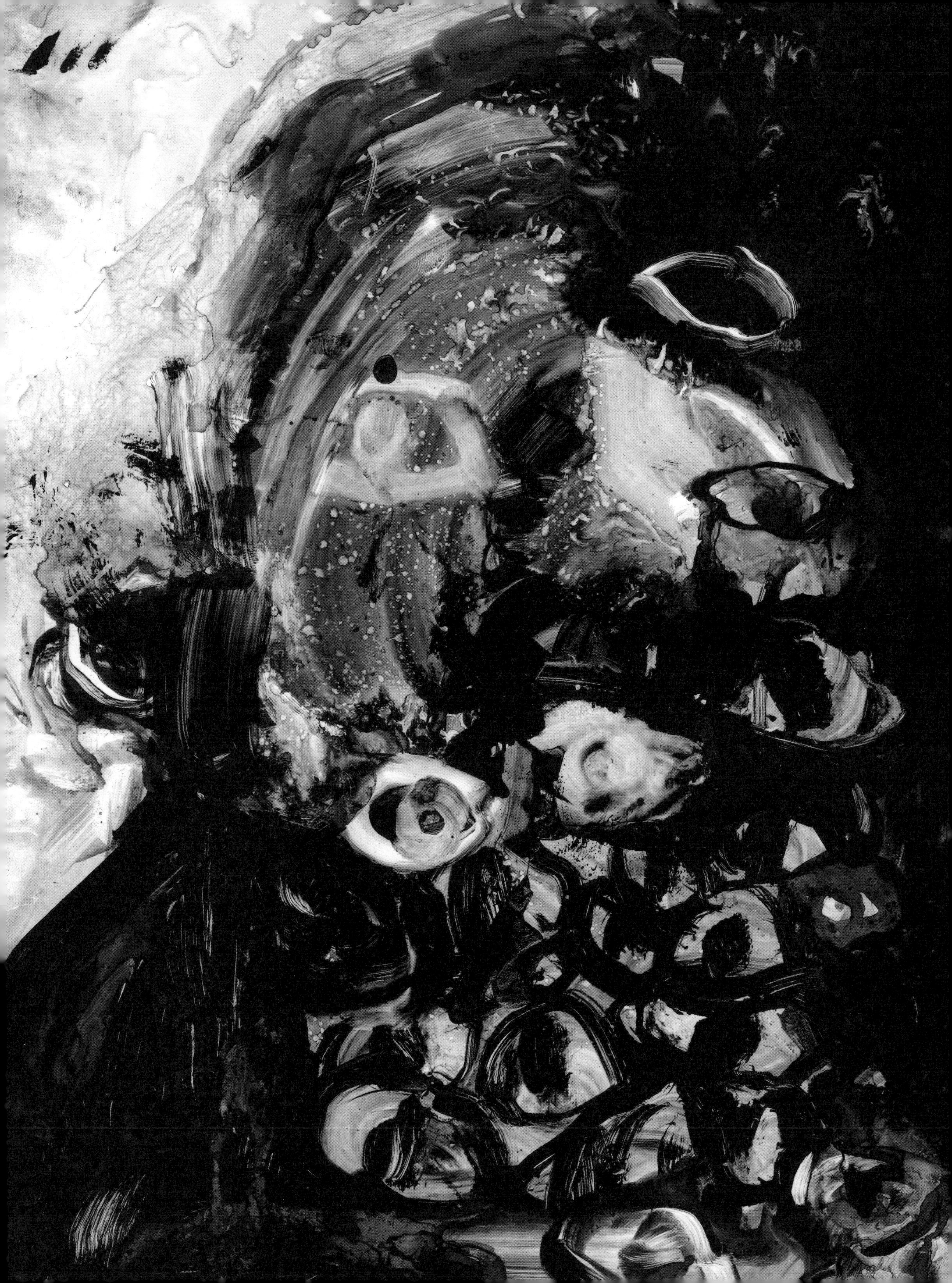

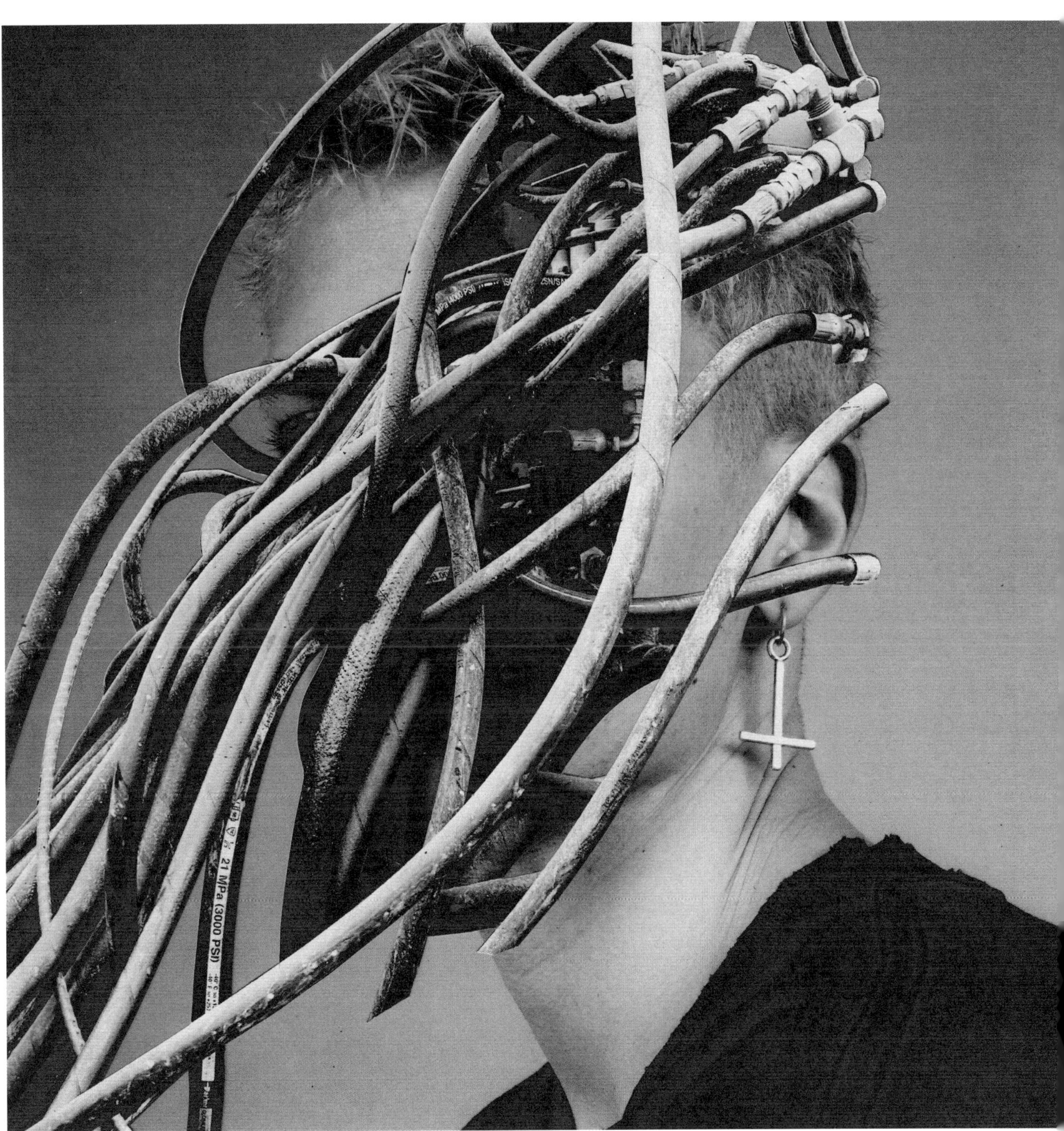
21 MPa (3000 PSI)

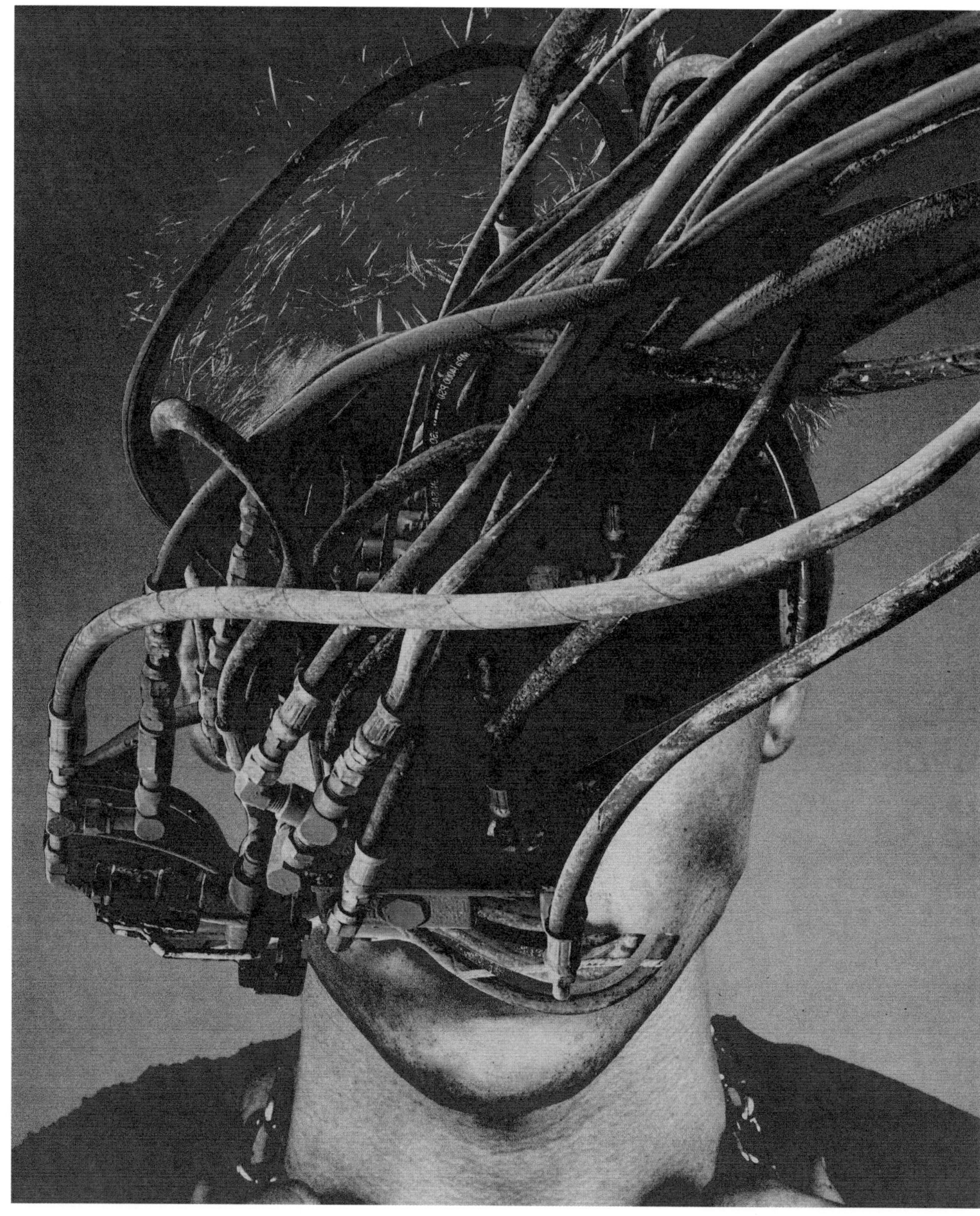

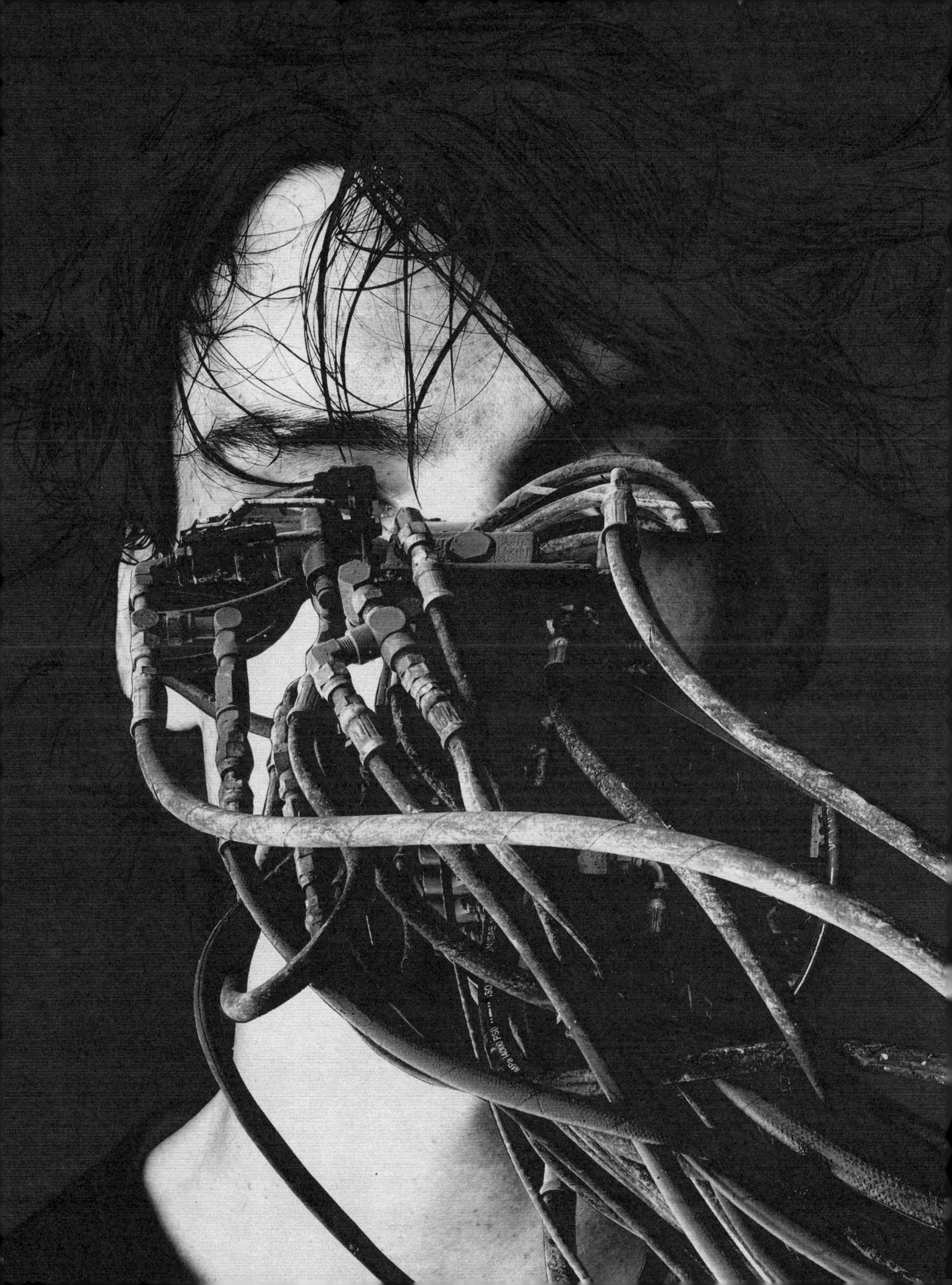

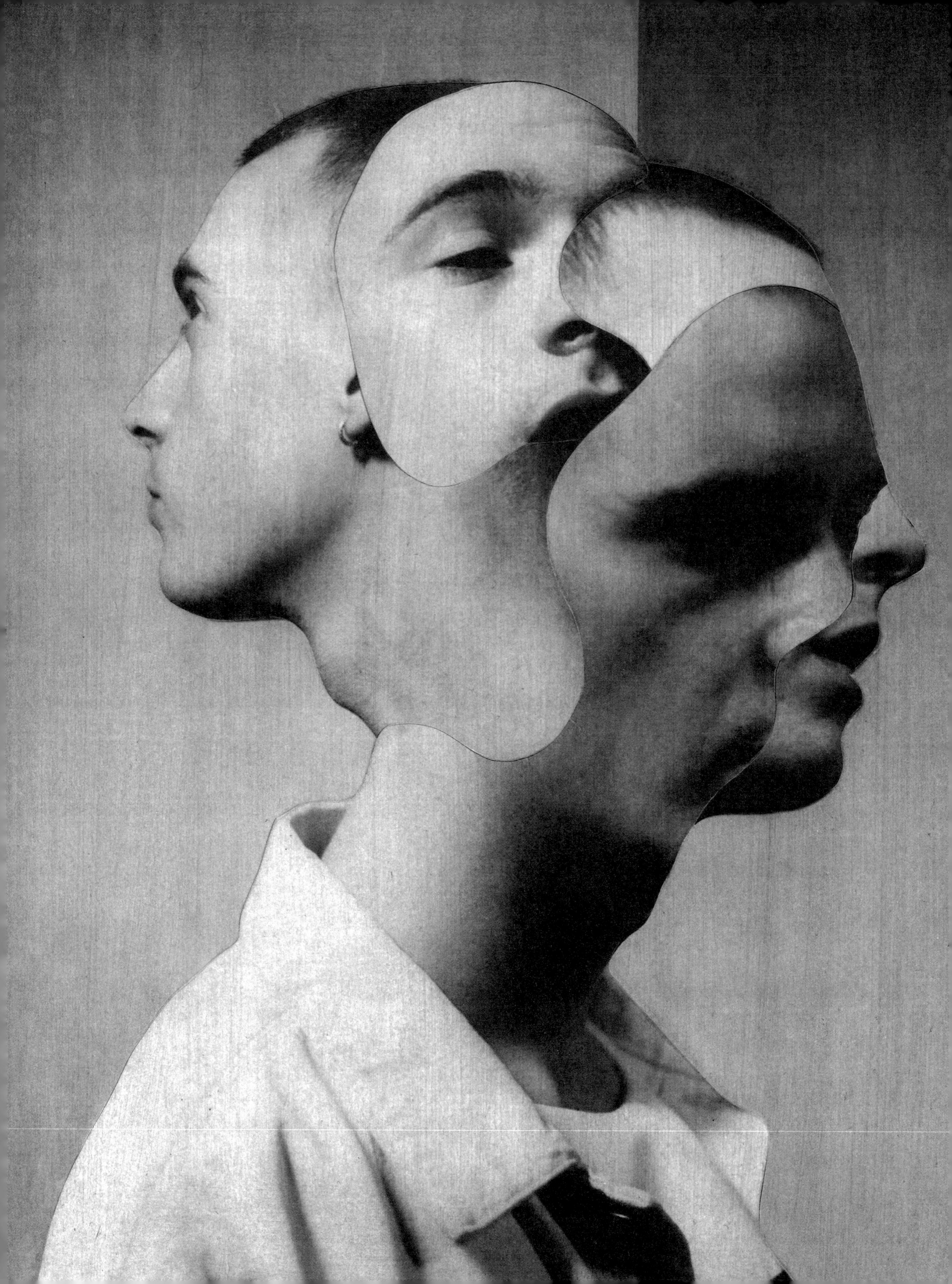

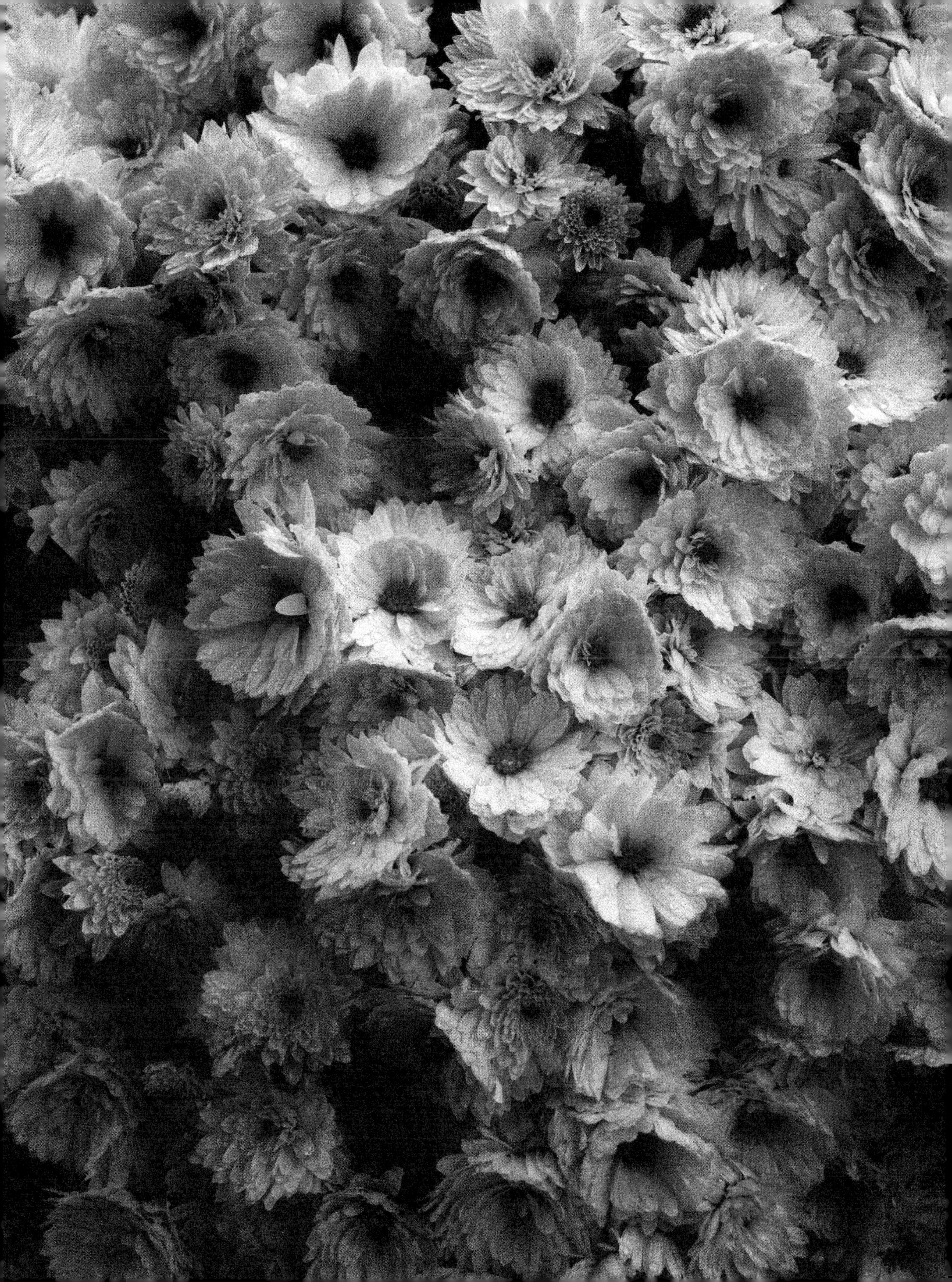

FTW

FOR THE WIN	FUCK THE WORLD
20%	80%

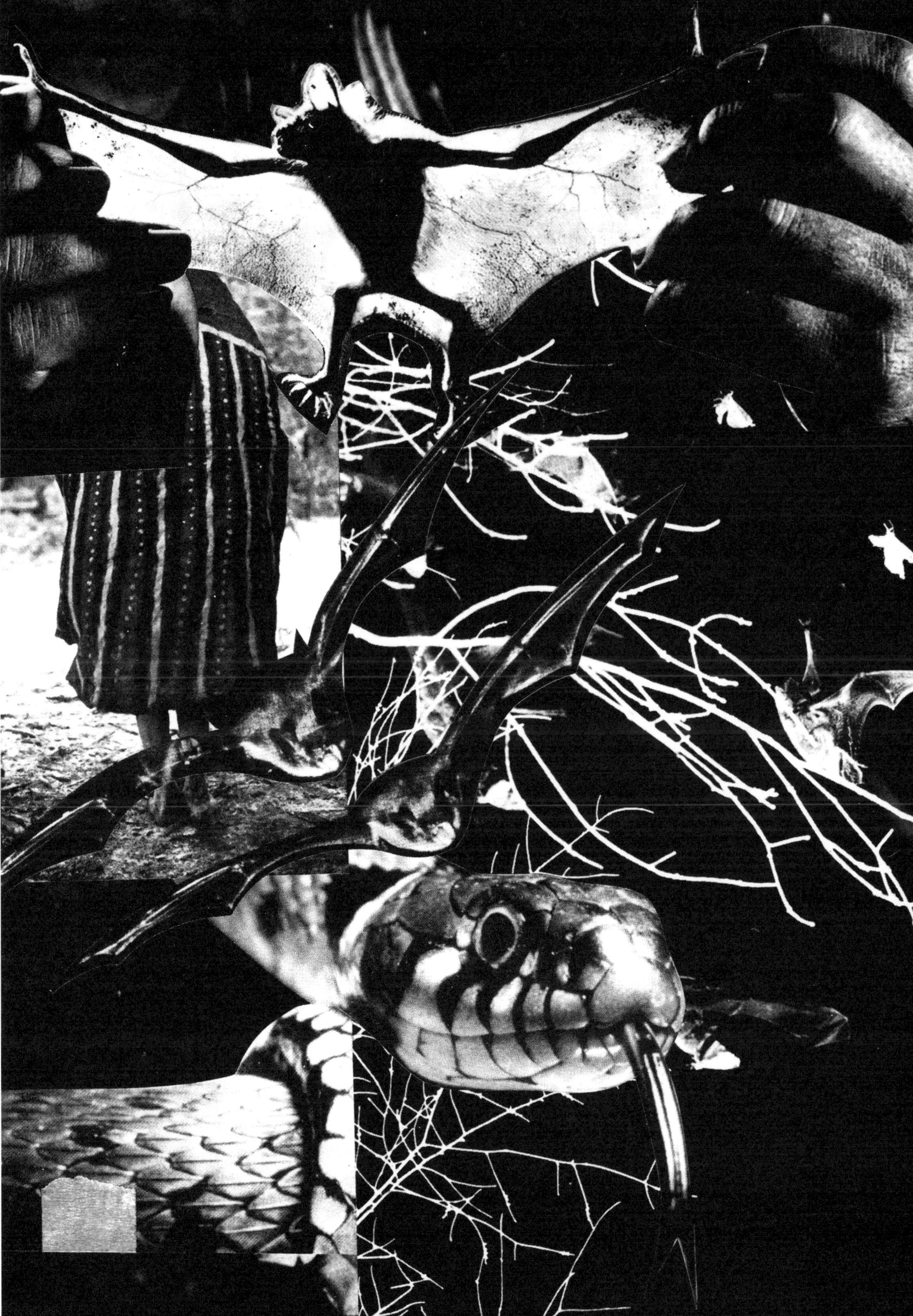

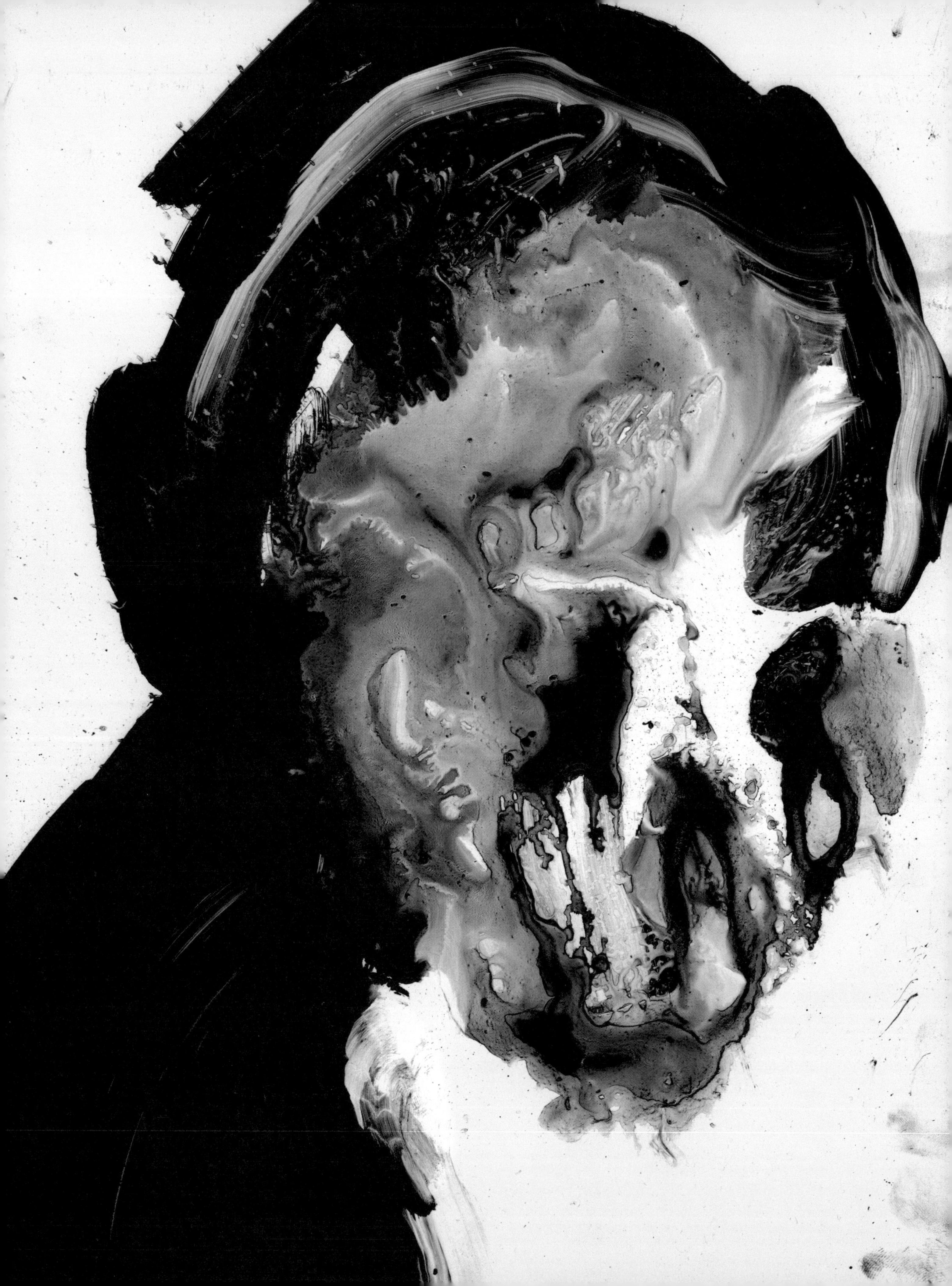

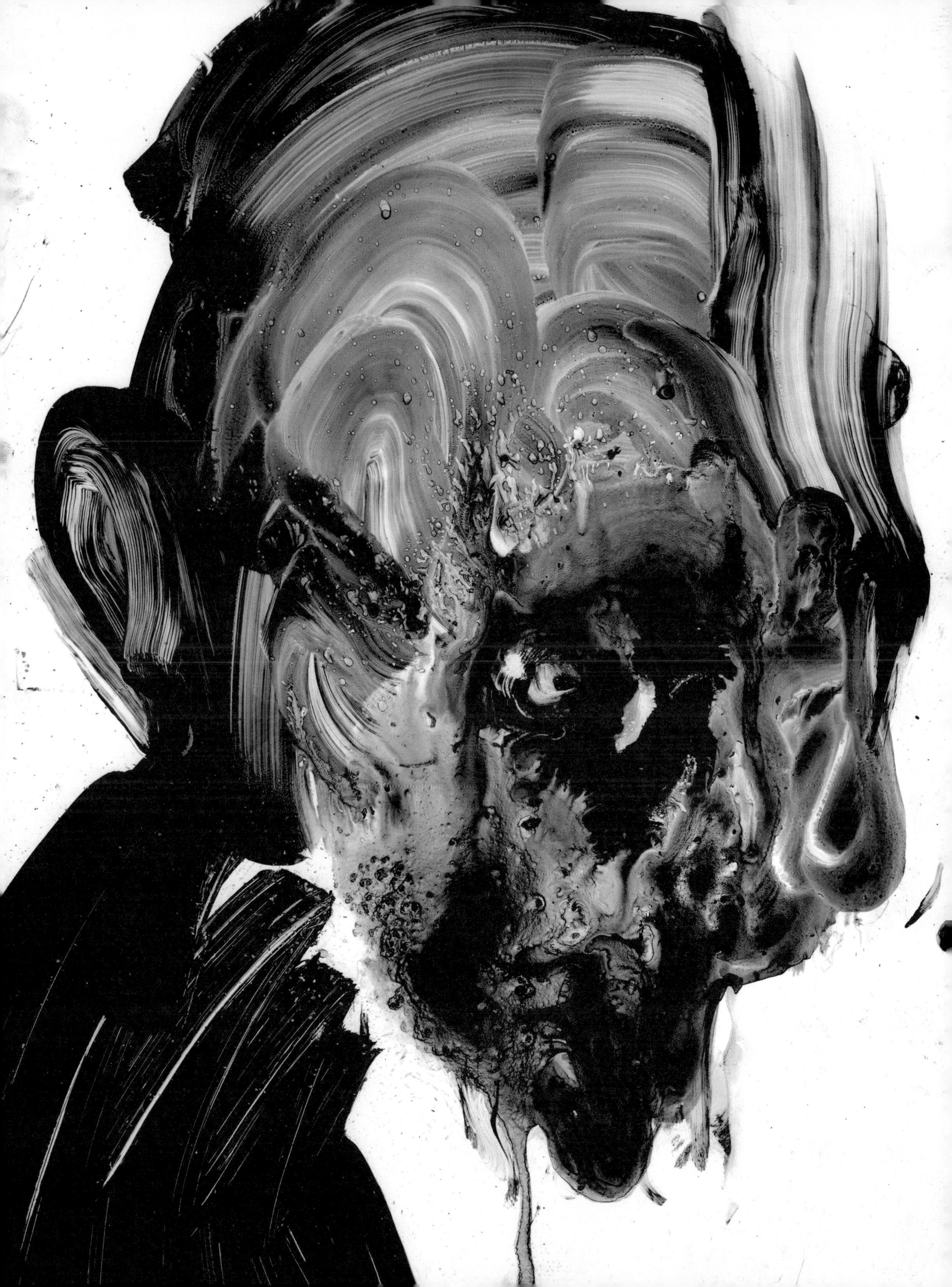

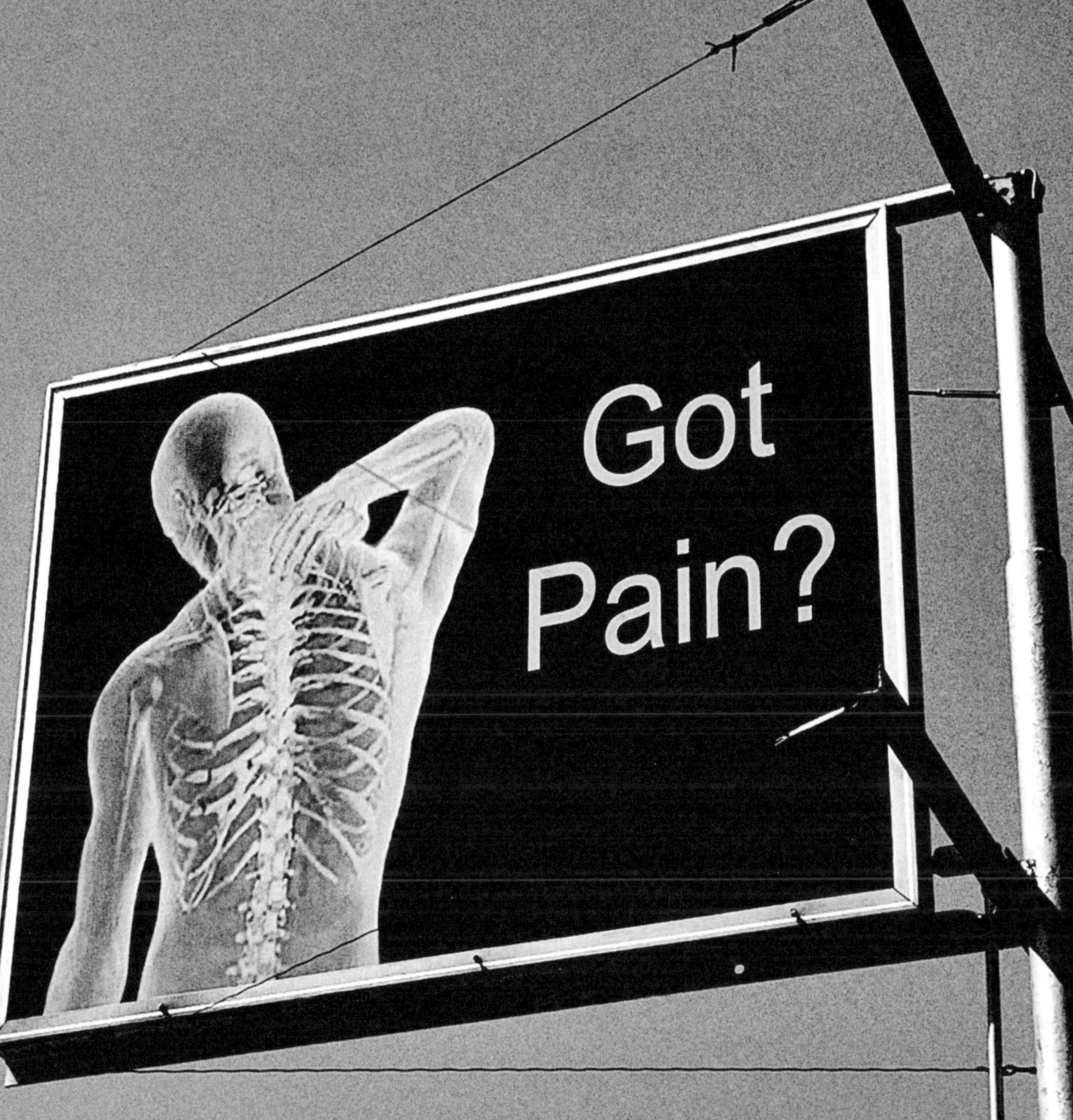
Got
Pain?

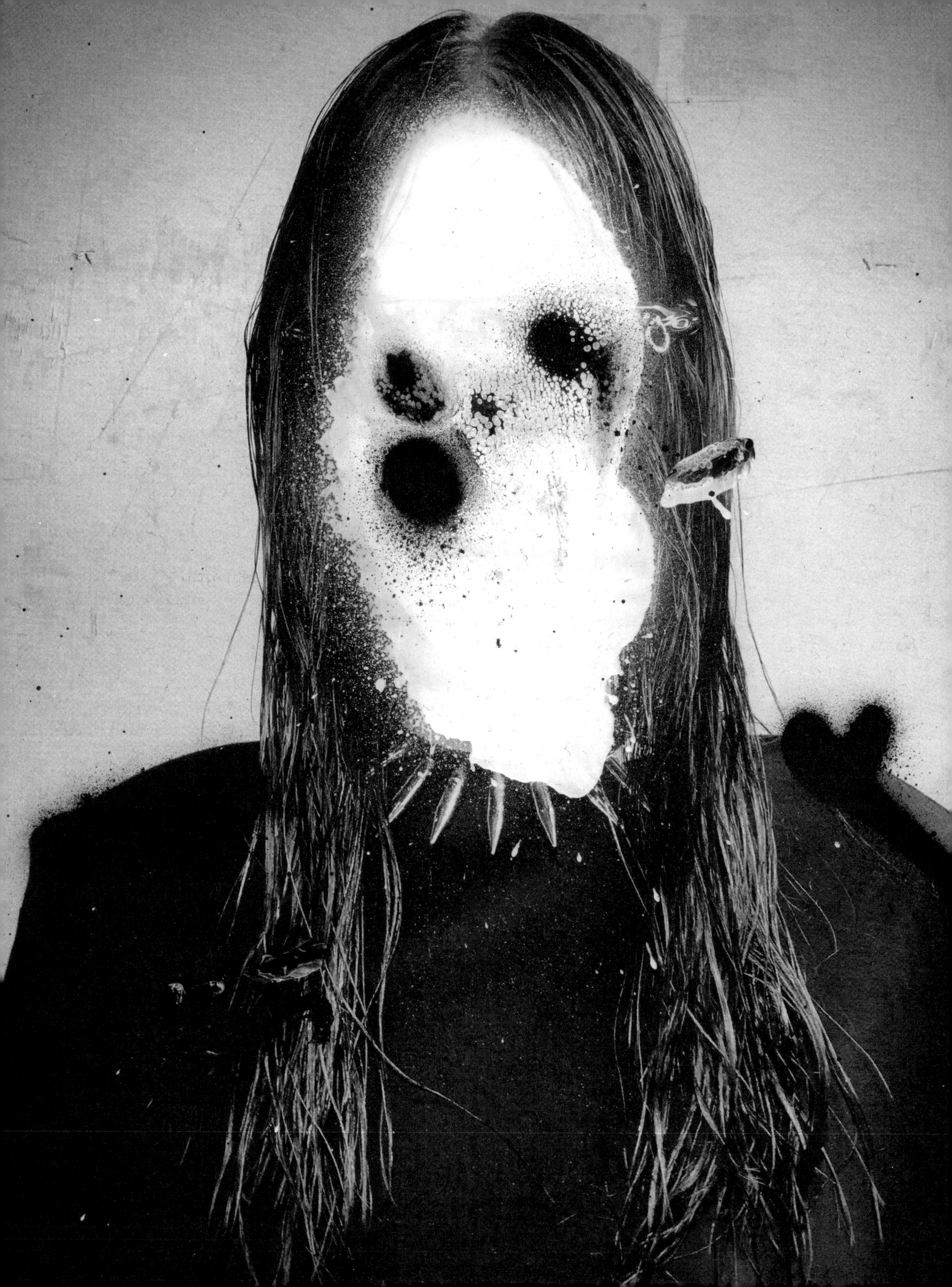

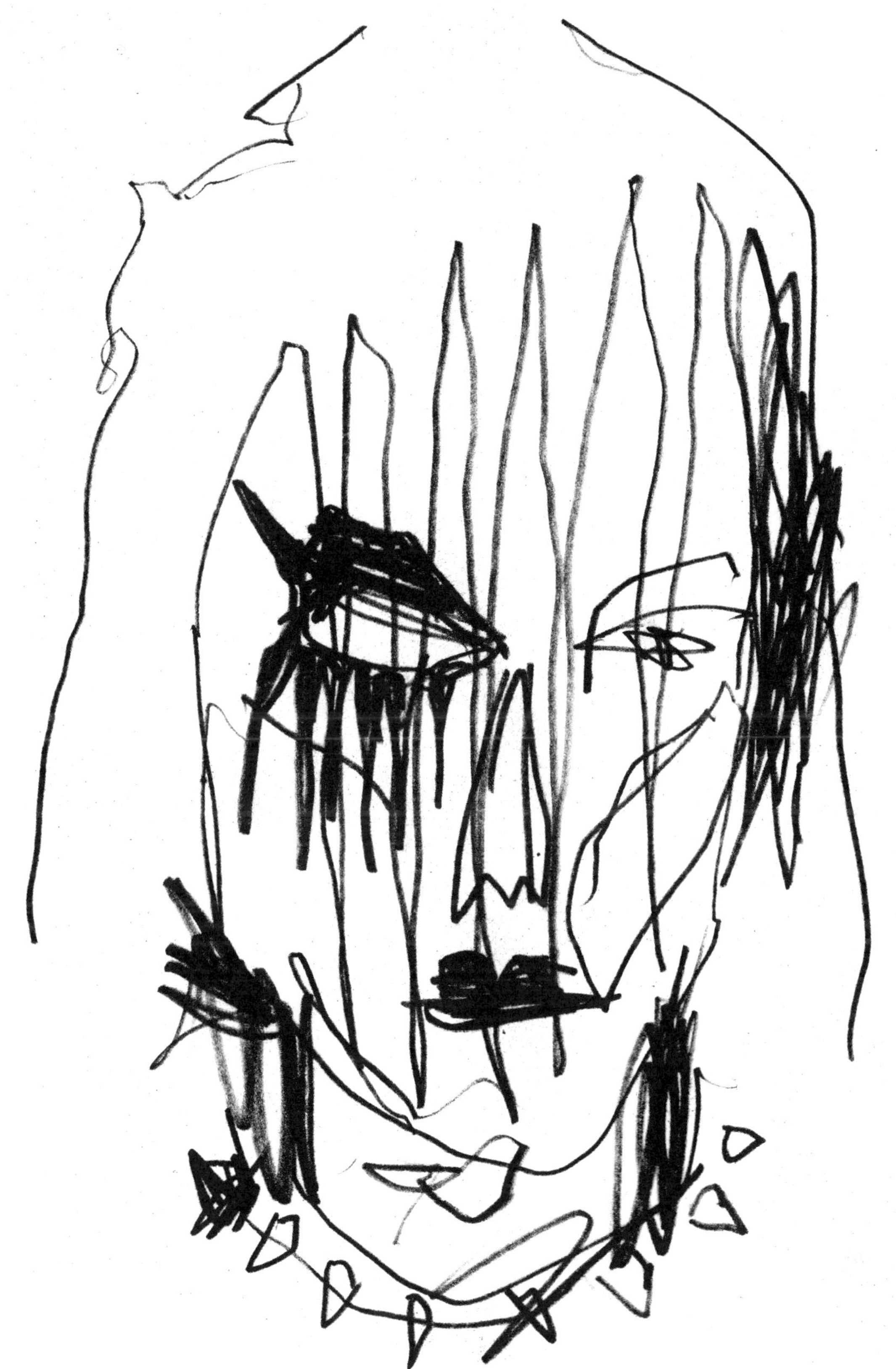

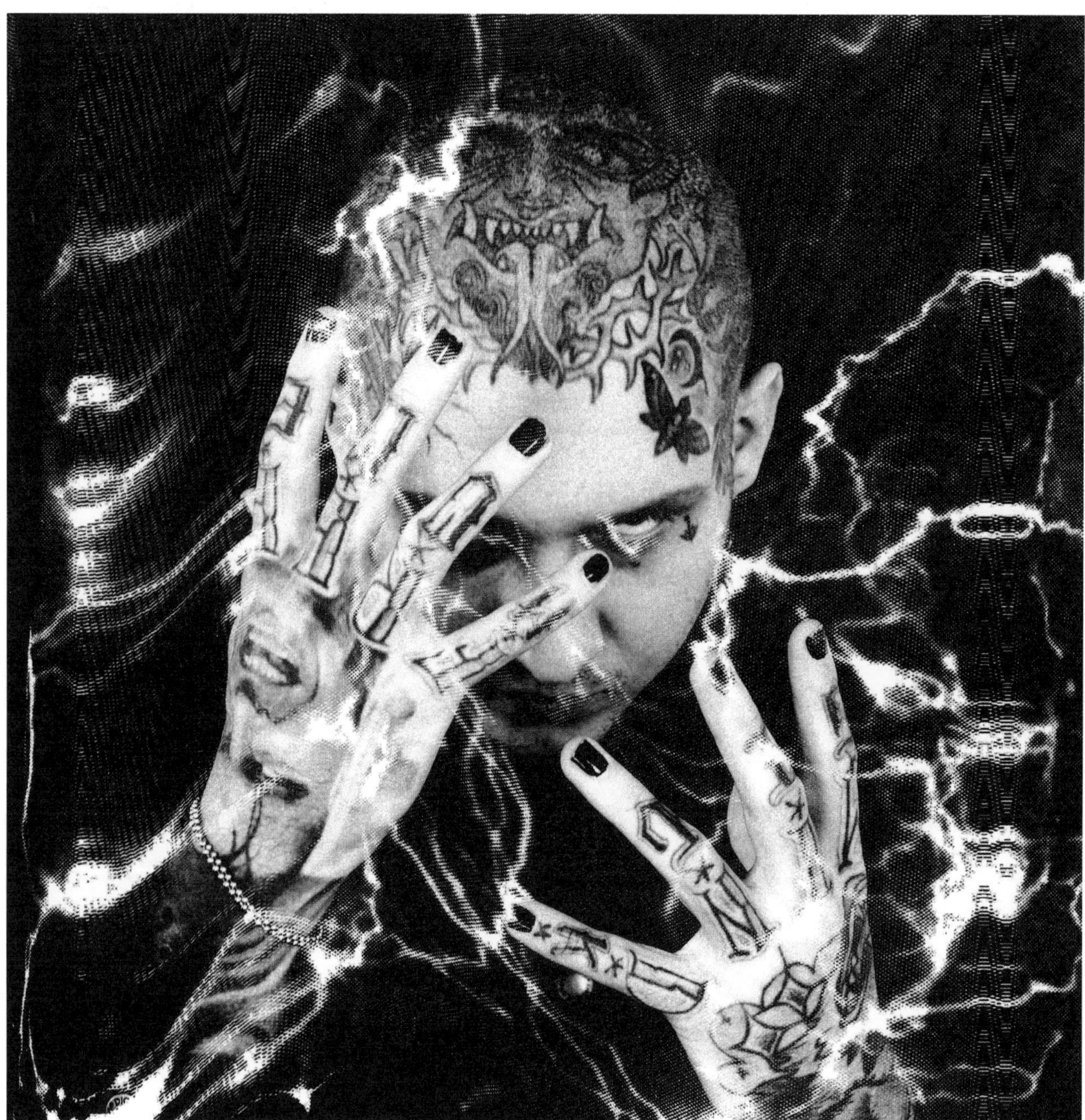

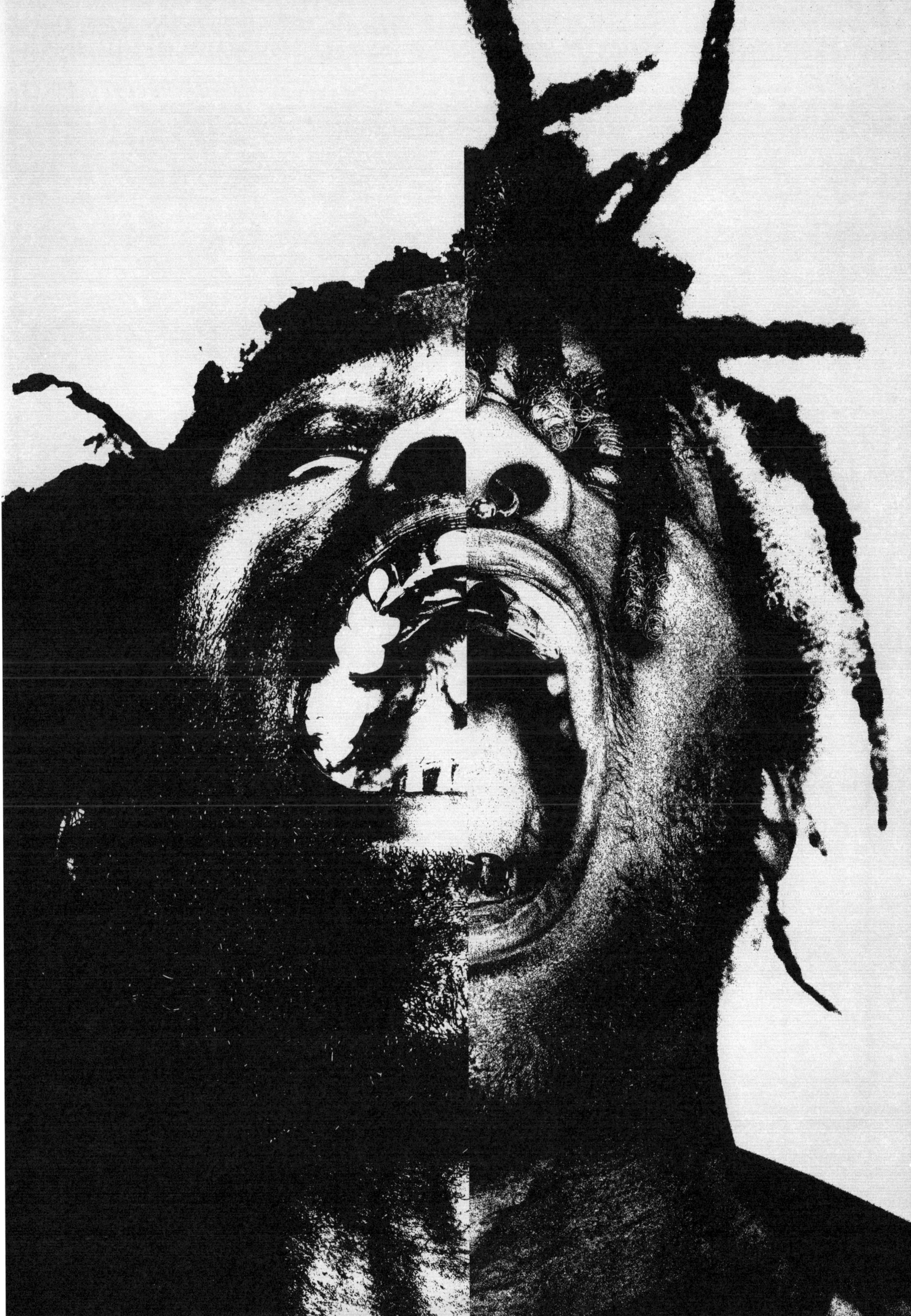

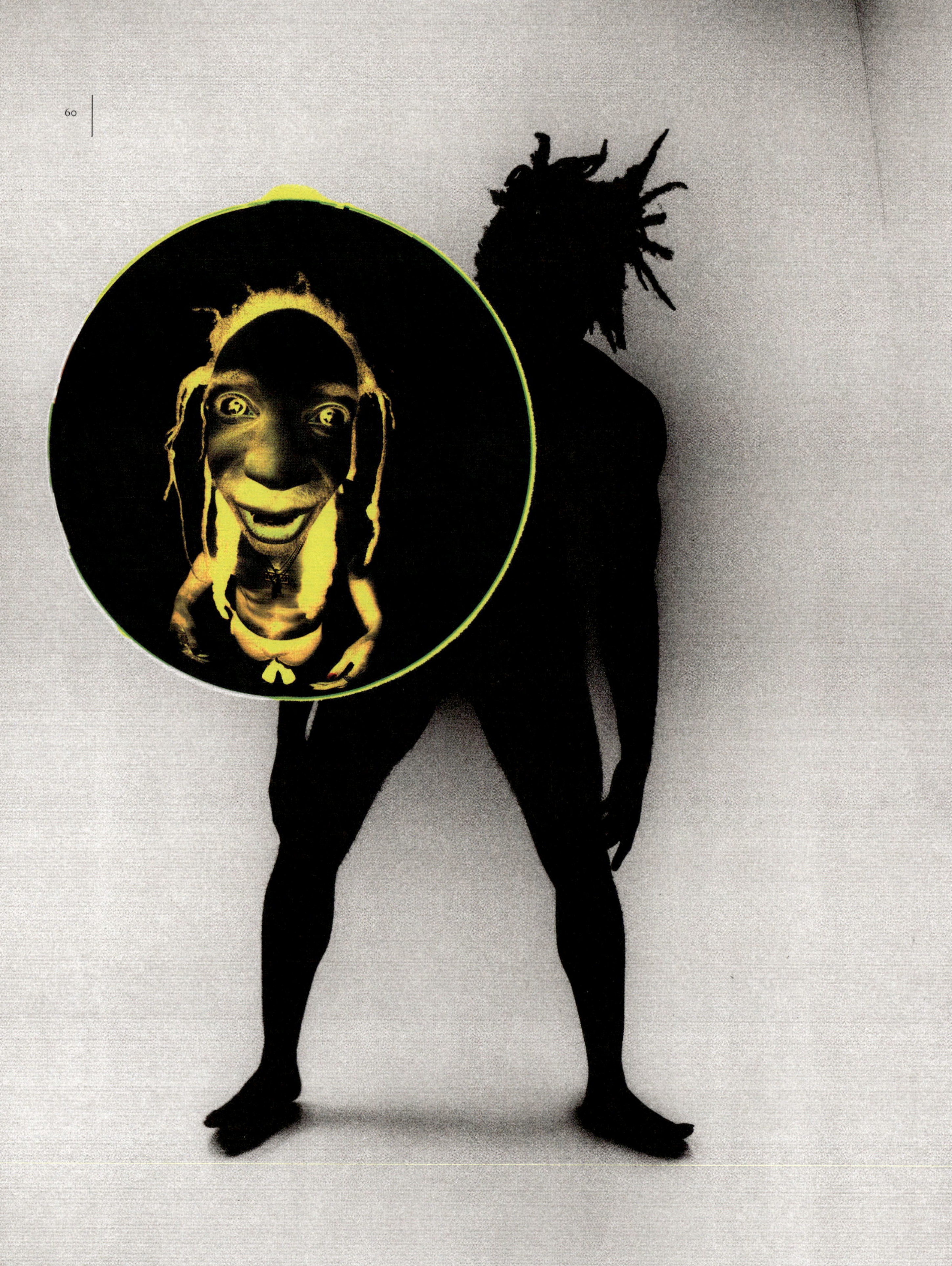

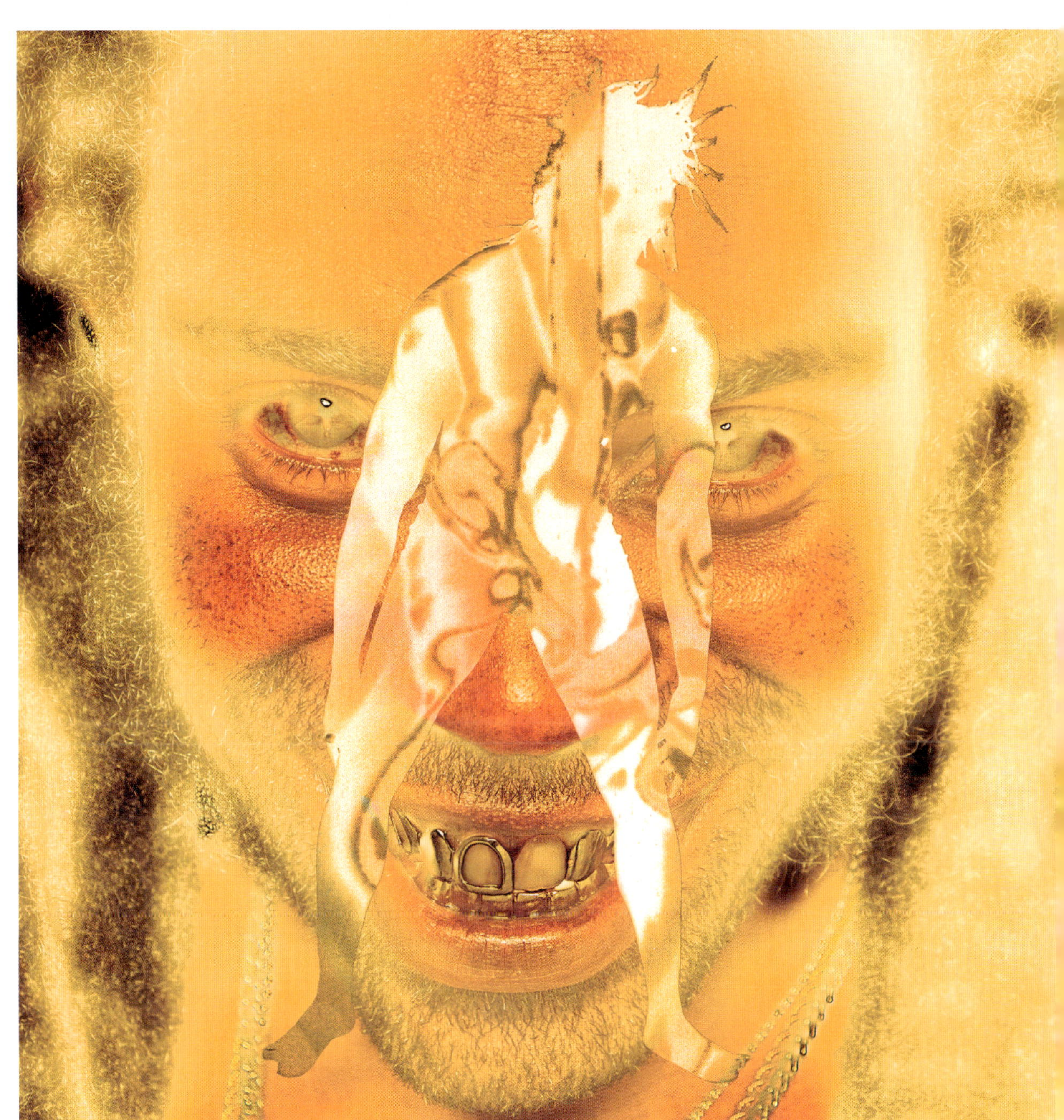

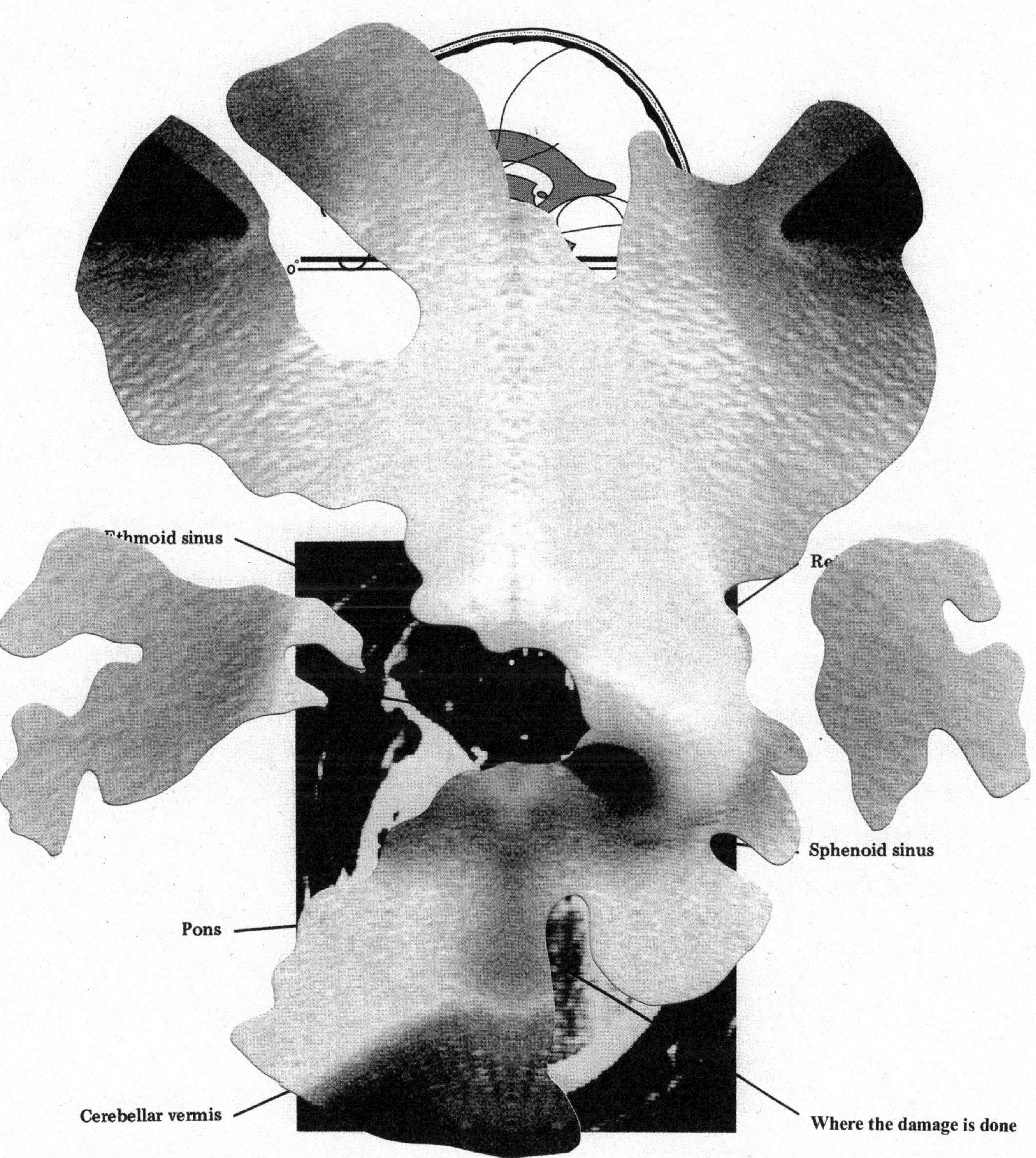
Ethmoid sinus
Sphenoid sinus
Pons
Cerebellar vermis
Where the damage is done
4

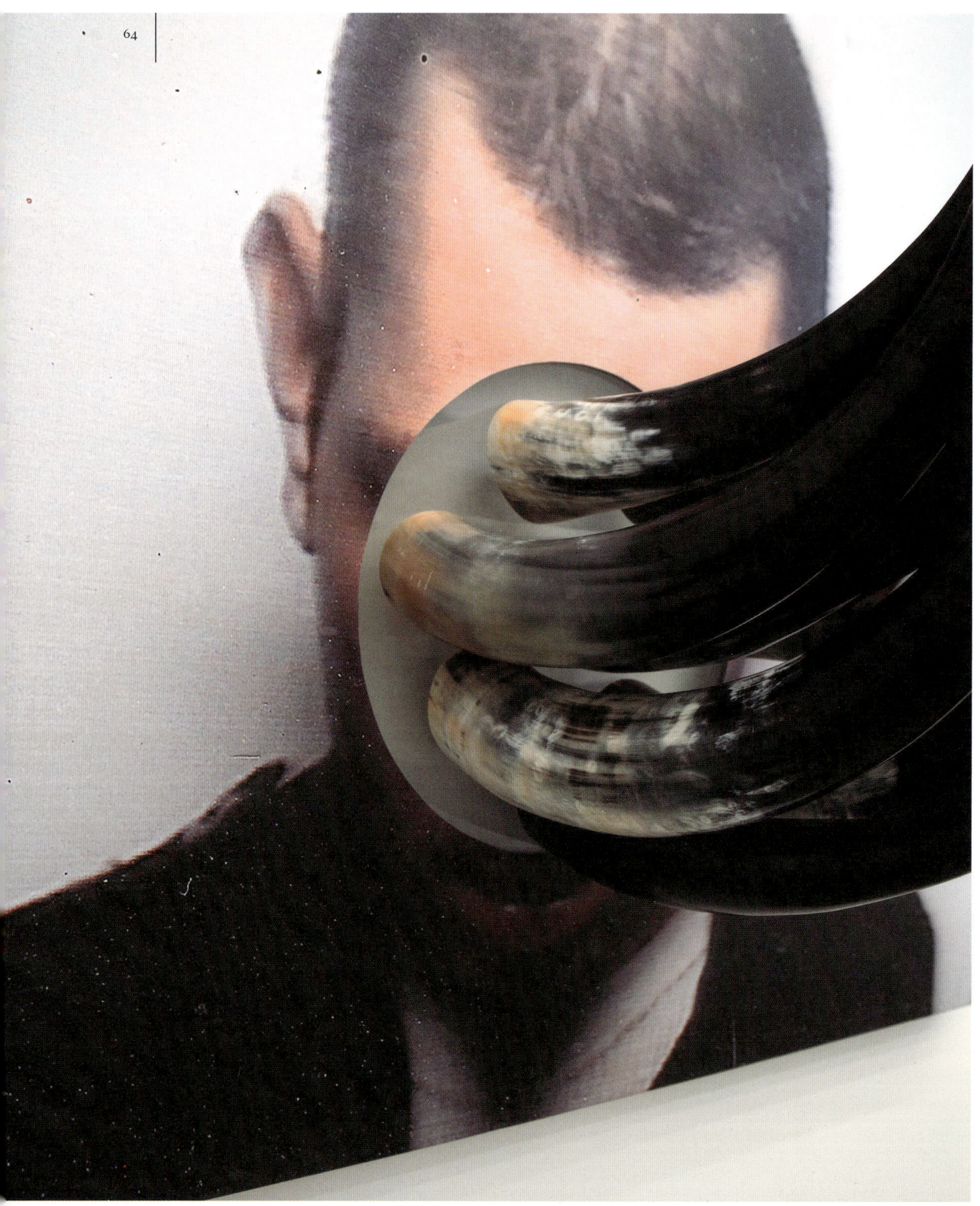

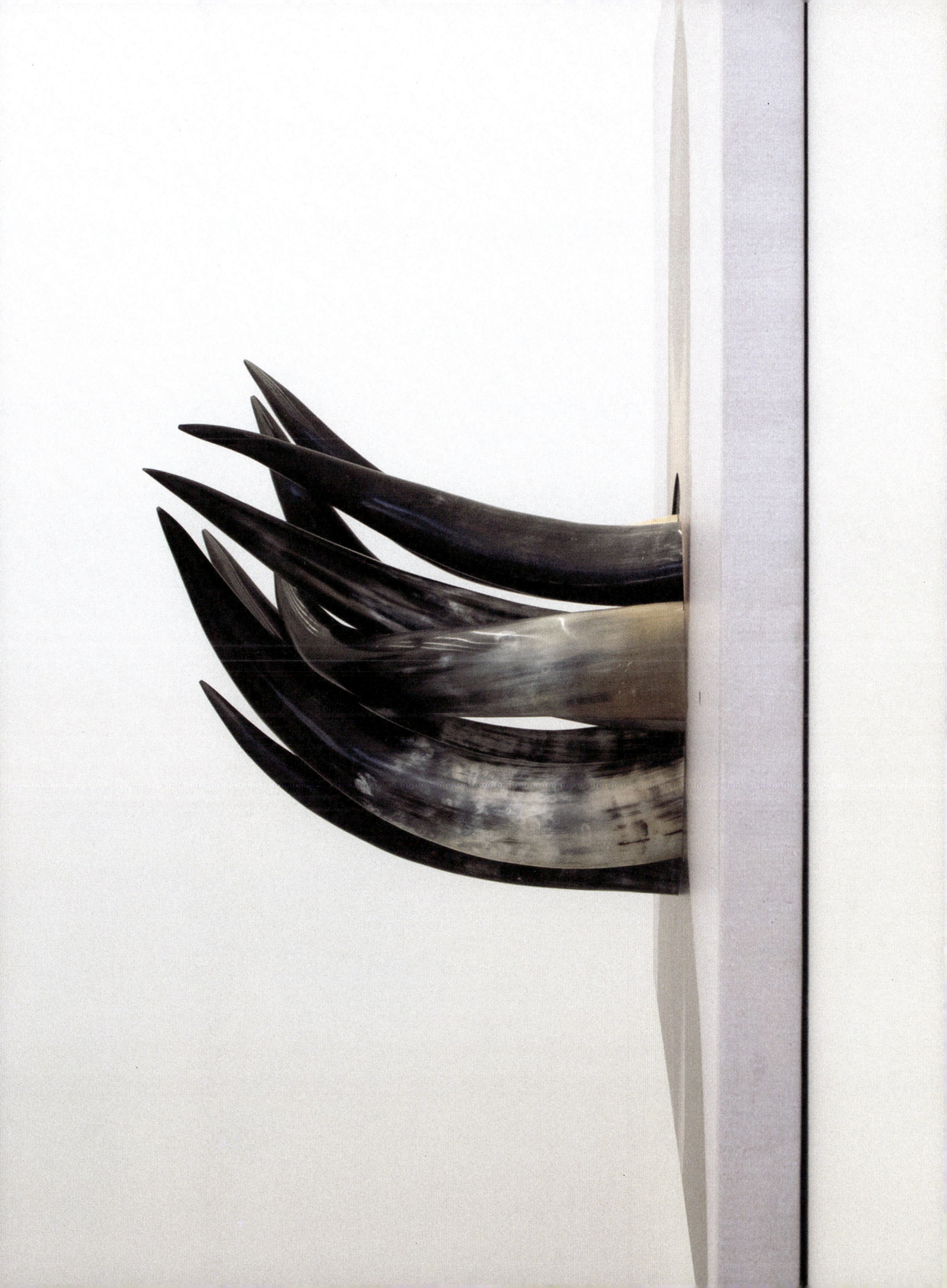

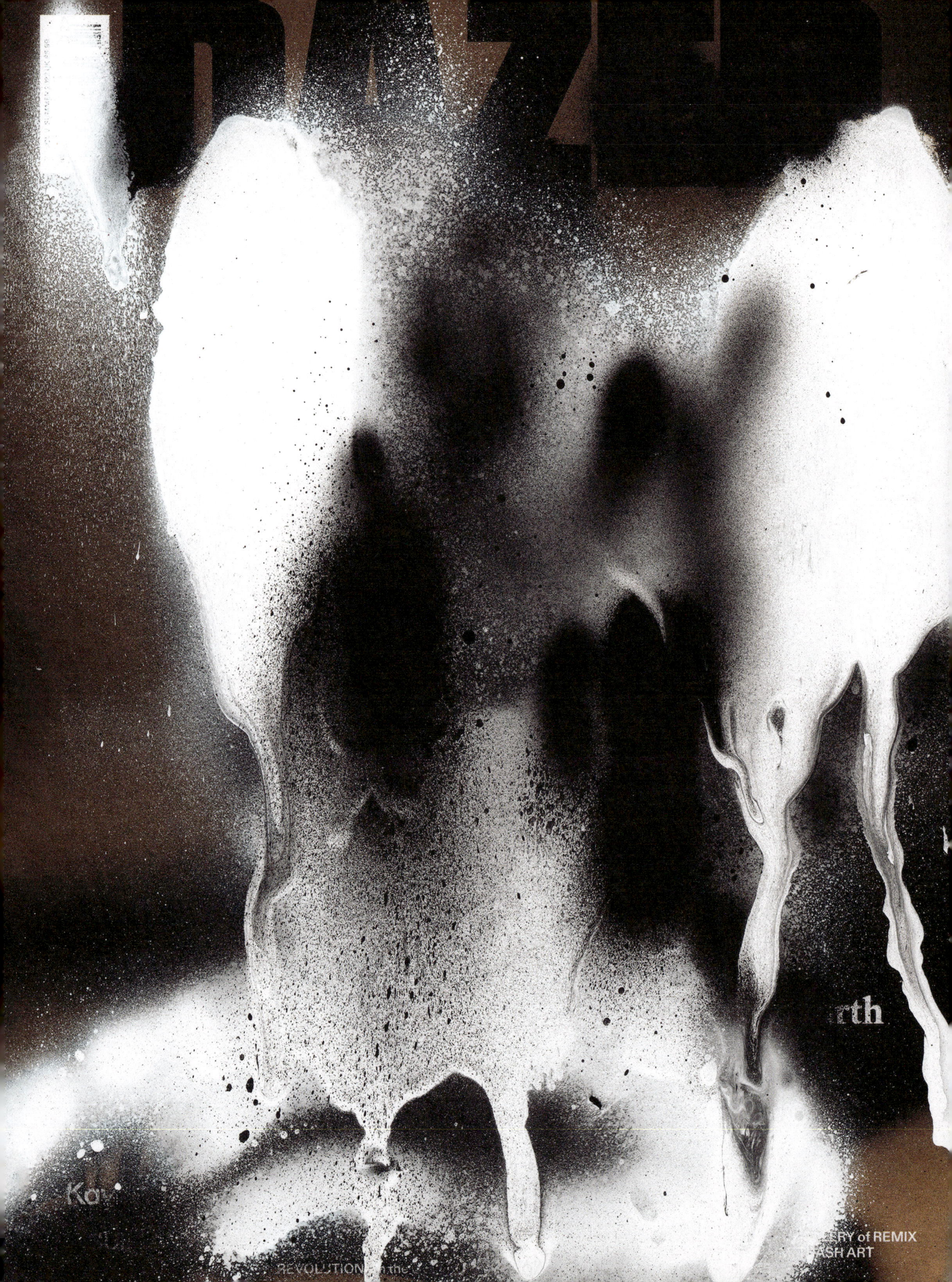
DAZED
rth
Ka
ERY of REMIX
ASH ART
REVOLUTION in the

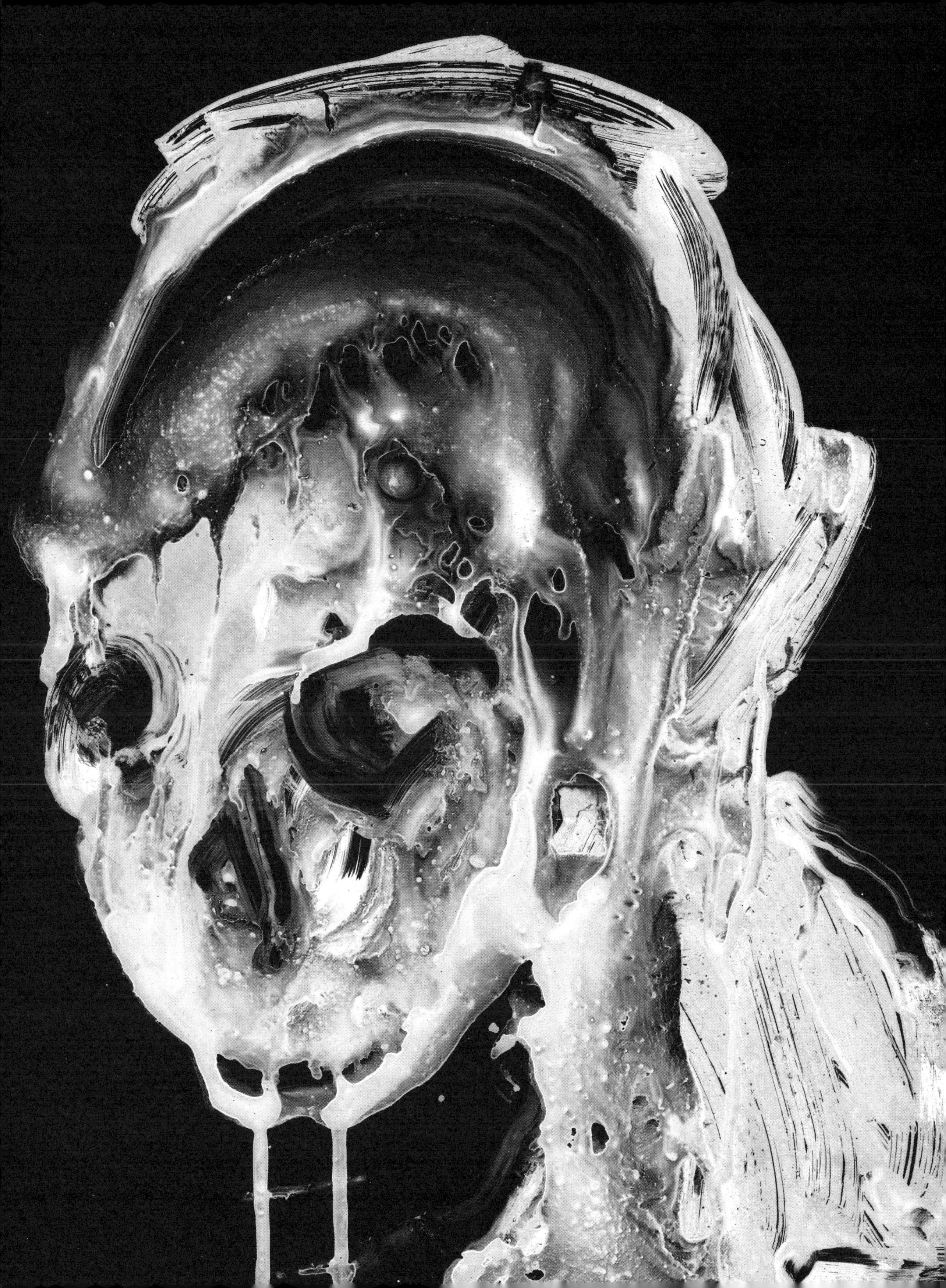

Alright so then I'm looking at the standard long wait after that for processing?

I'd like to frame this differently for you. I'm helping you get paid [redacted] from a major corporation.

If you do as we ask, you will get paid and it will not be a long wait

i will call you in a moment

Read 12:24 PM

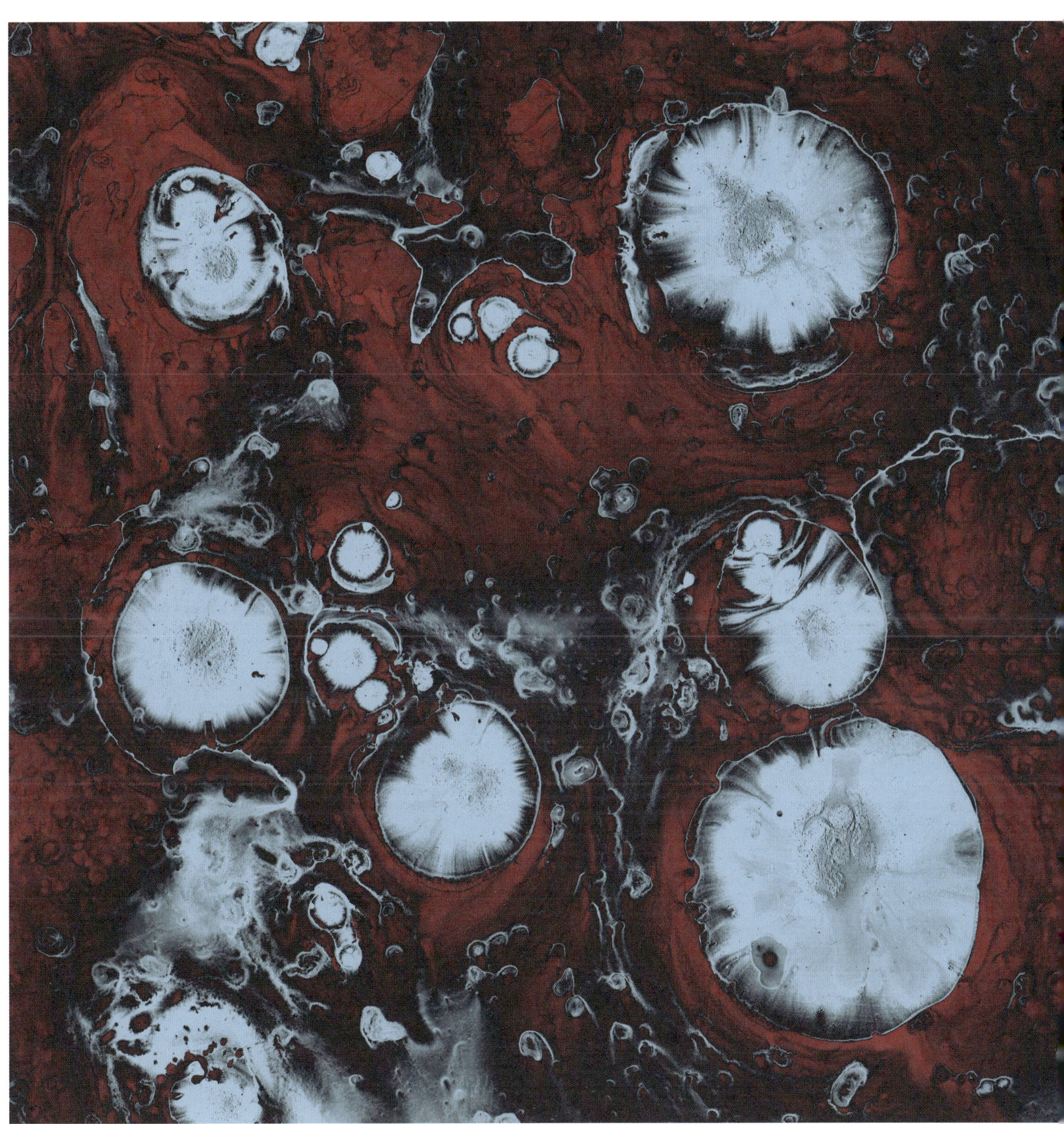

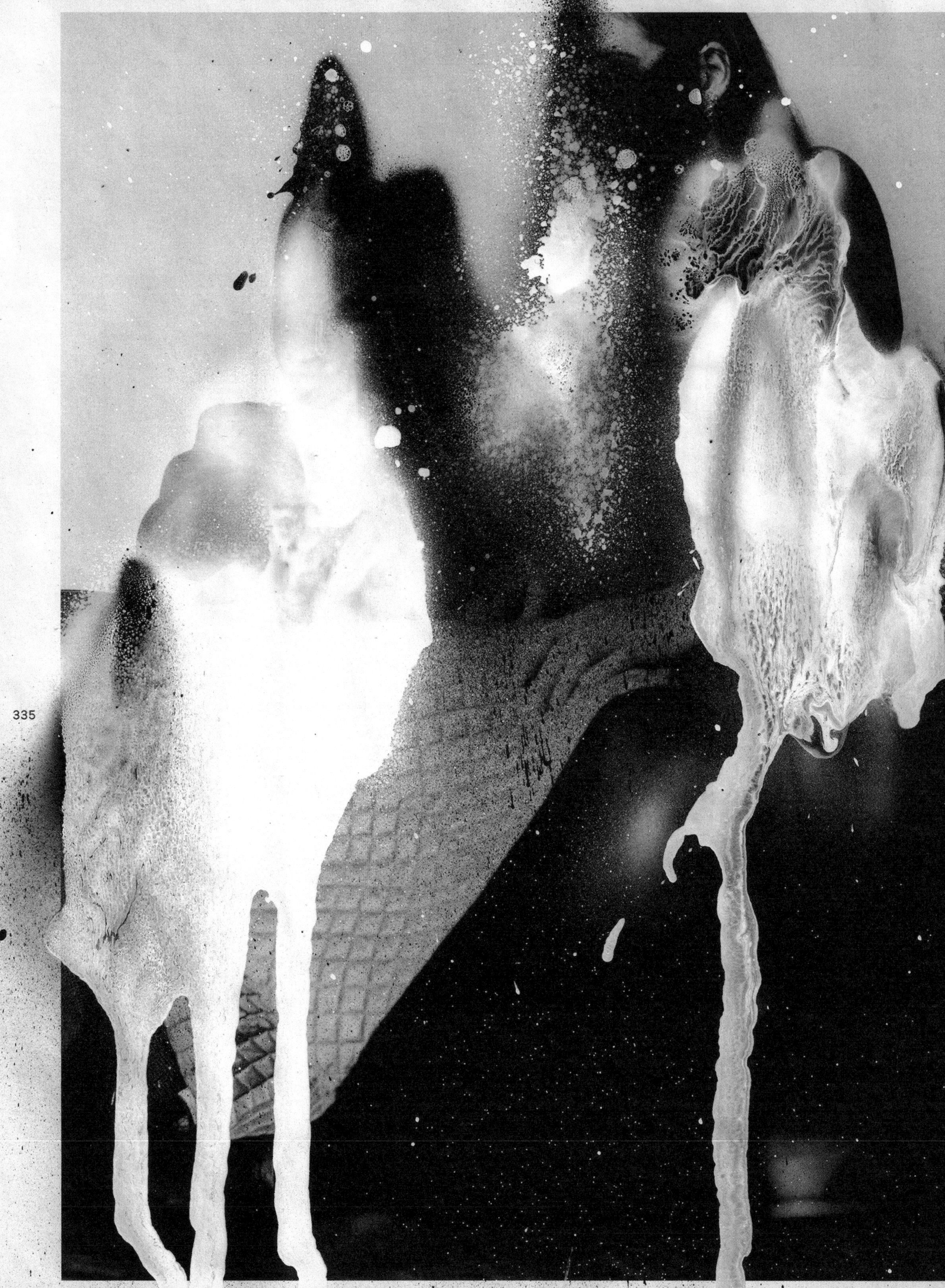

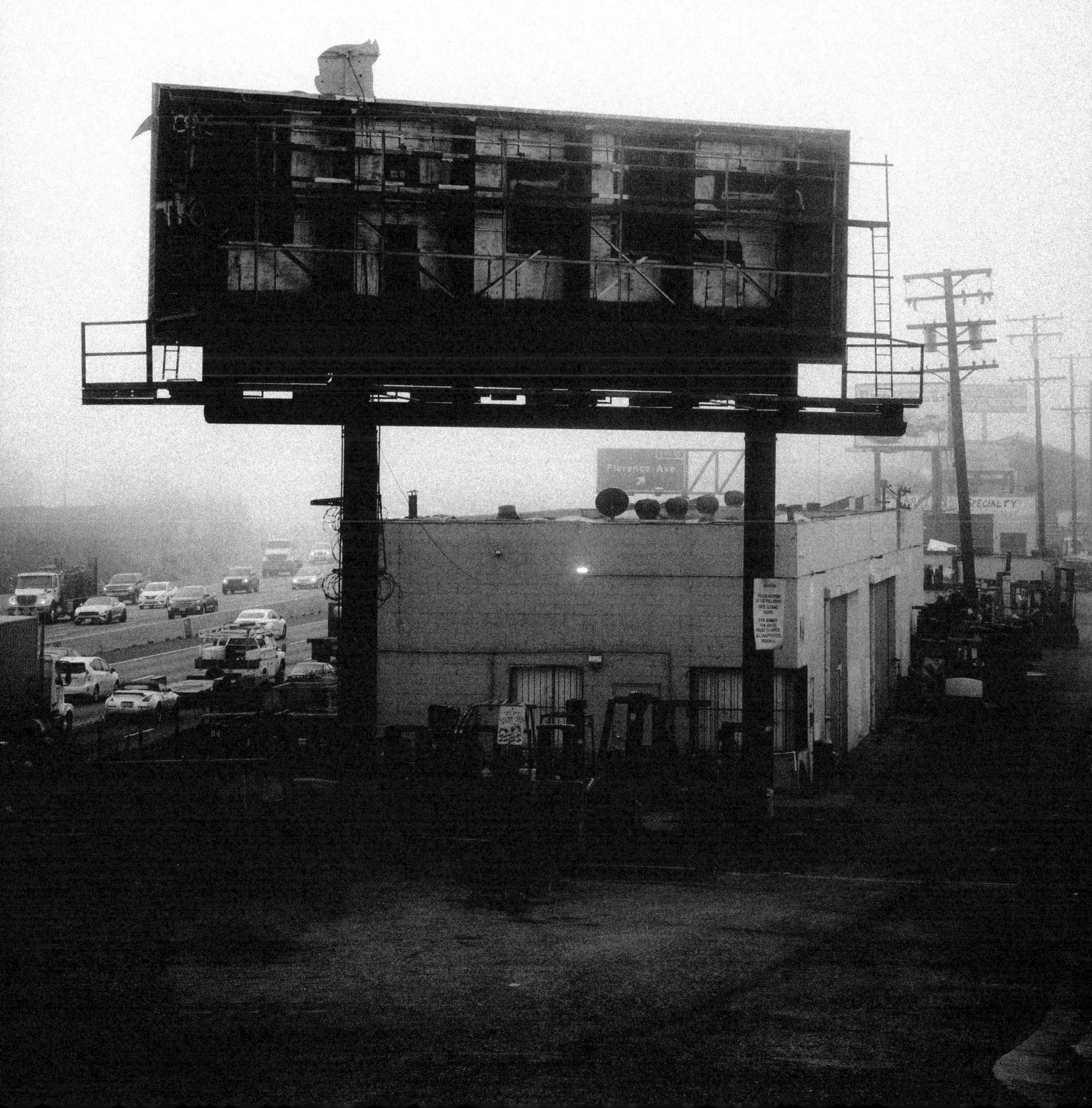
Florence Ave
SPECIALTY

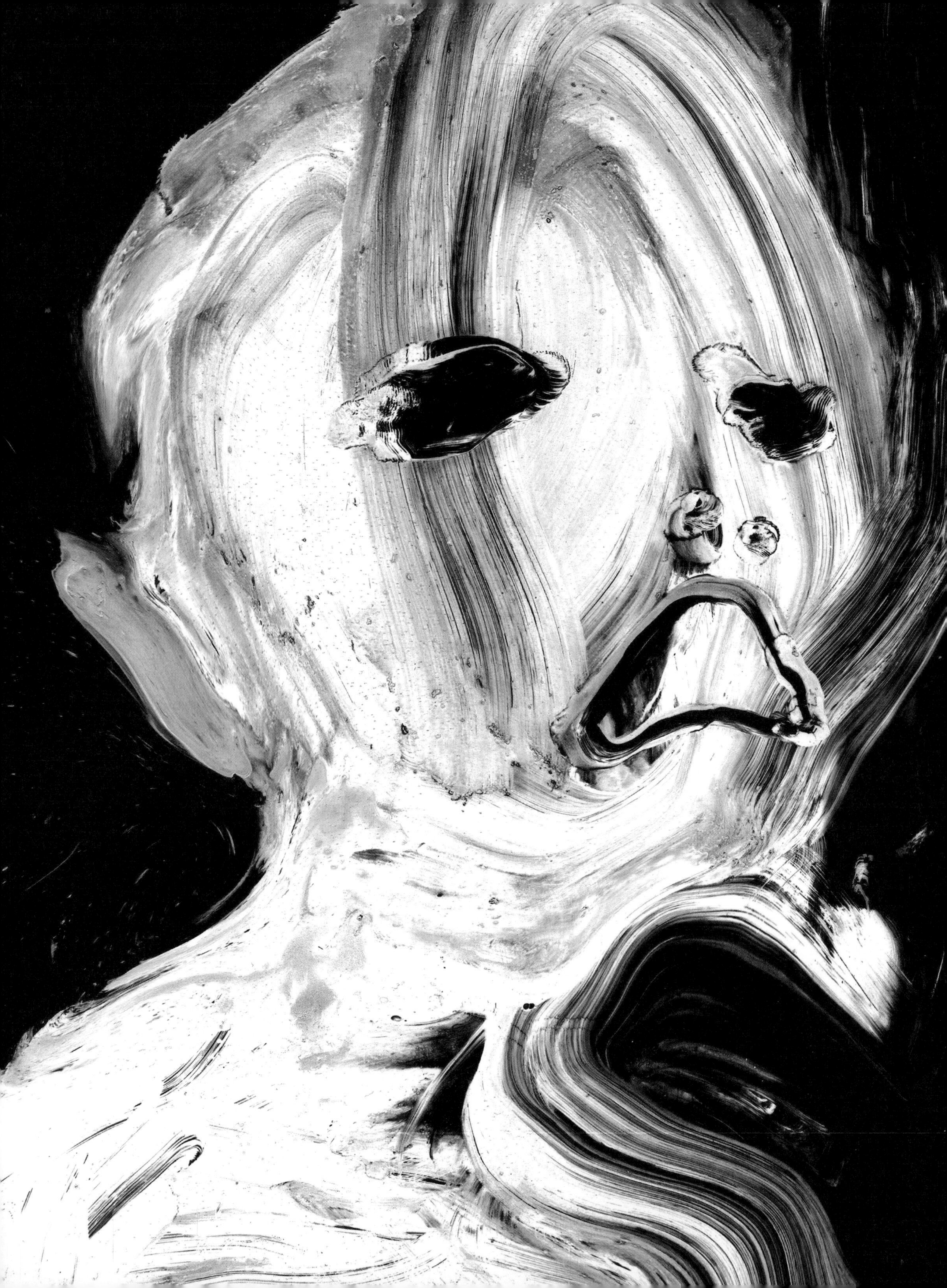

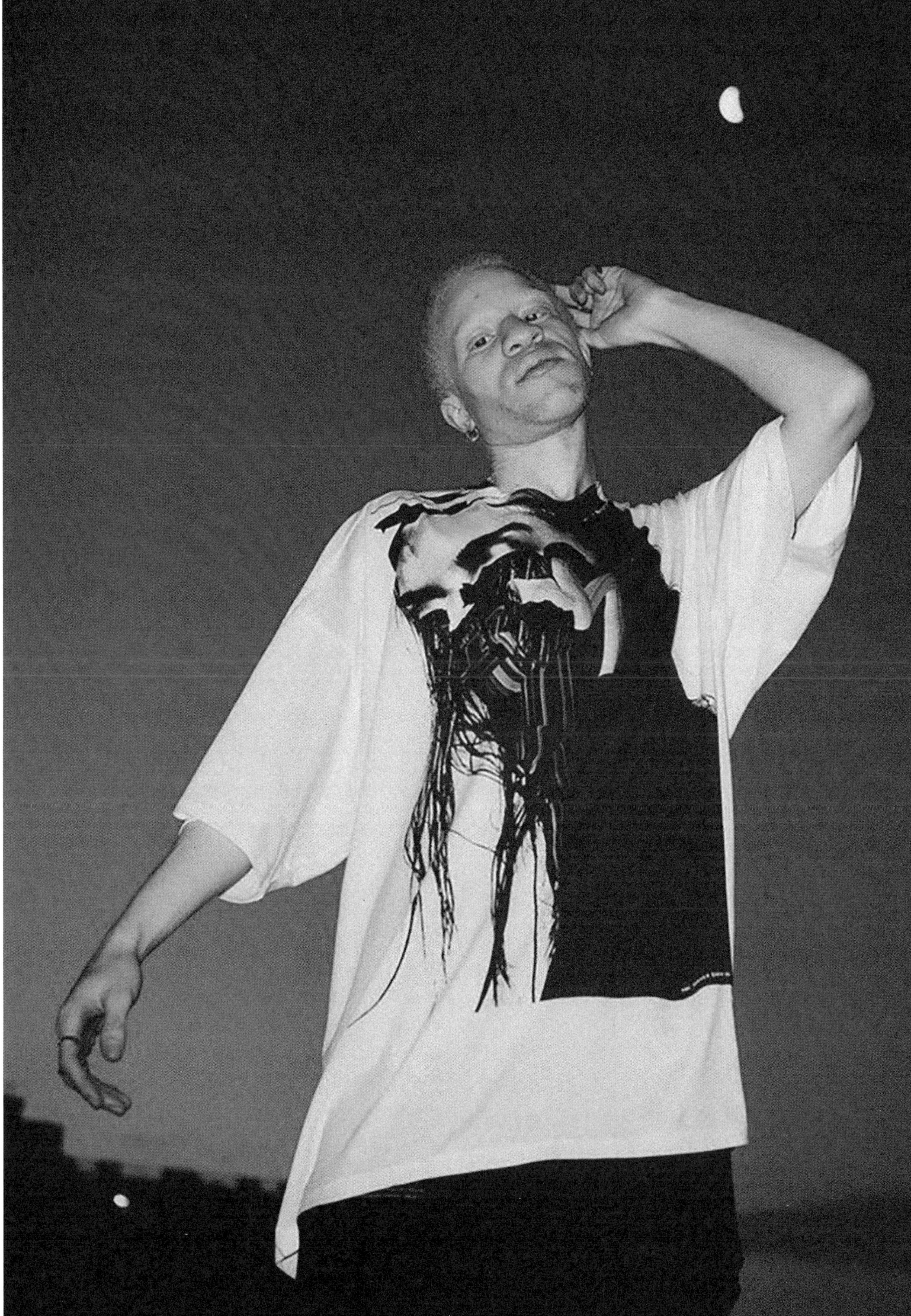

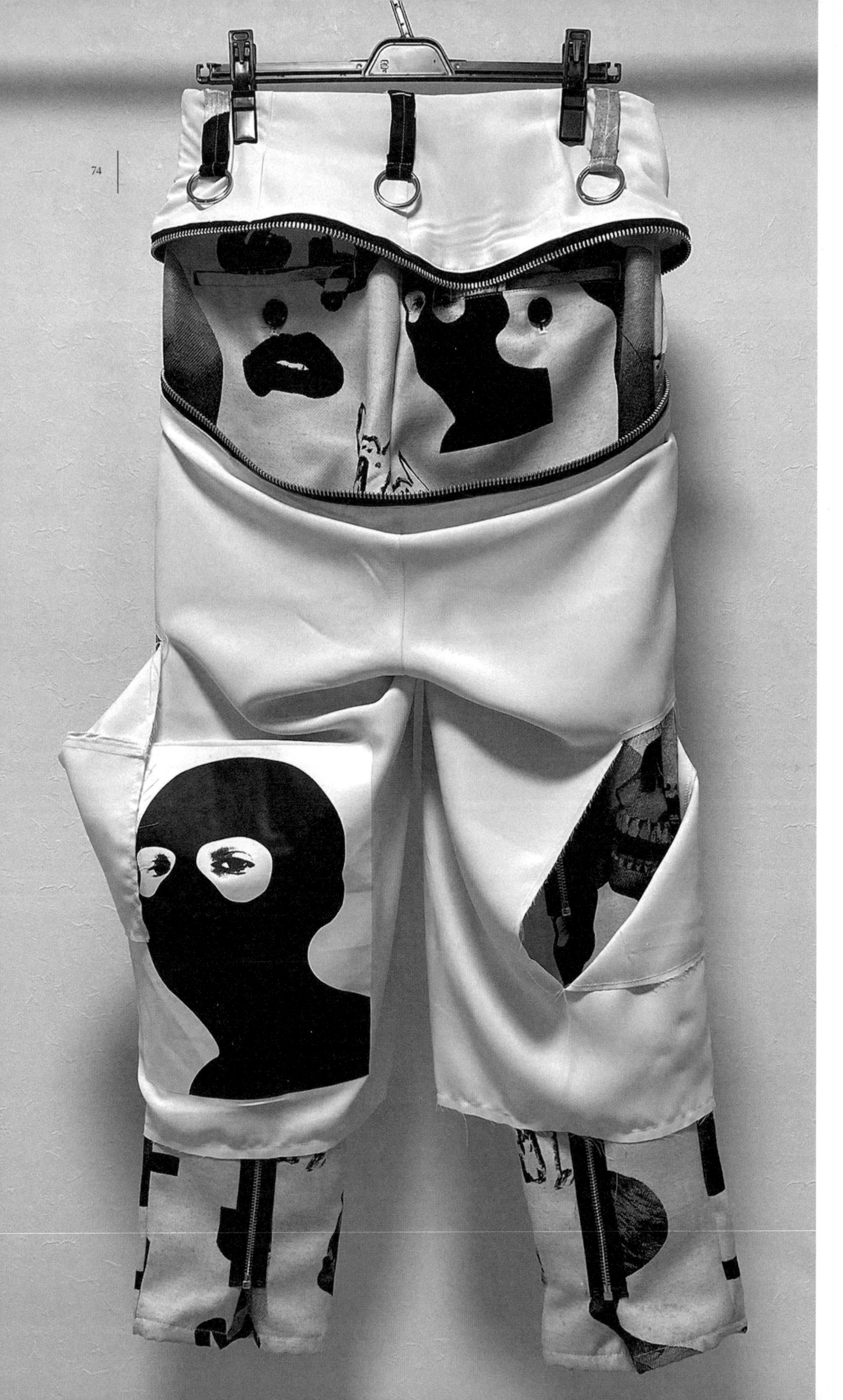

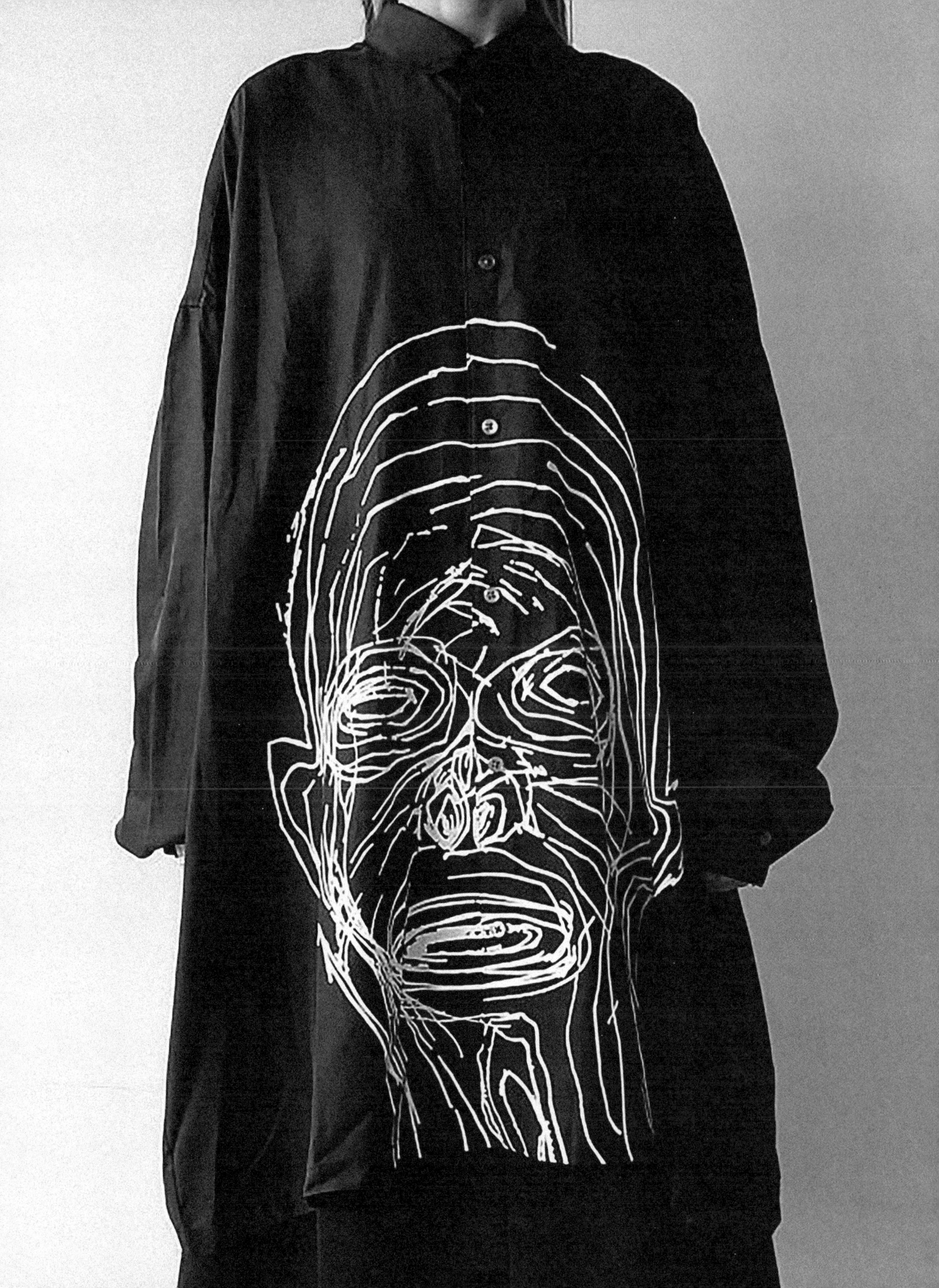

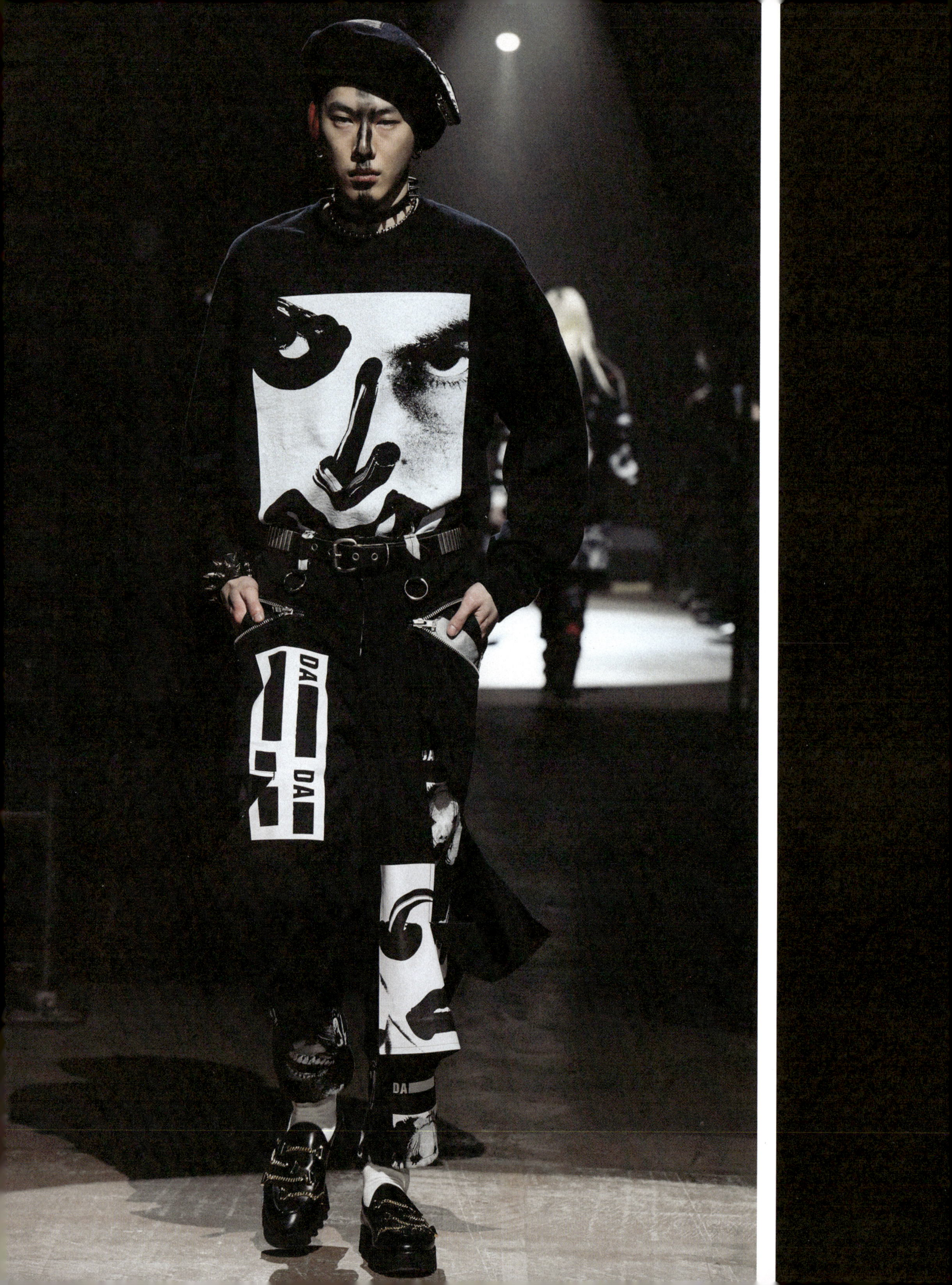
DA
DA
DA

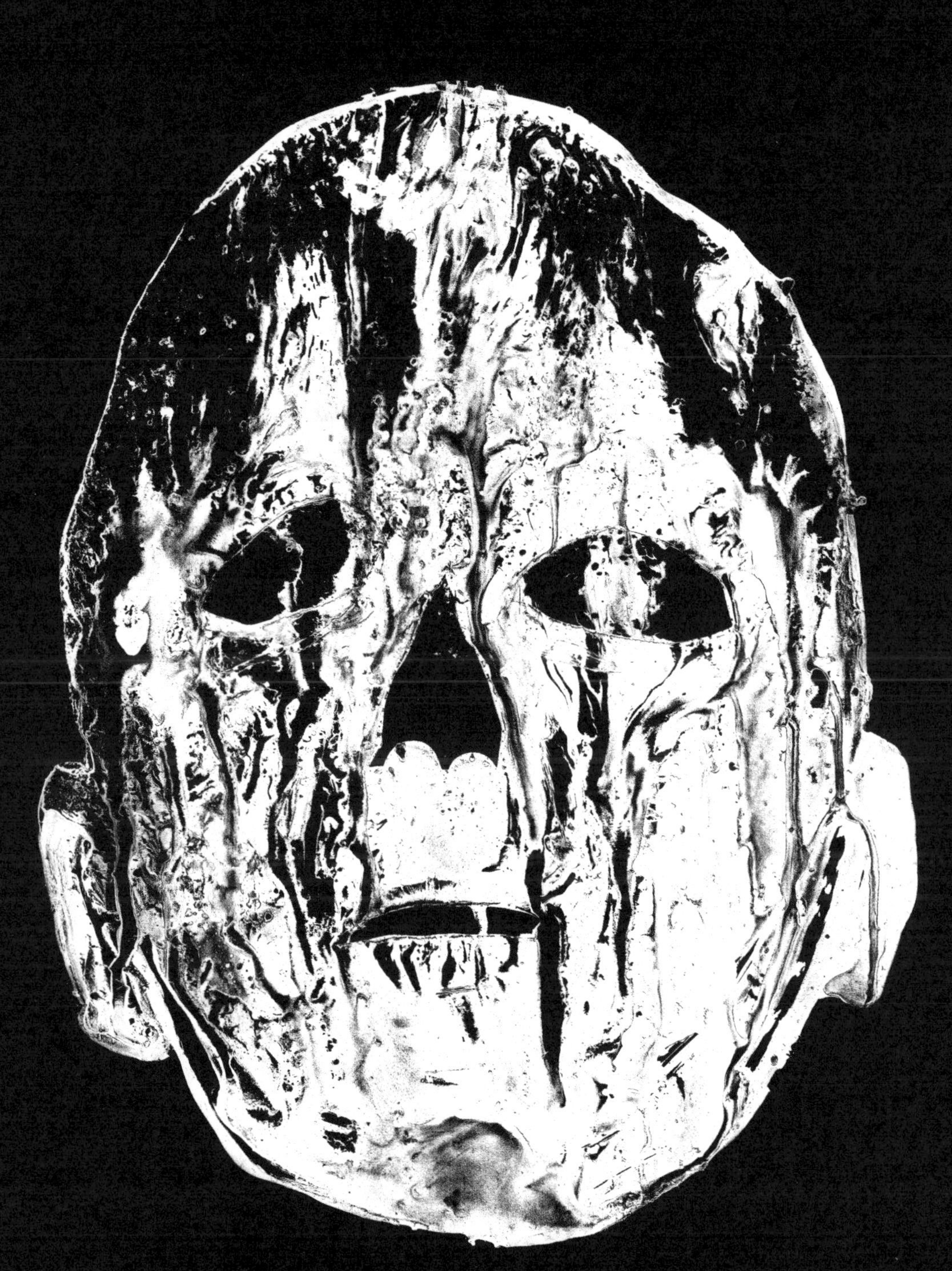

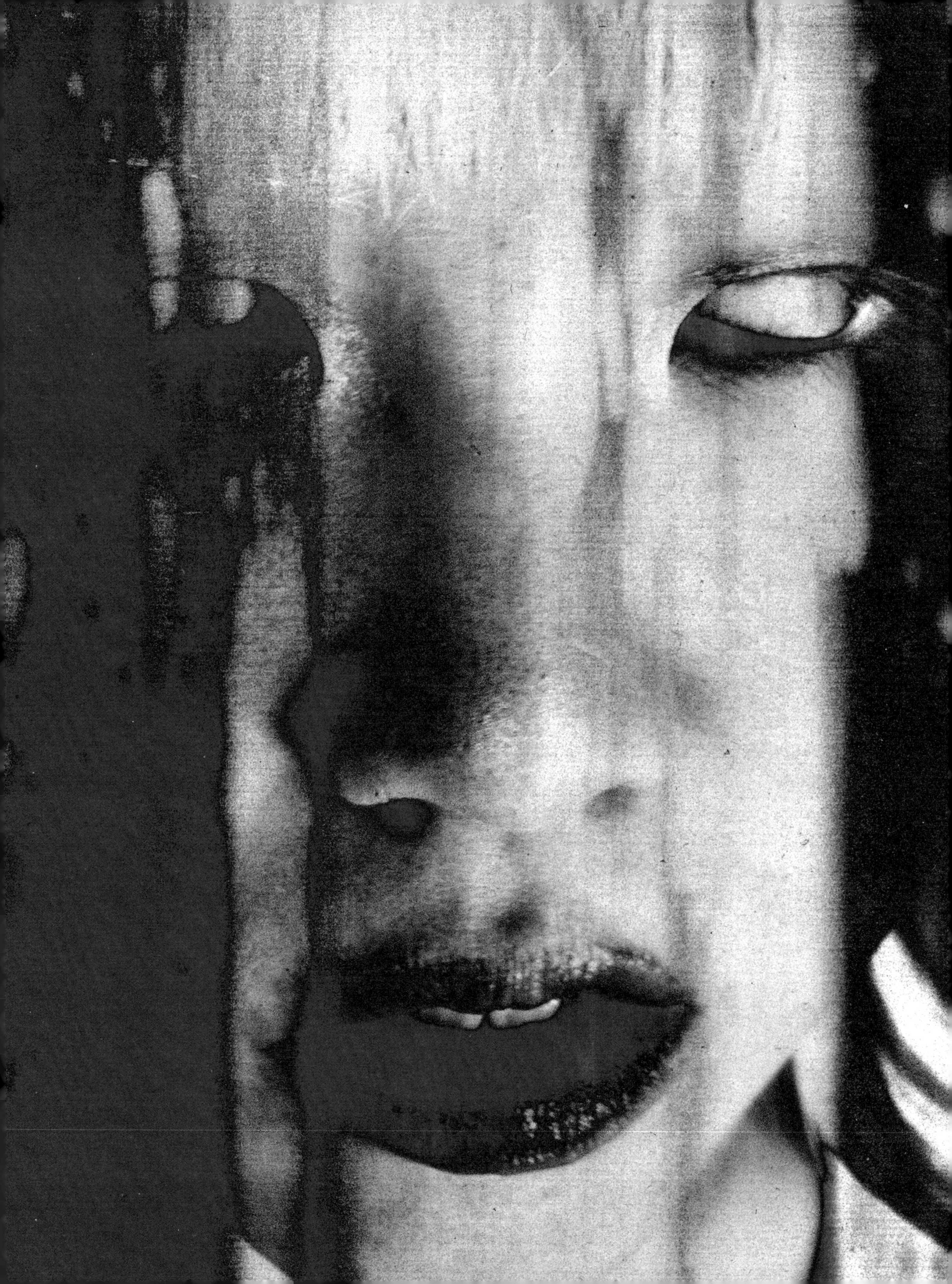

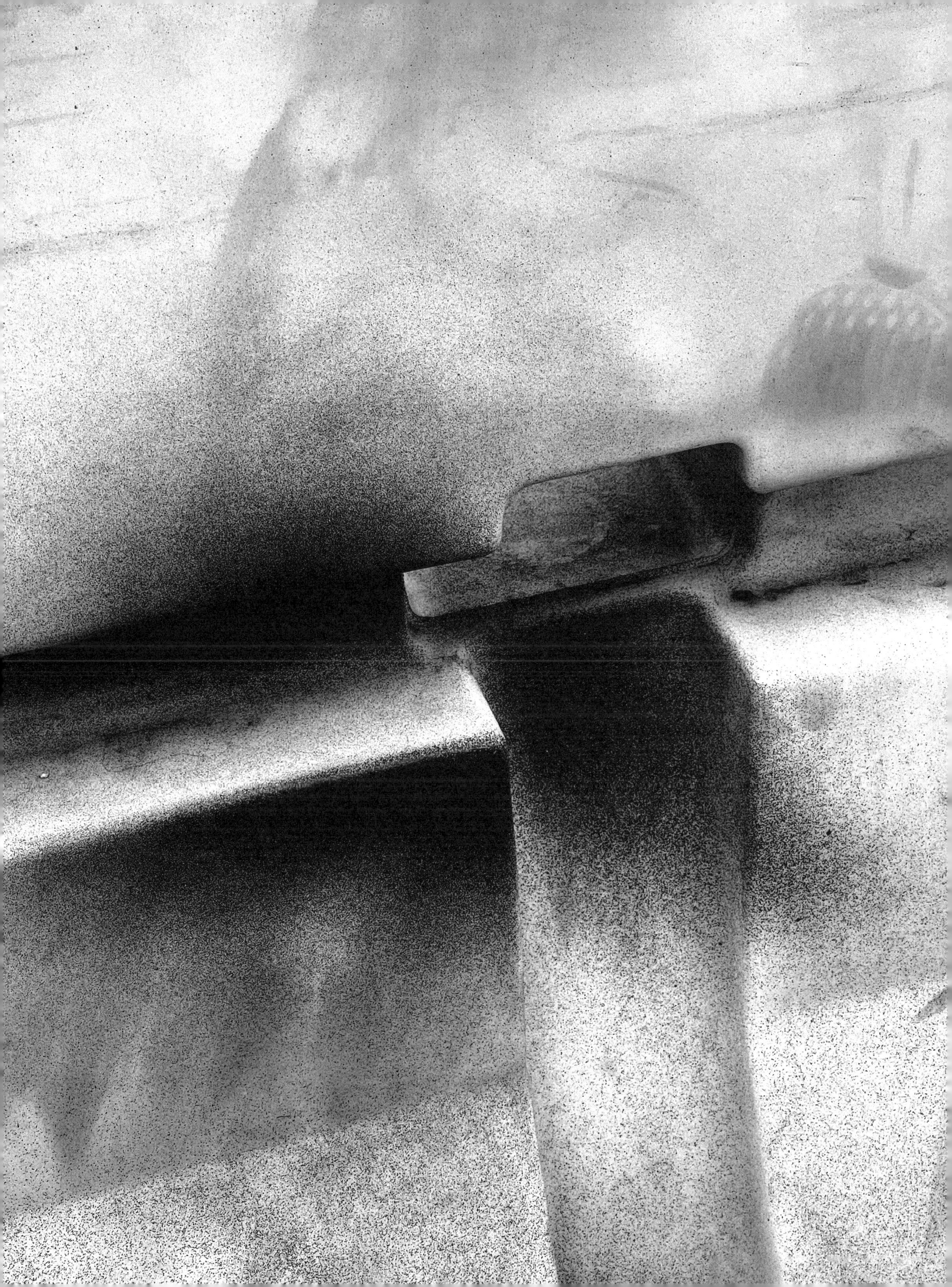

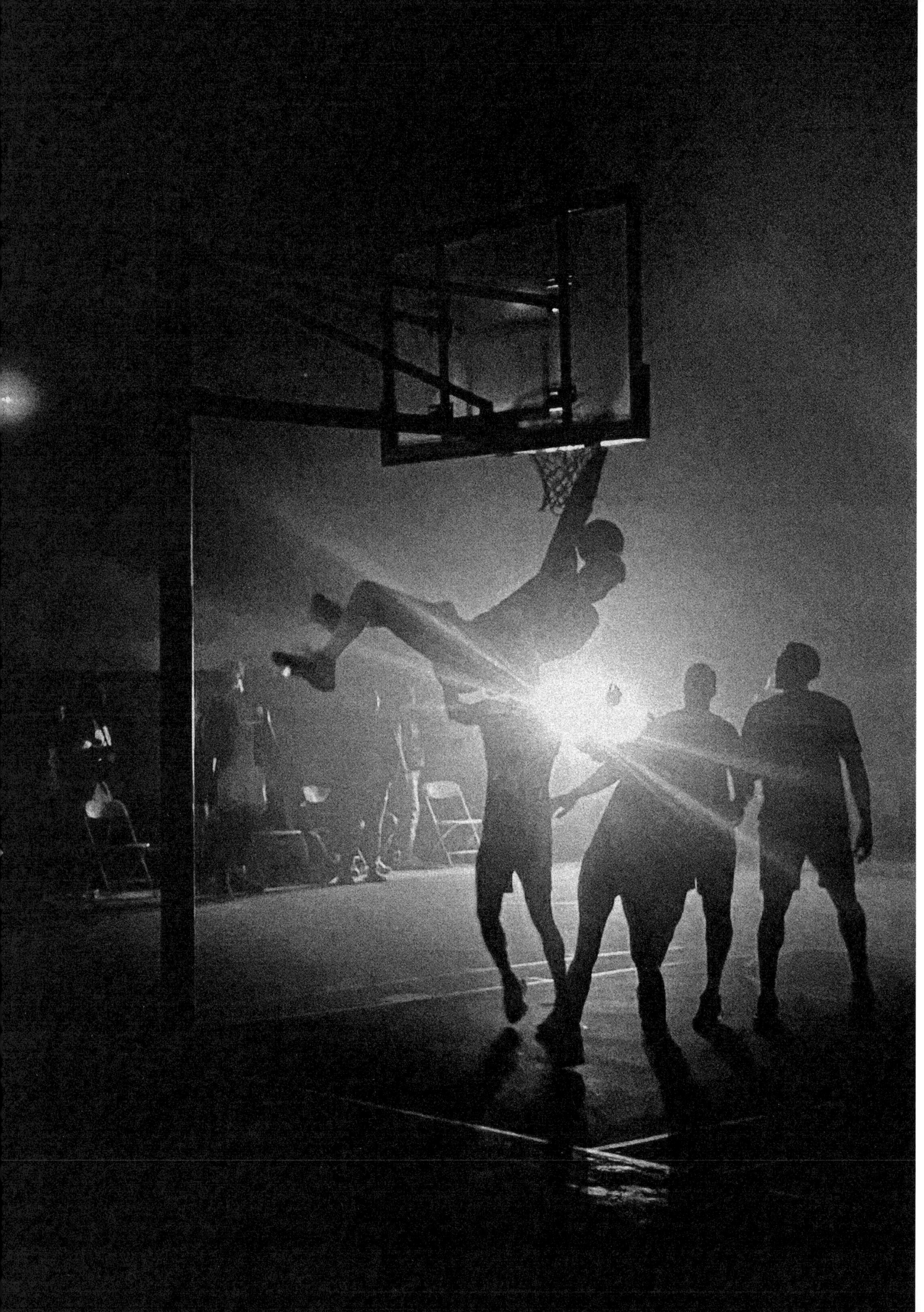

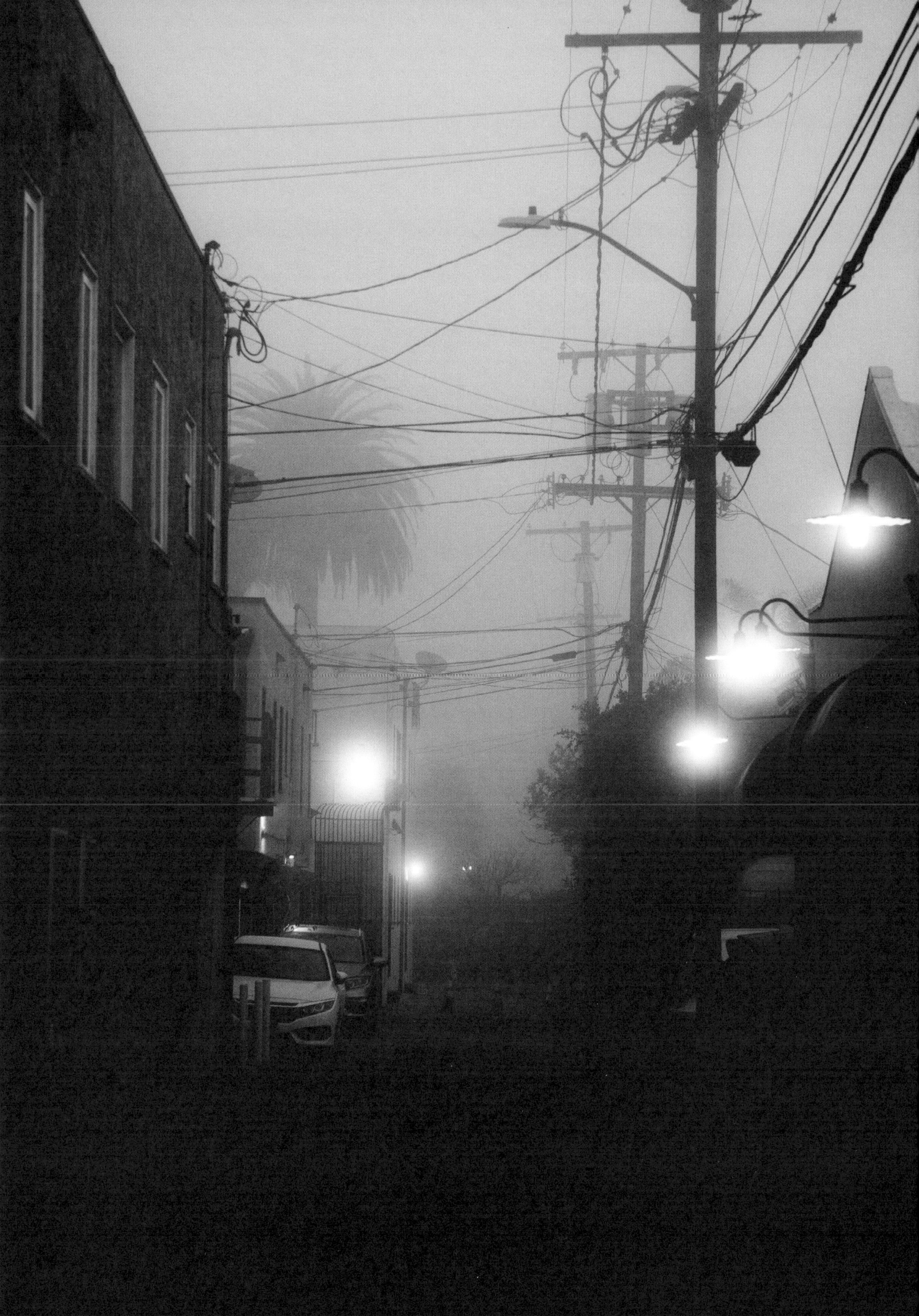

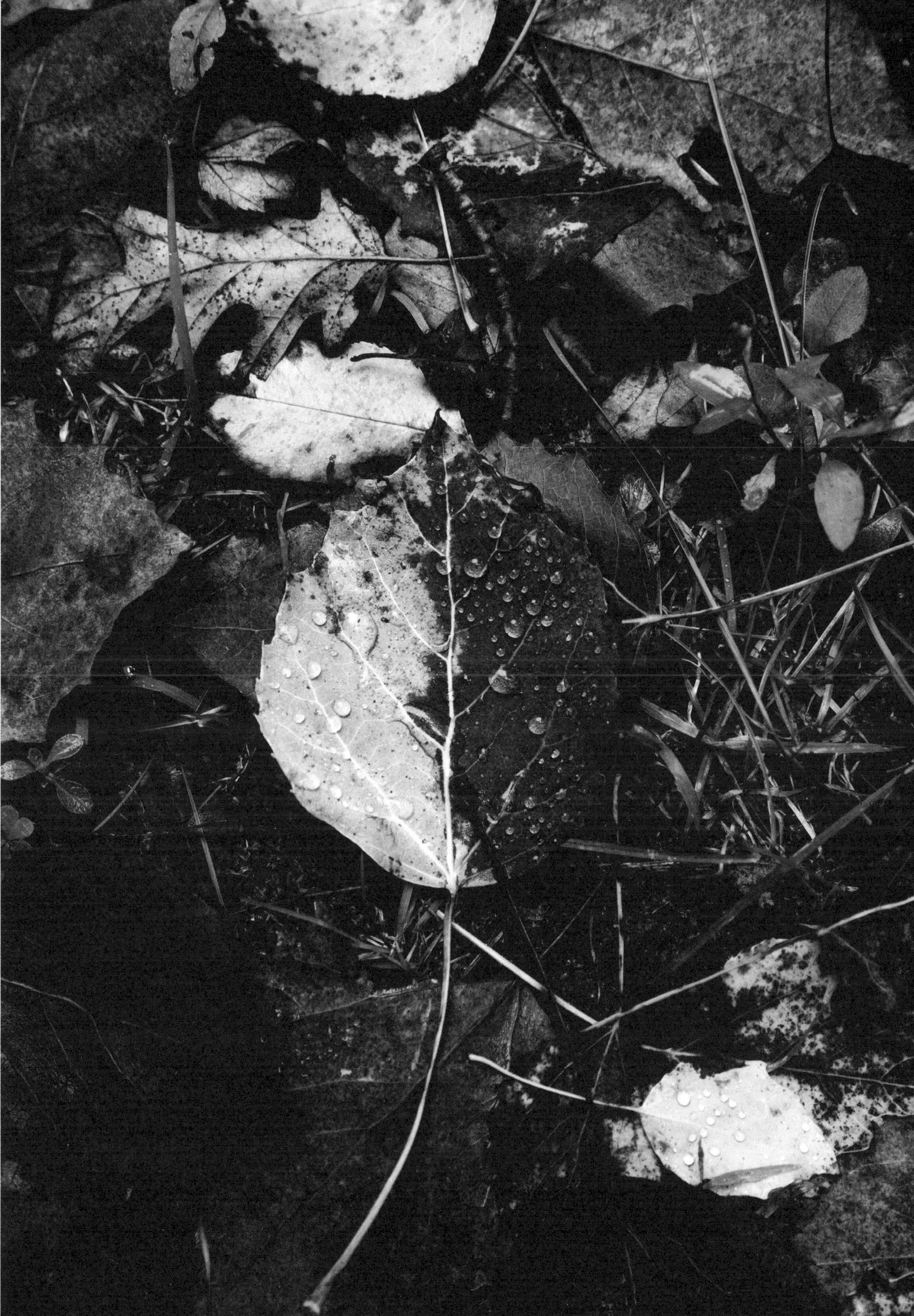

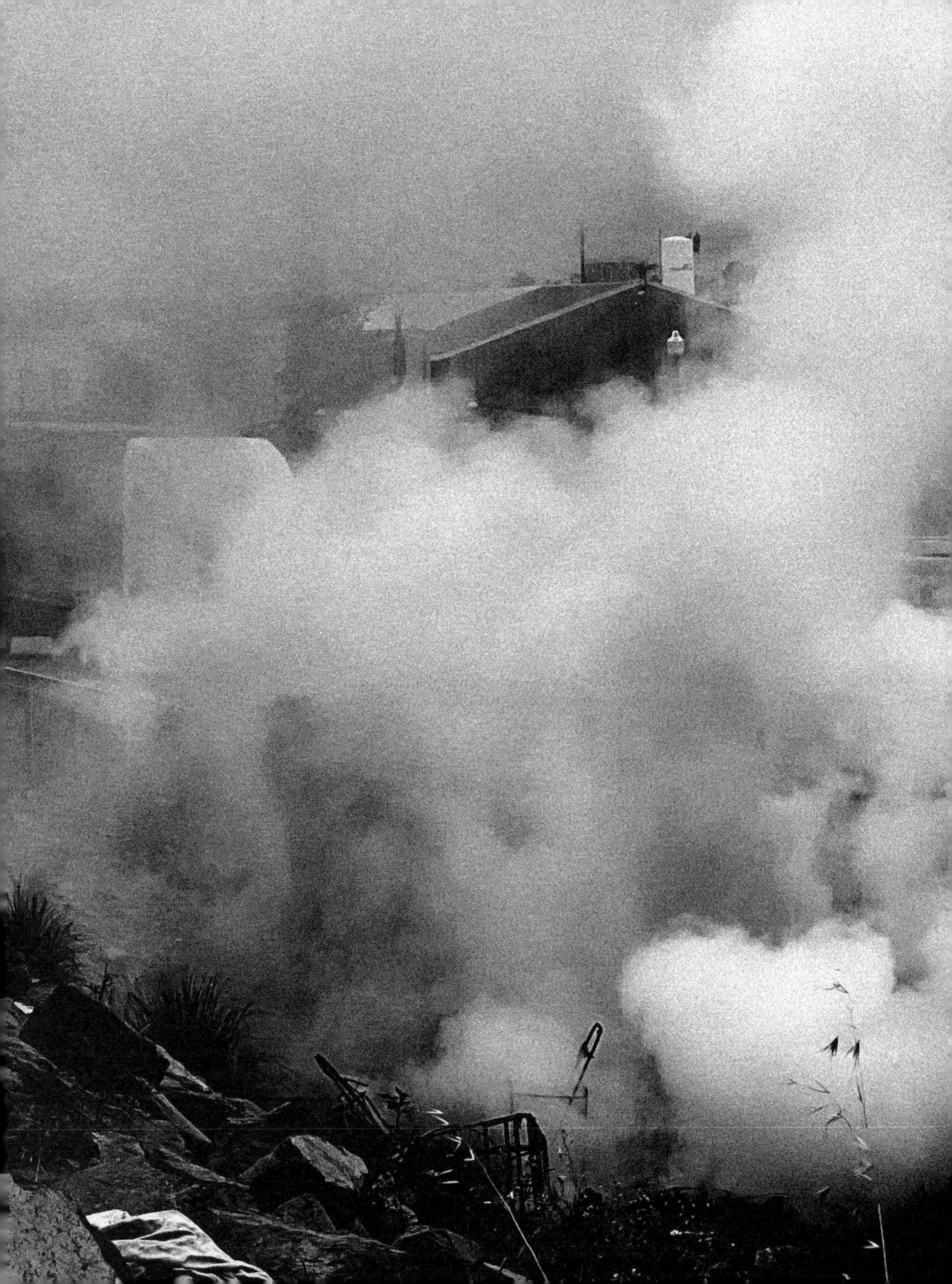

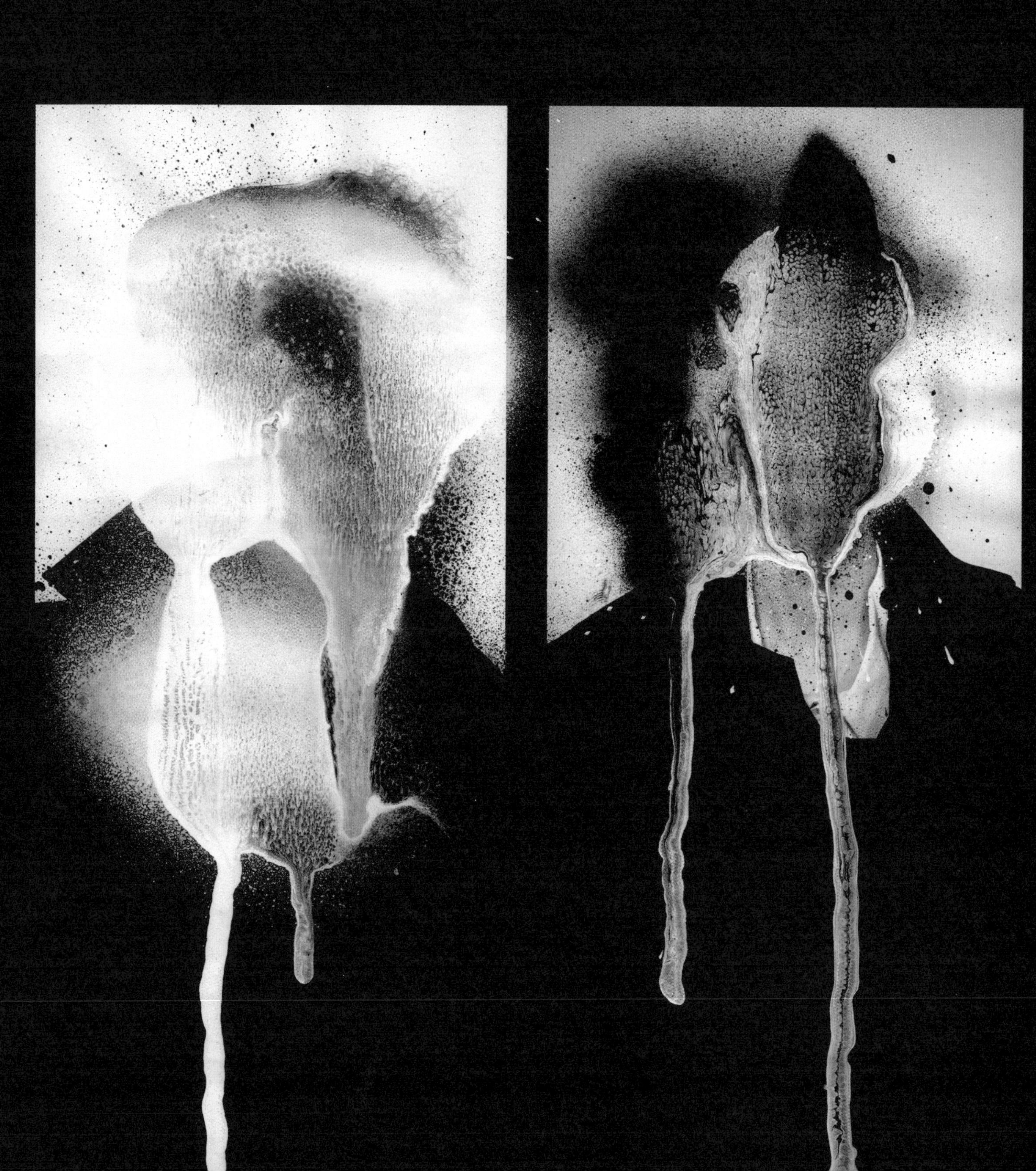

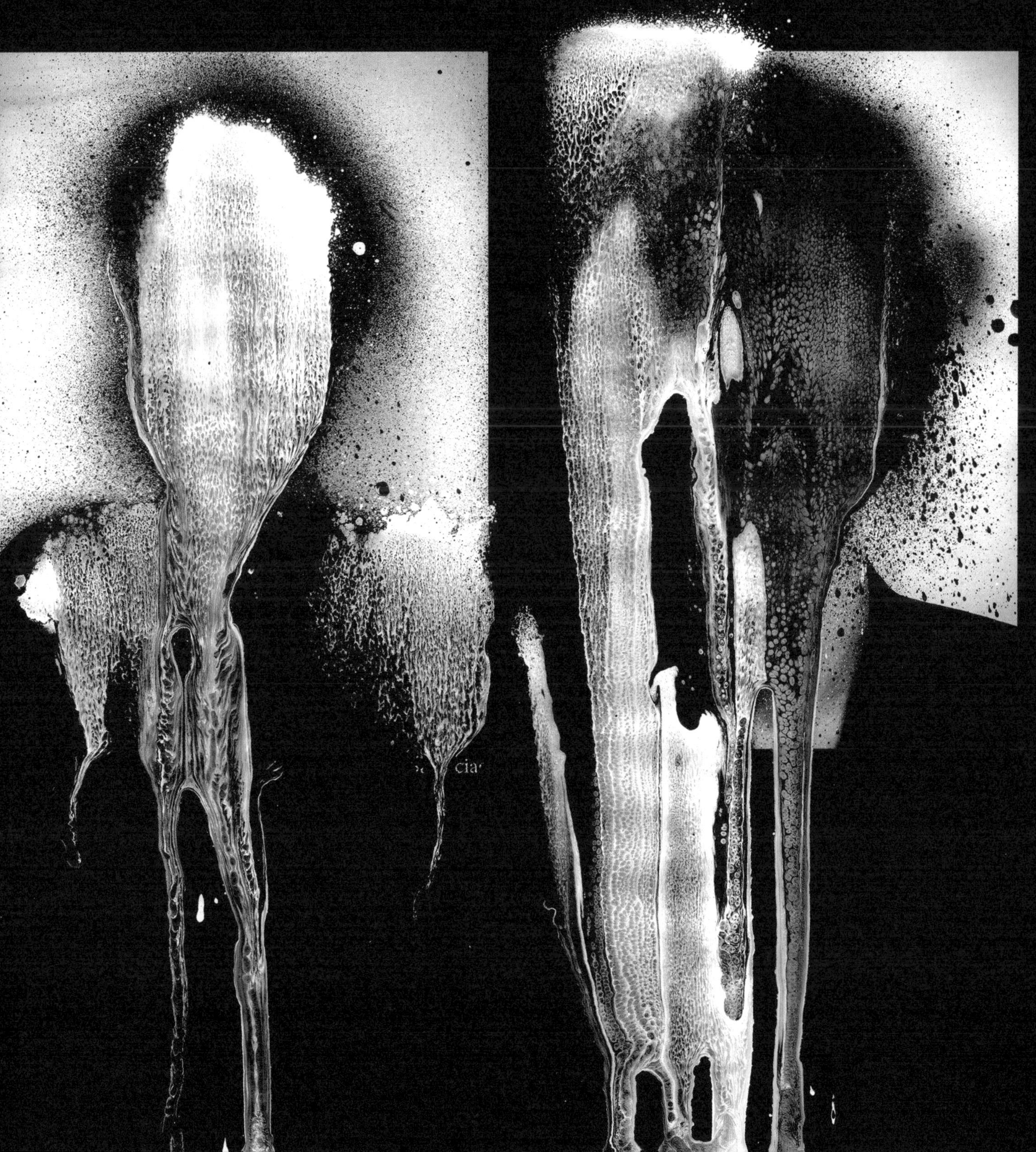

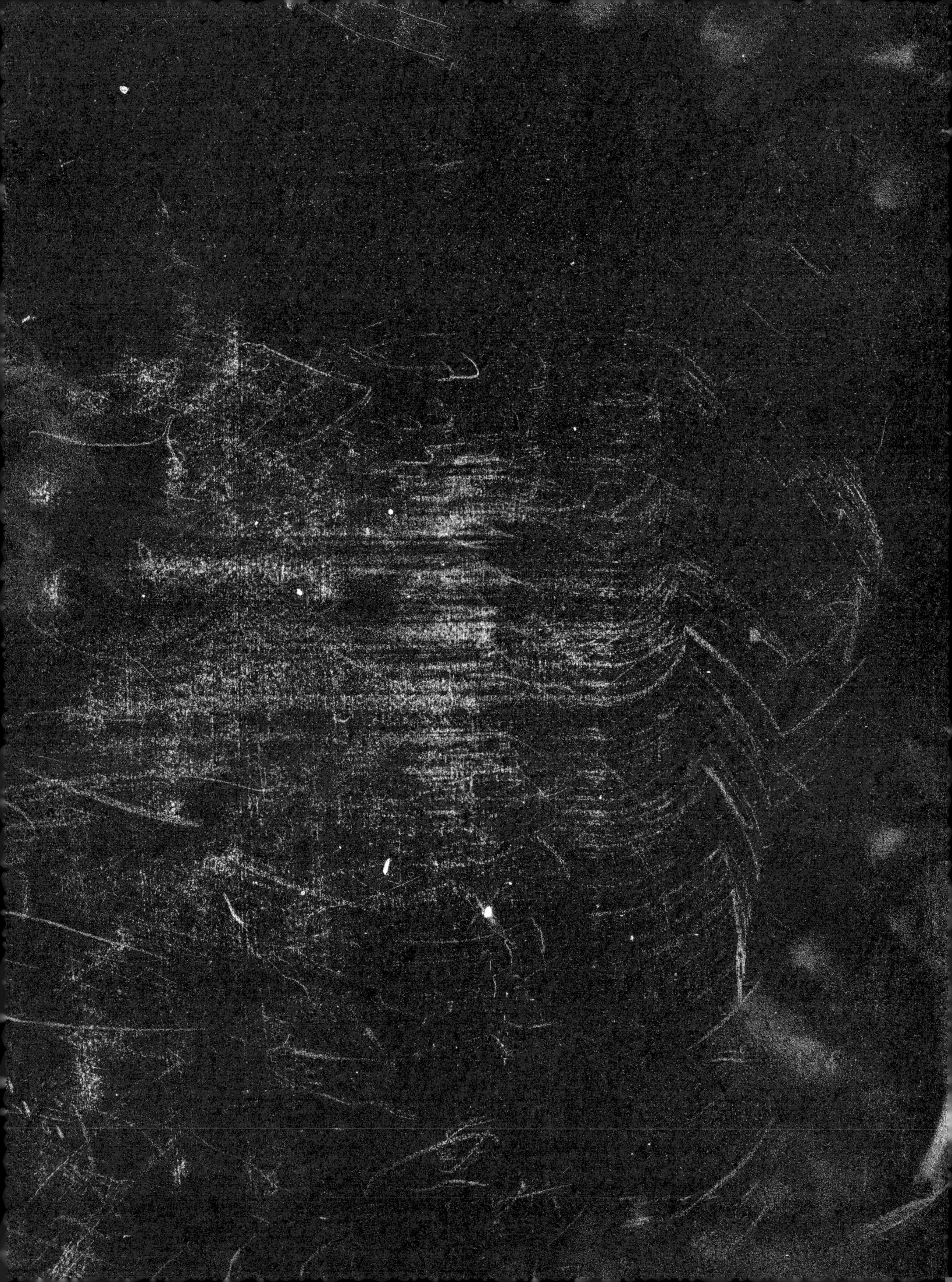

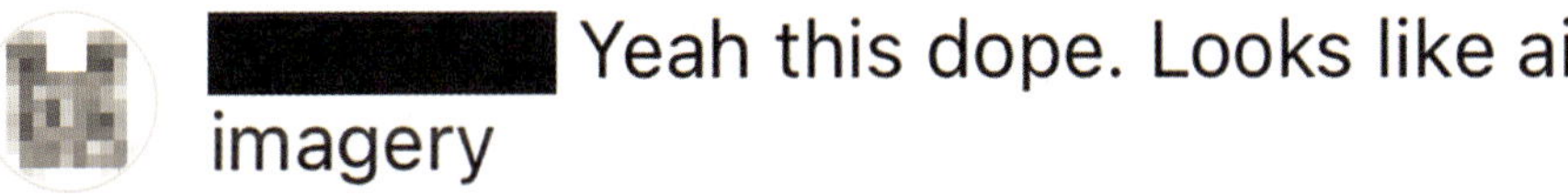

jessedraxler i think you mean to say that ai imagery looks like mine

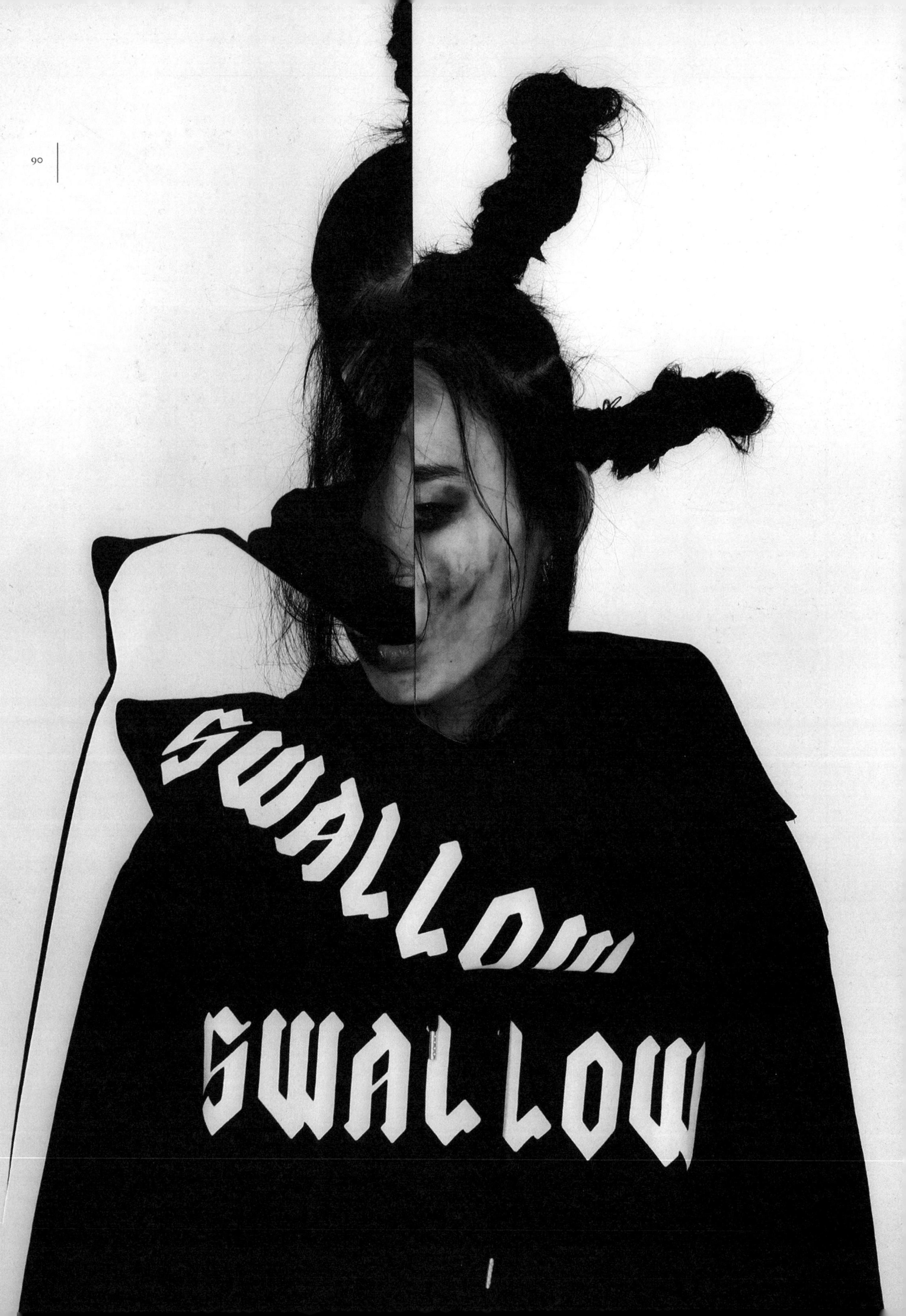

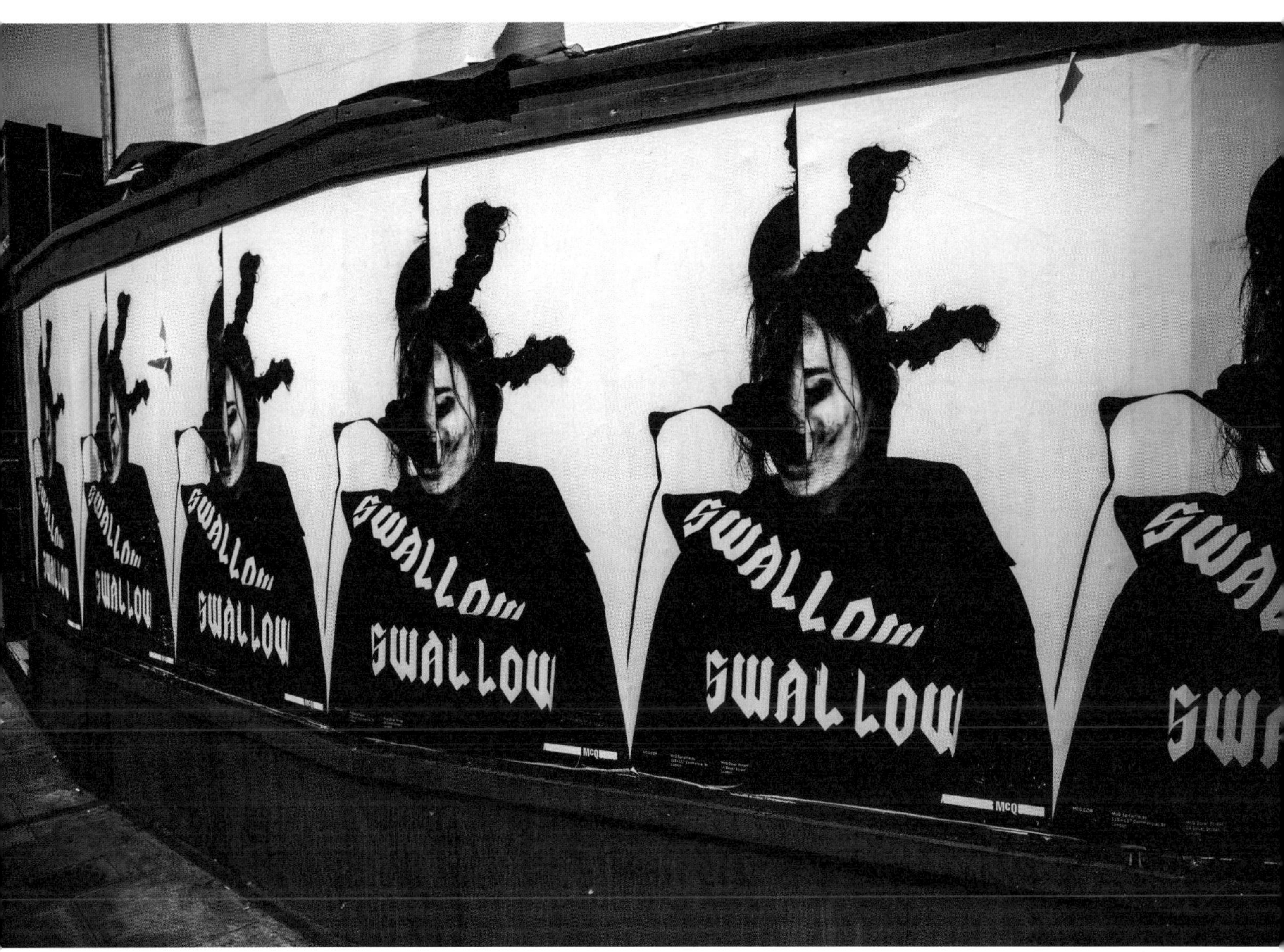
SWALLOW
SWALLOW
MCQ

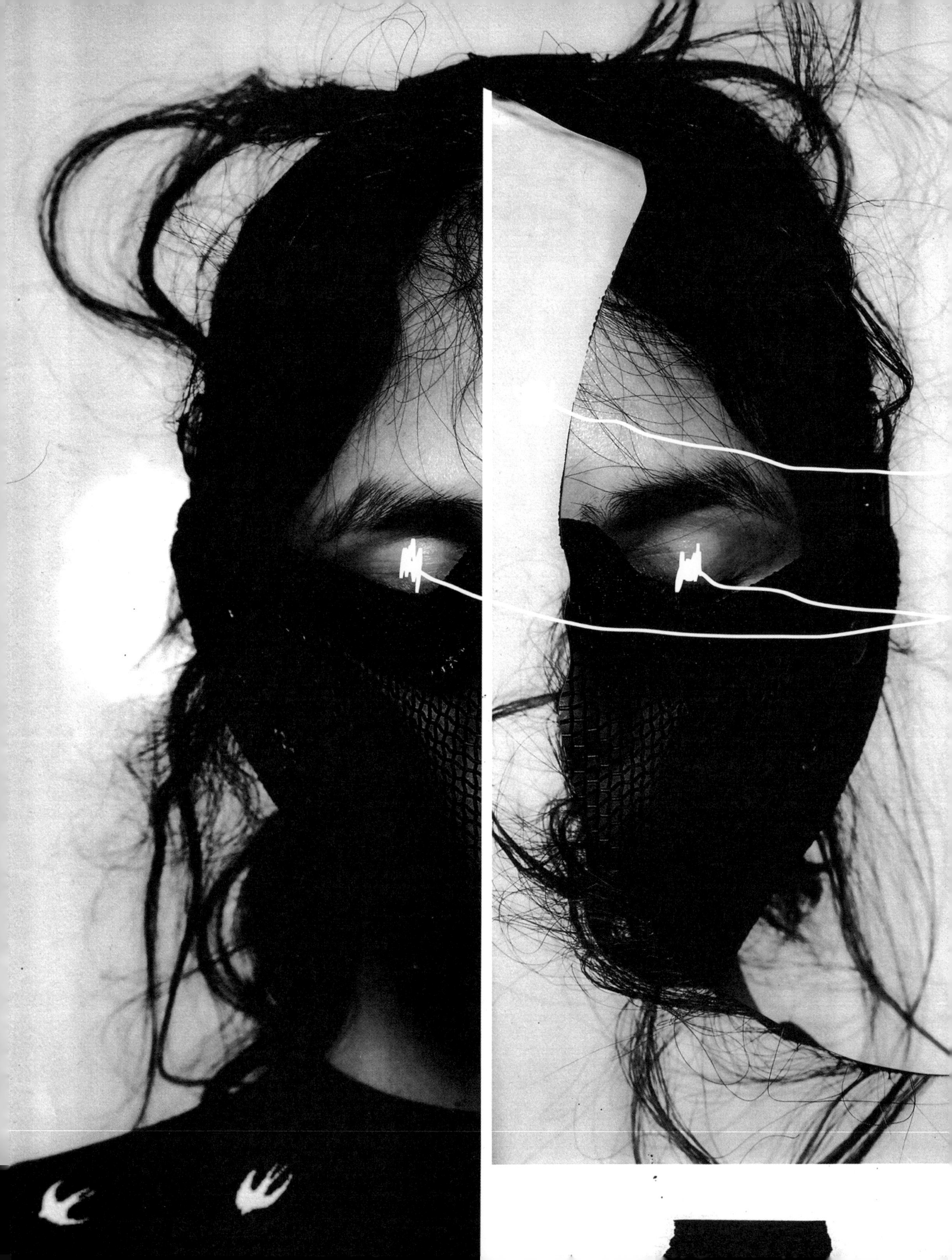

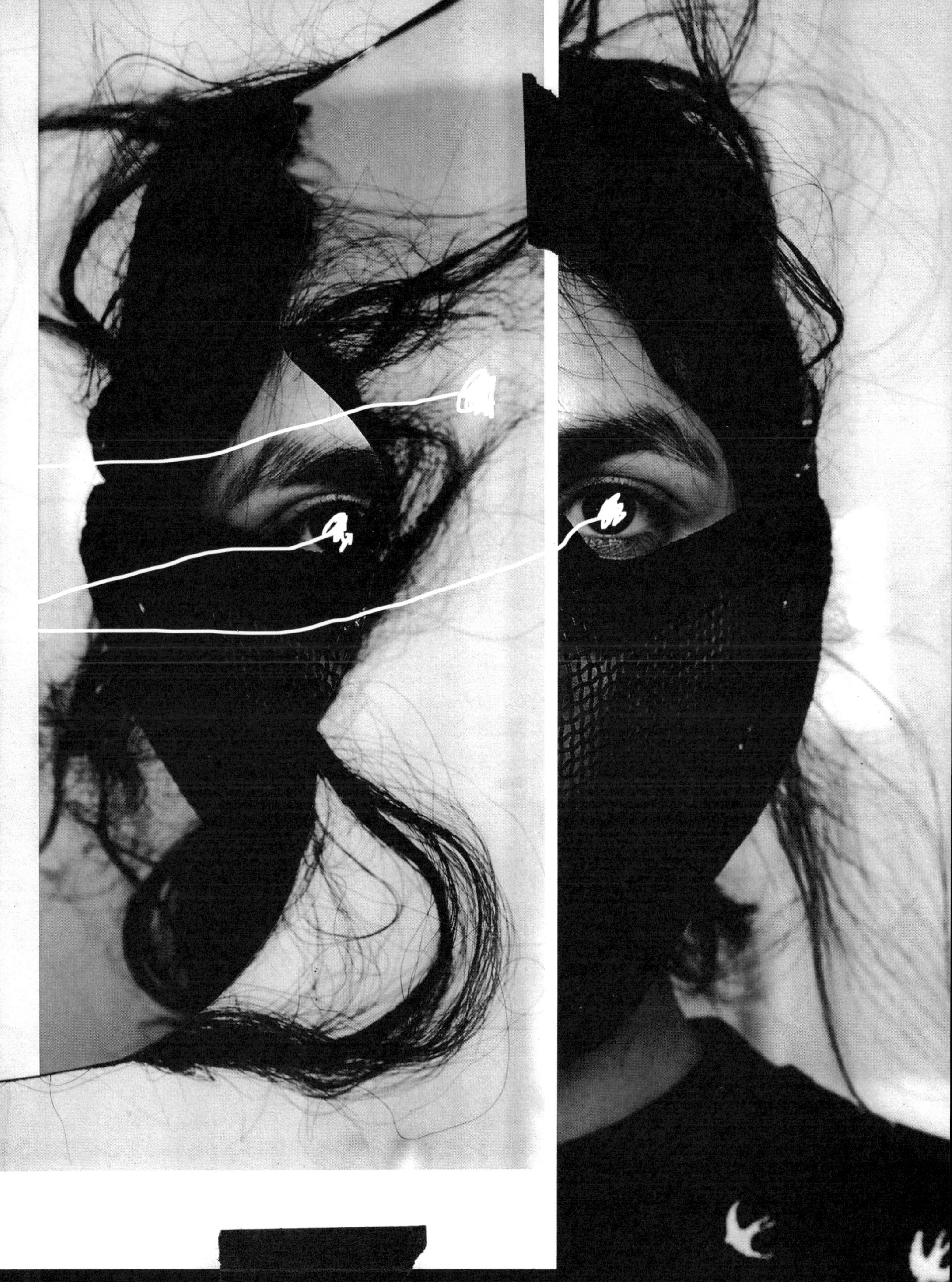

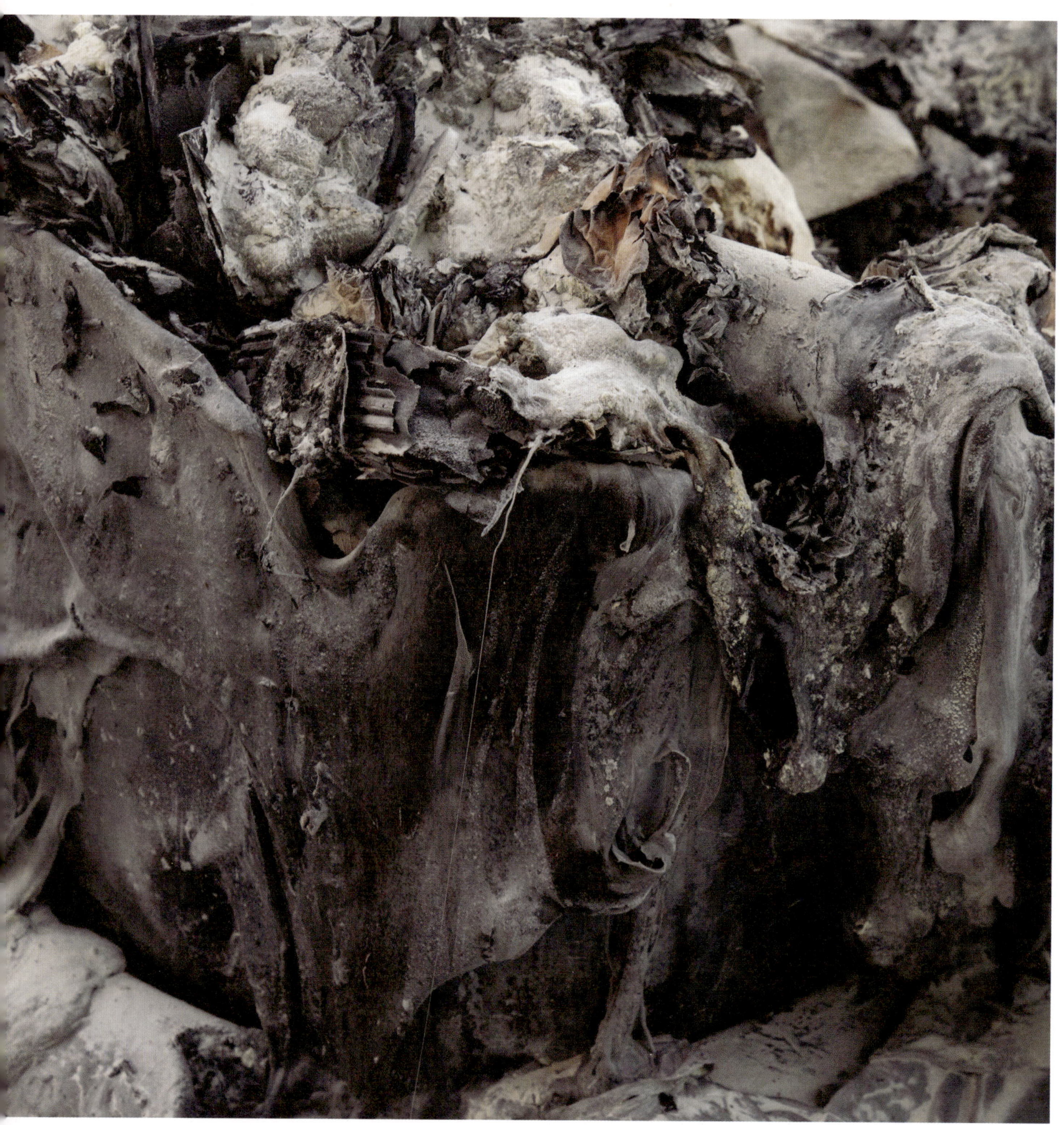

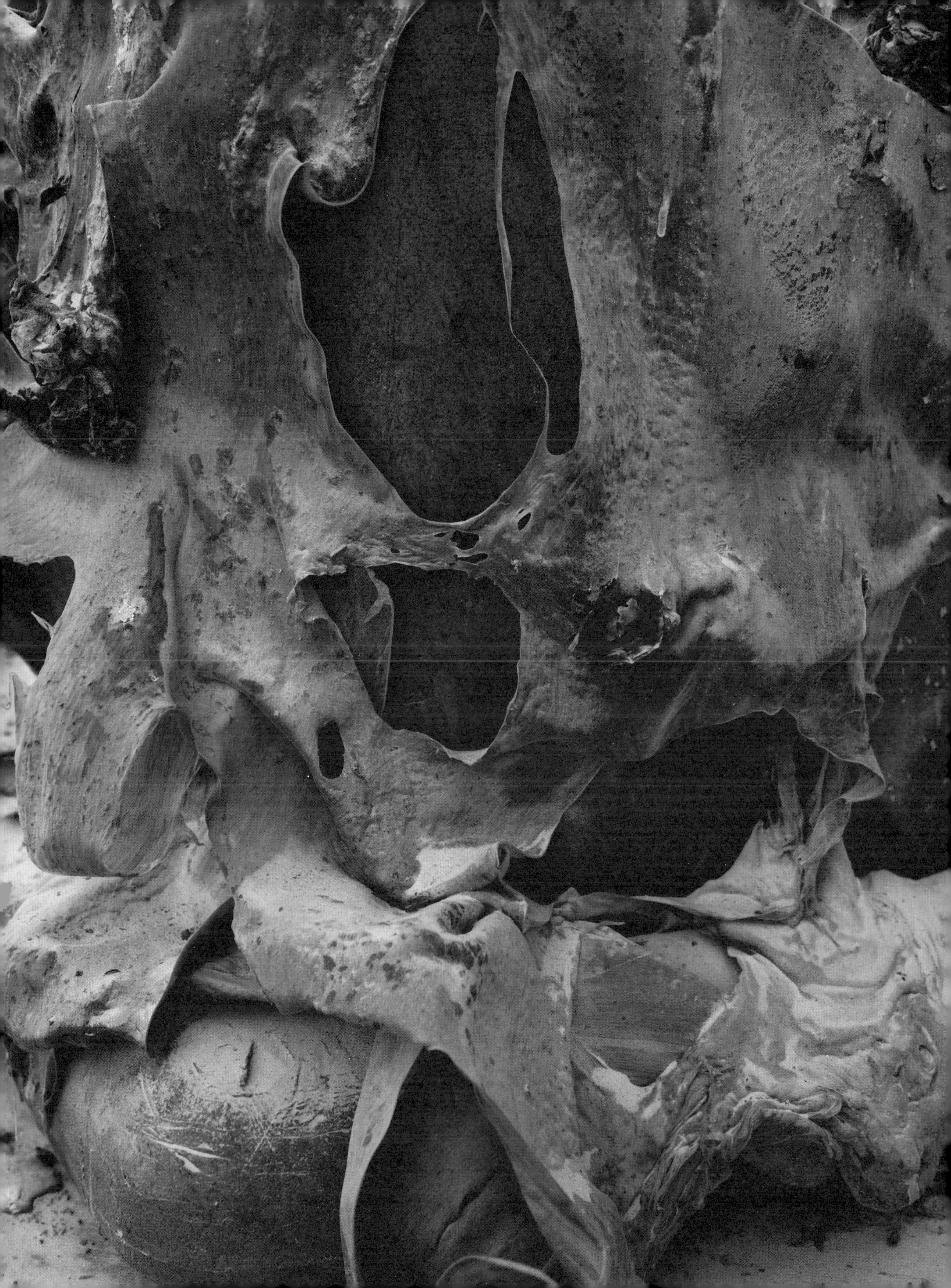

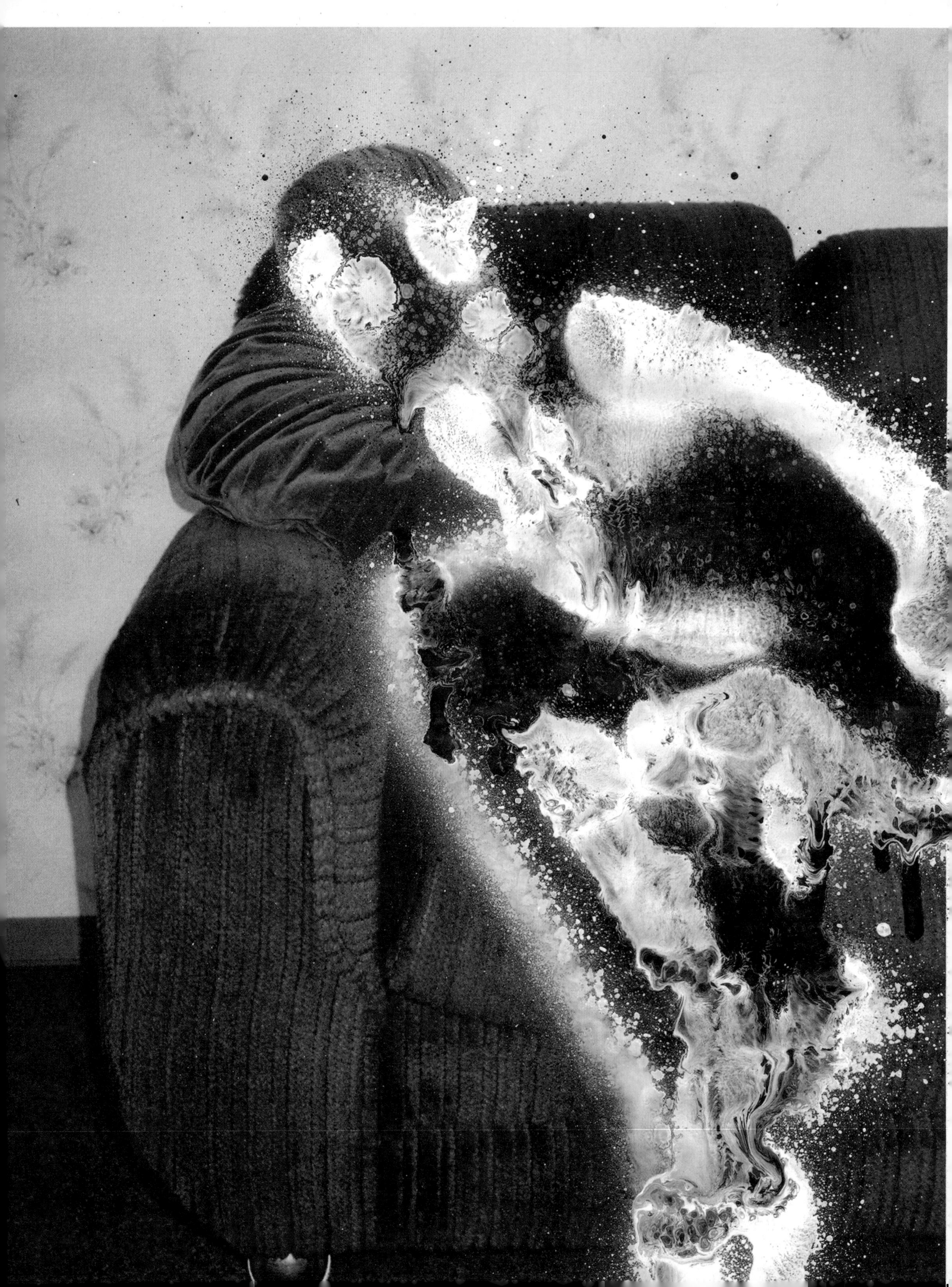

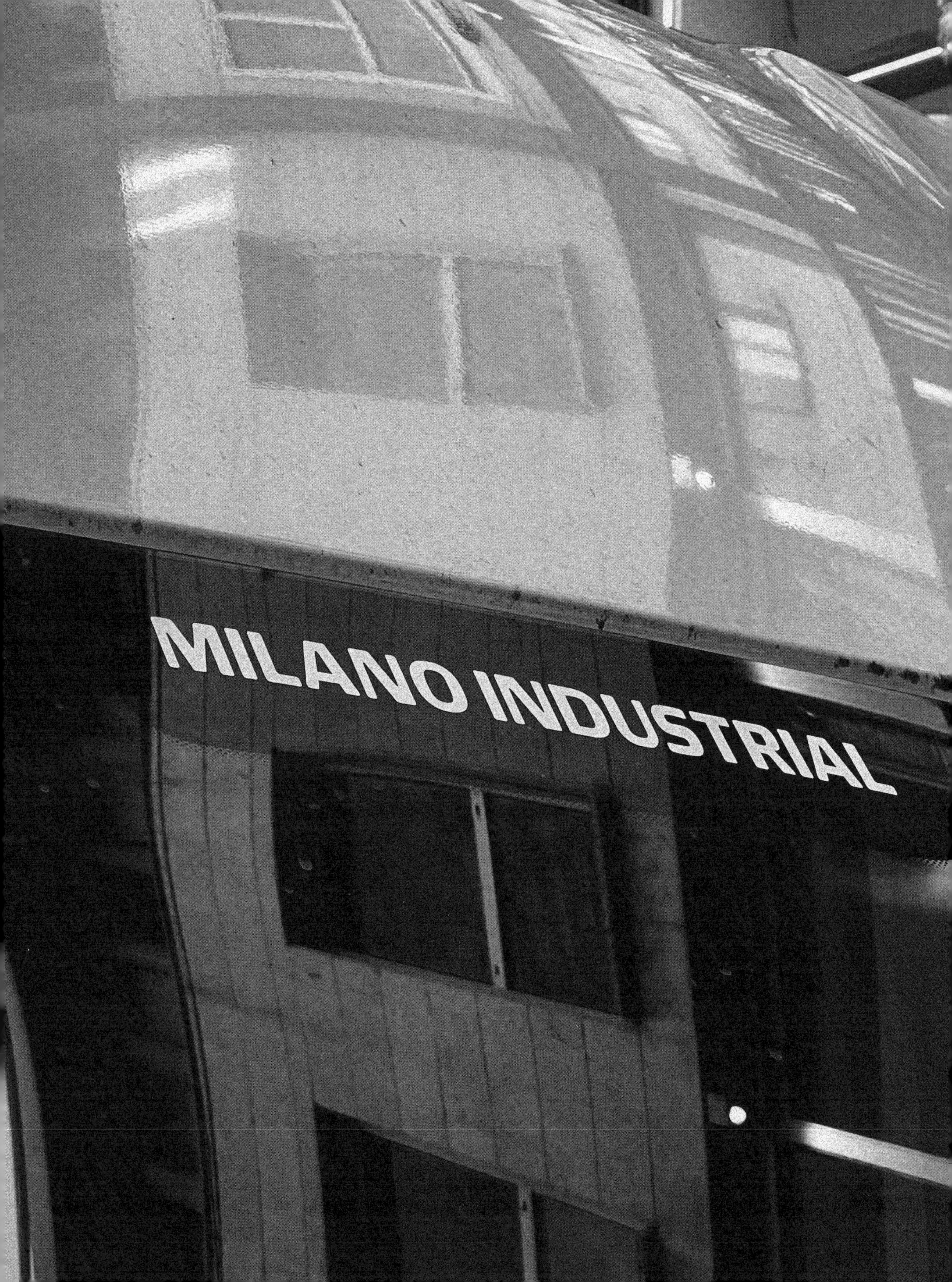
MILANO INDUSTRIAL

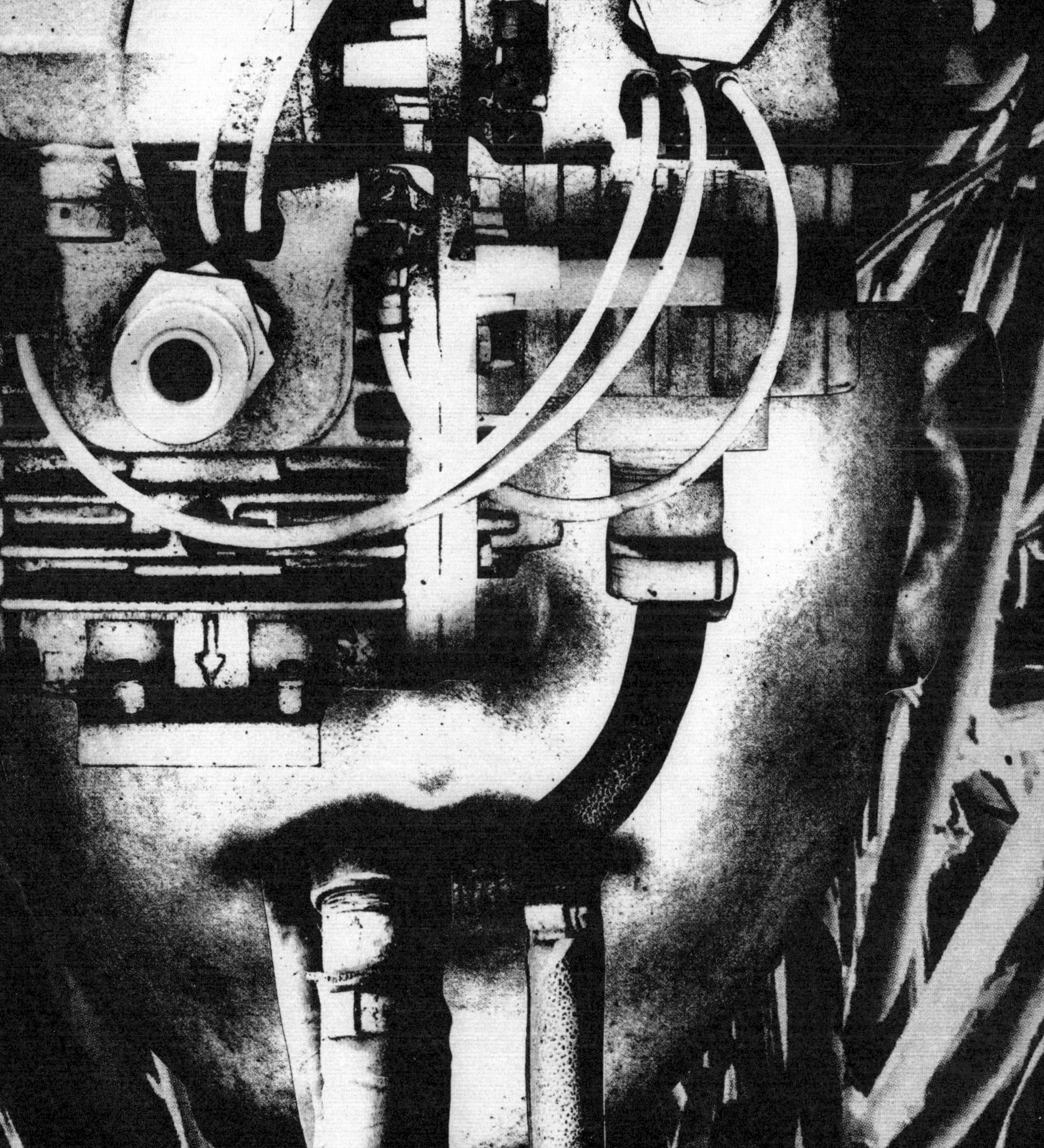
SYNTHETIC OIL
HD 10W-30

I JUST WOKE UP FROM
A NAP –
WHEN I WOKE I HAD
FORGOTTEN MY FORM –
I DID NOT OPEN
MY EYES BUT IMAGINED
ALL THE SHAPES I
COULD BE.

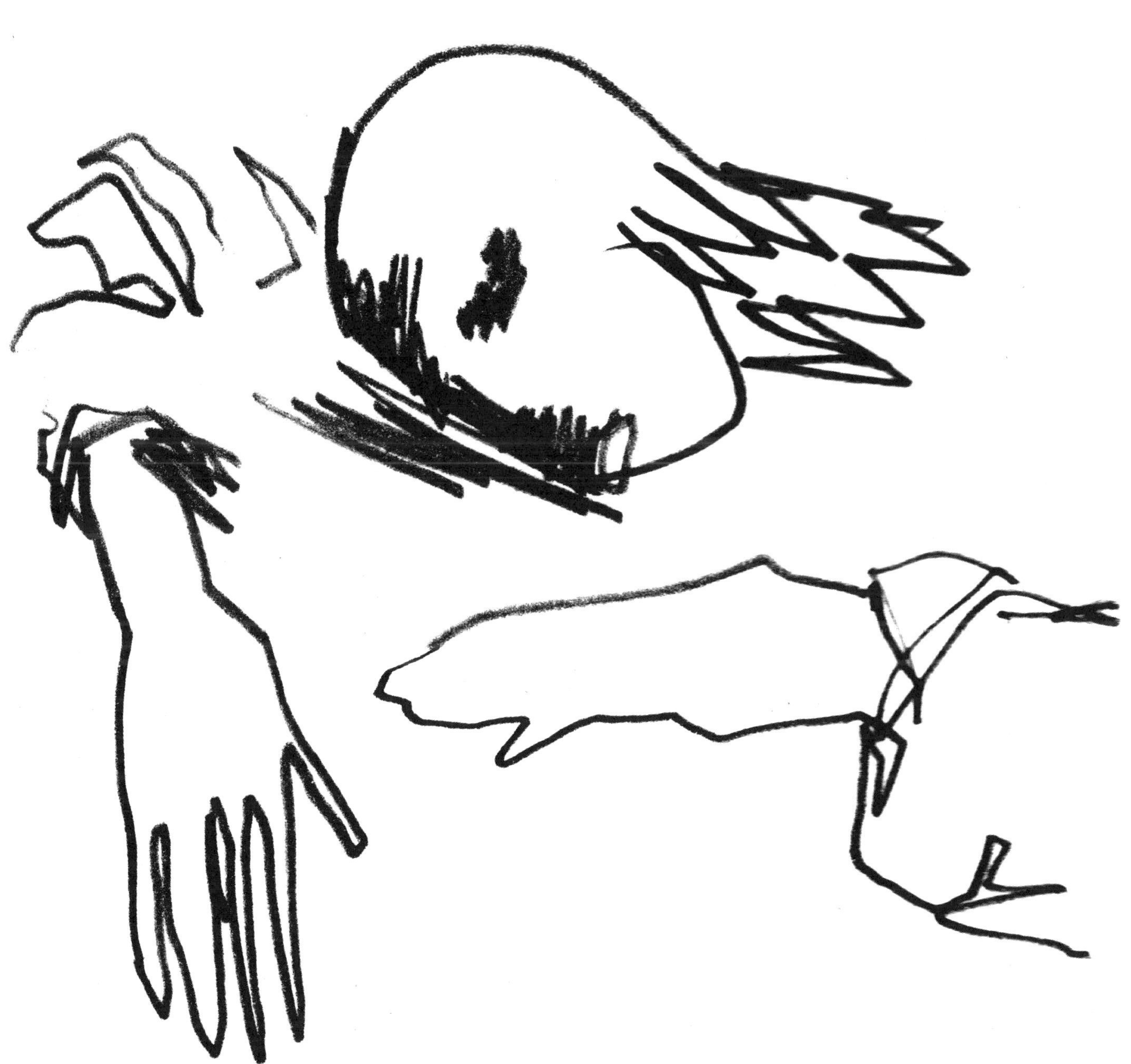

THE BODY IS OBSOLETE

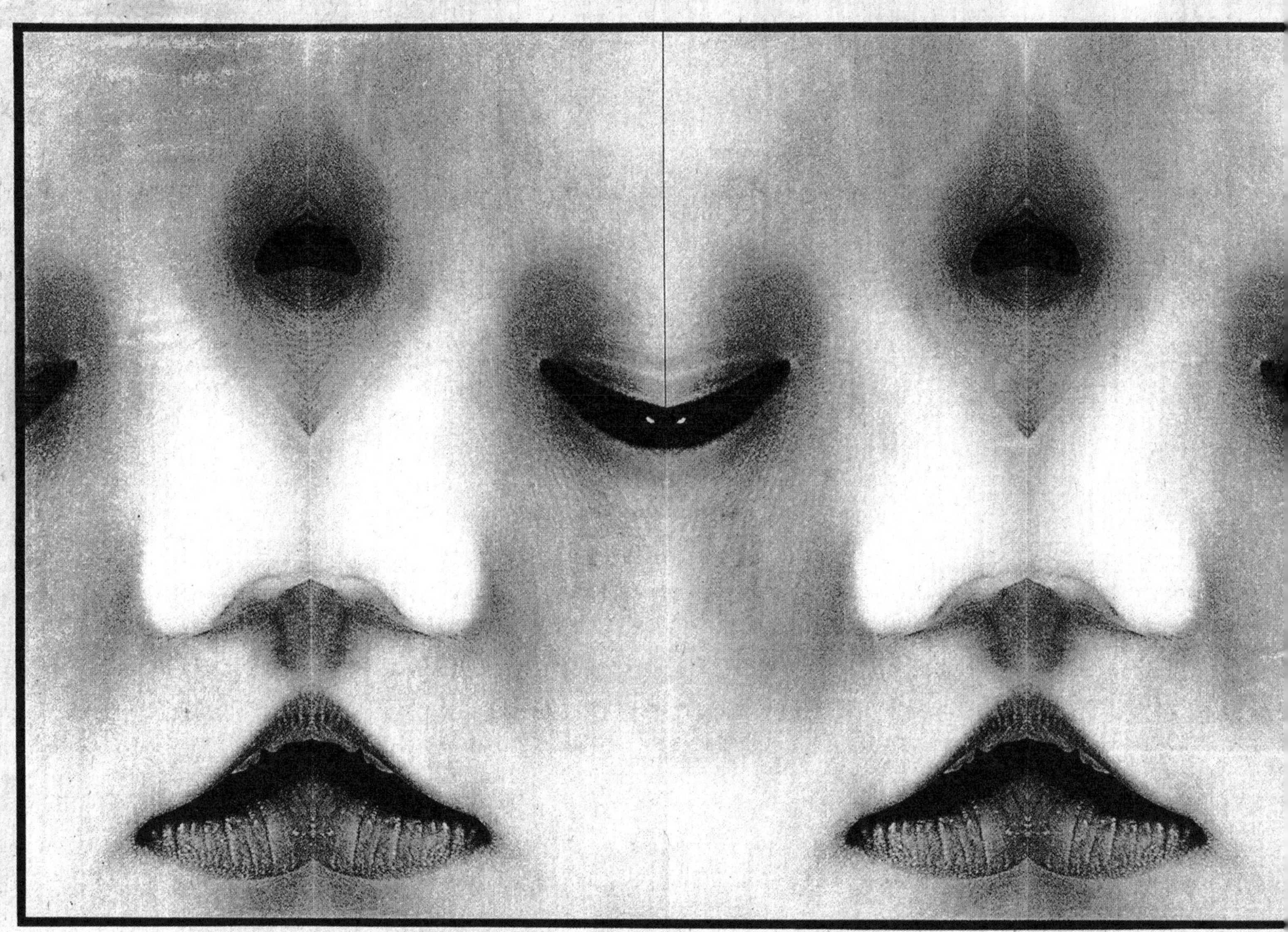

THE END OF

EVOLUTION IS AT HAND

No data in the grid

10 09 18
THE ANTHEM
WASHINGTON DC
nin

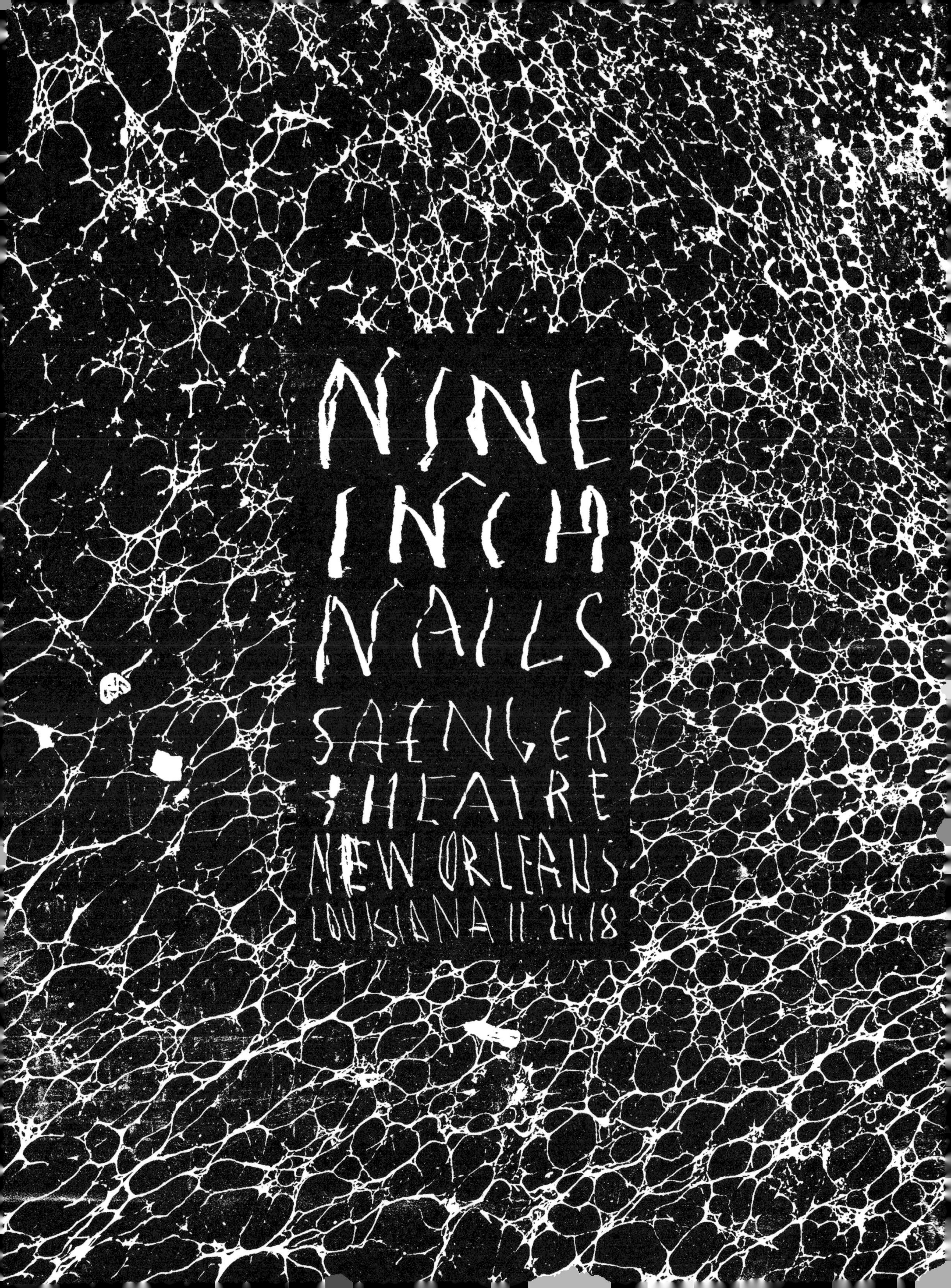
NINE
INCH
NAILS
SAENGER
THEATRE
NEW ORLEANS
LOUISIANA 11.24.18

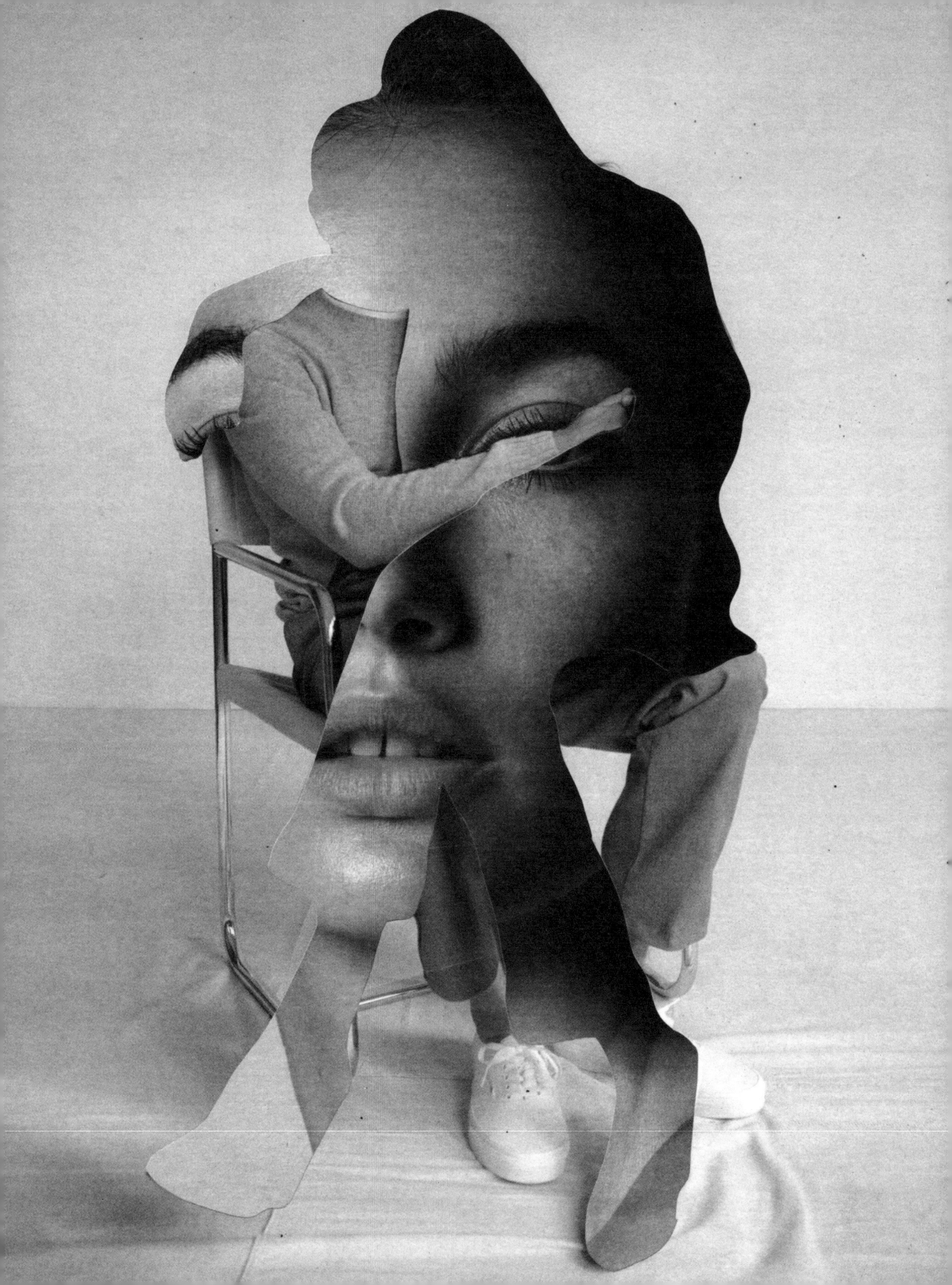

Nothing I

(attachment to emptiness)

No form, no emptiness.

1x0=0

1000x0=0

Freedom I

(attachment to freedom)

Freedom form, freedom emptiness.

1+2=3000

100x1000=-4

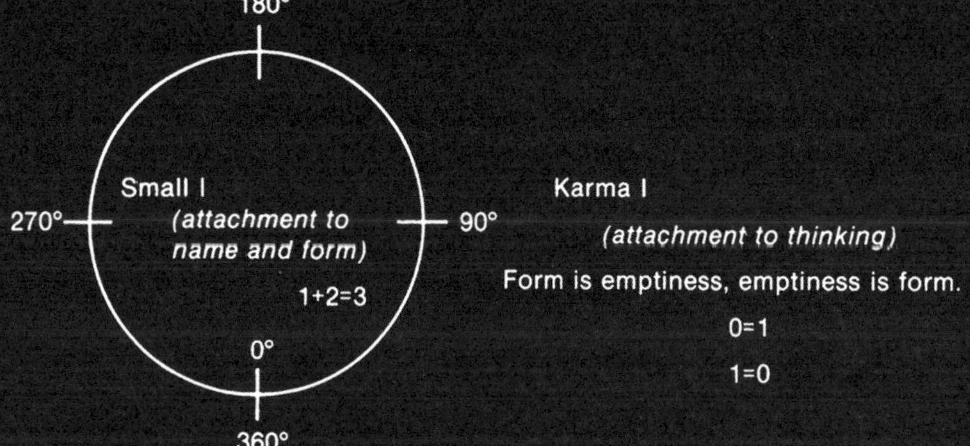

Big I

(no-attachment thinking)

Form is form, emptiness is emptiness.

3x3=9

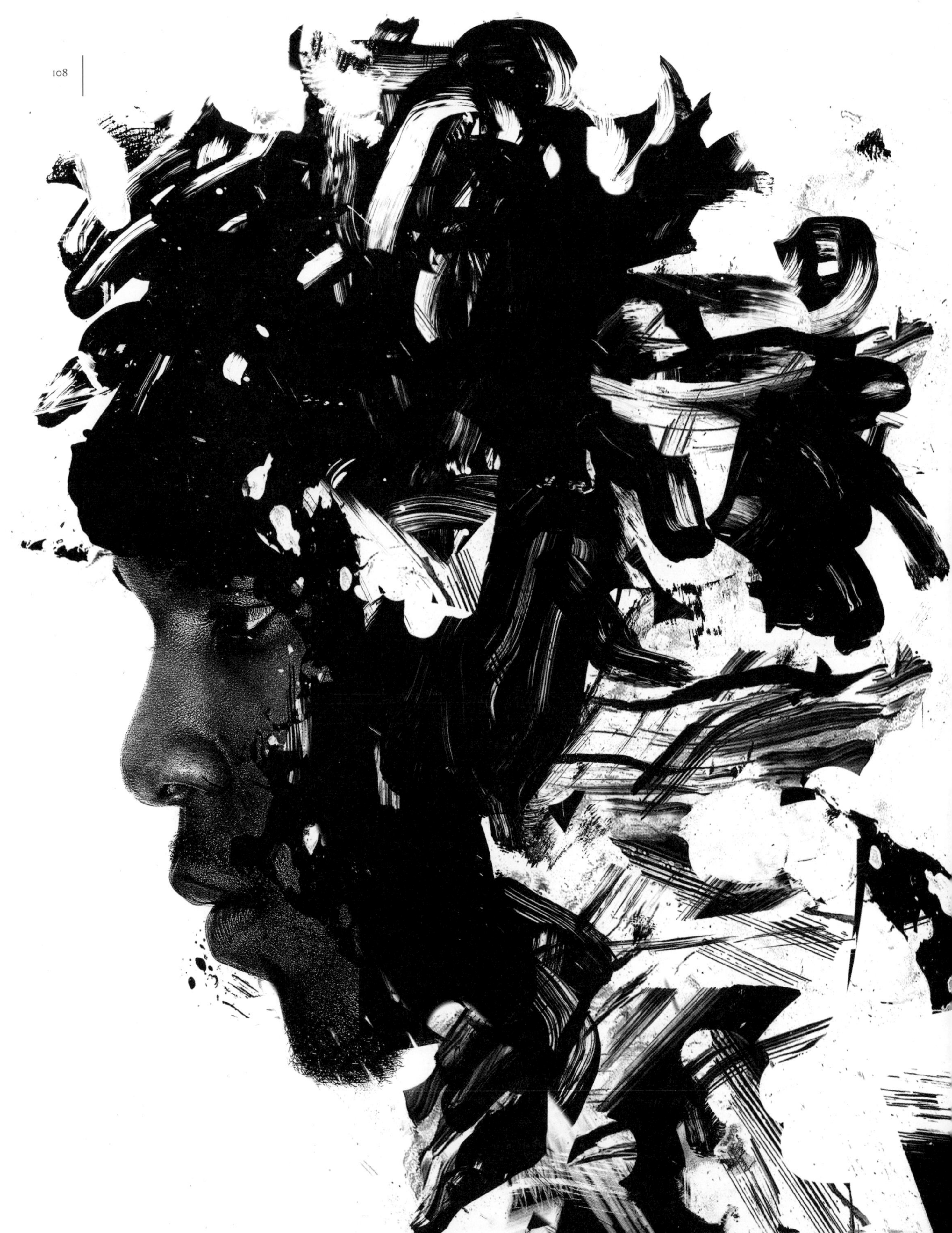

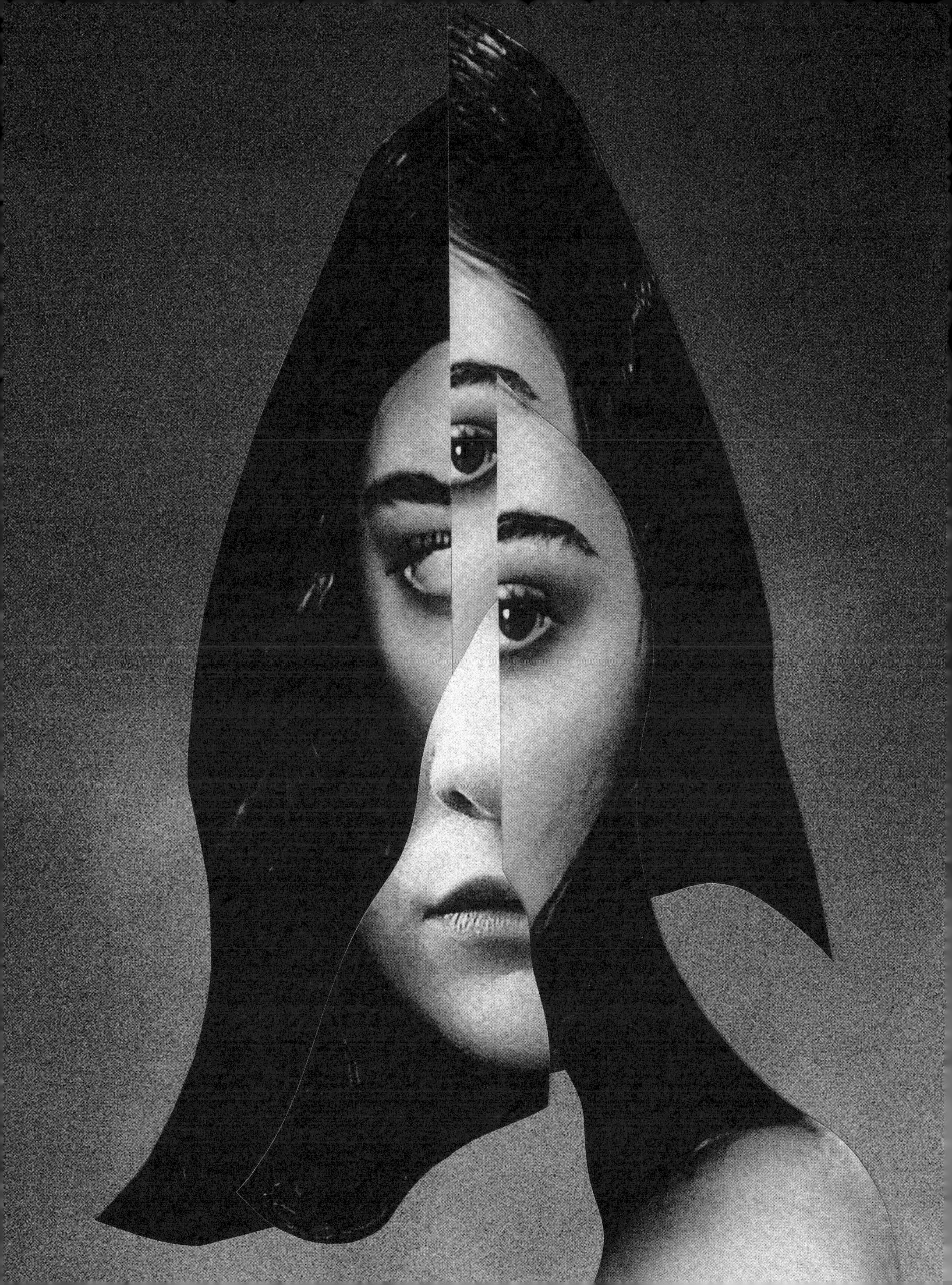

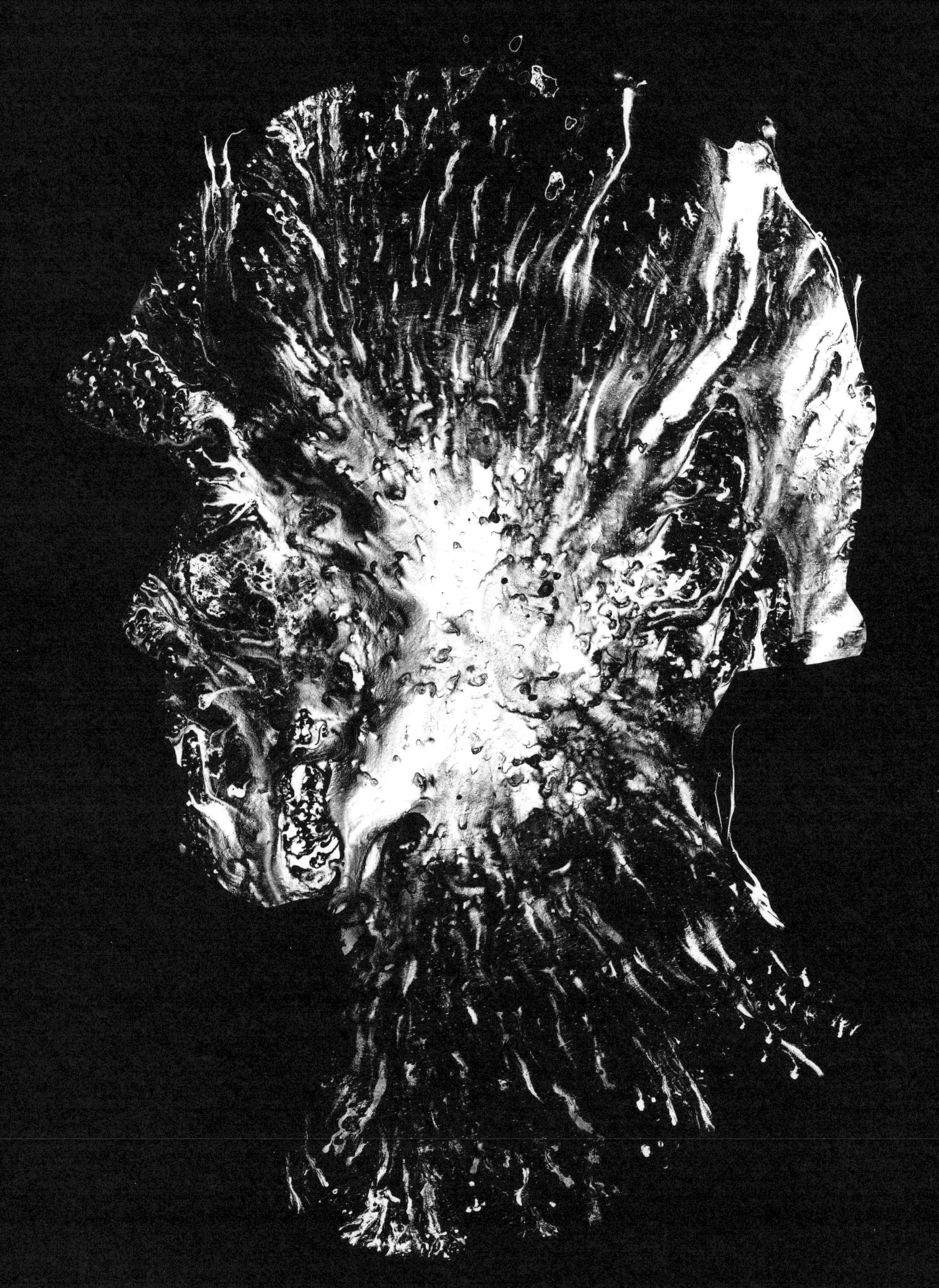

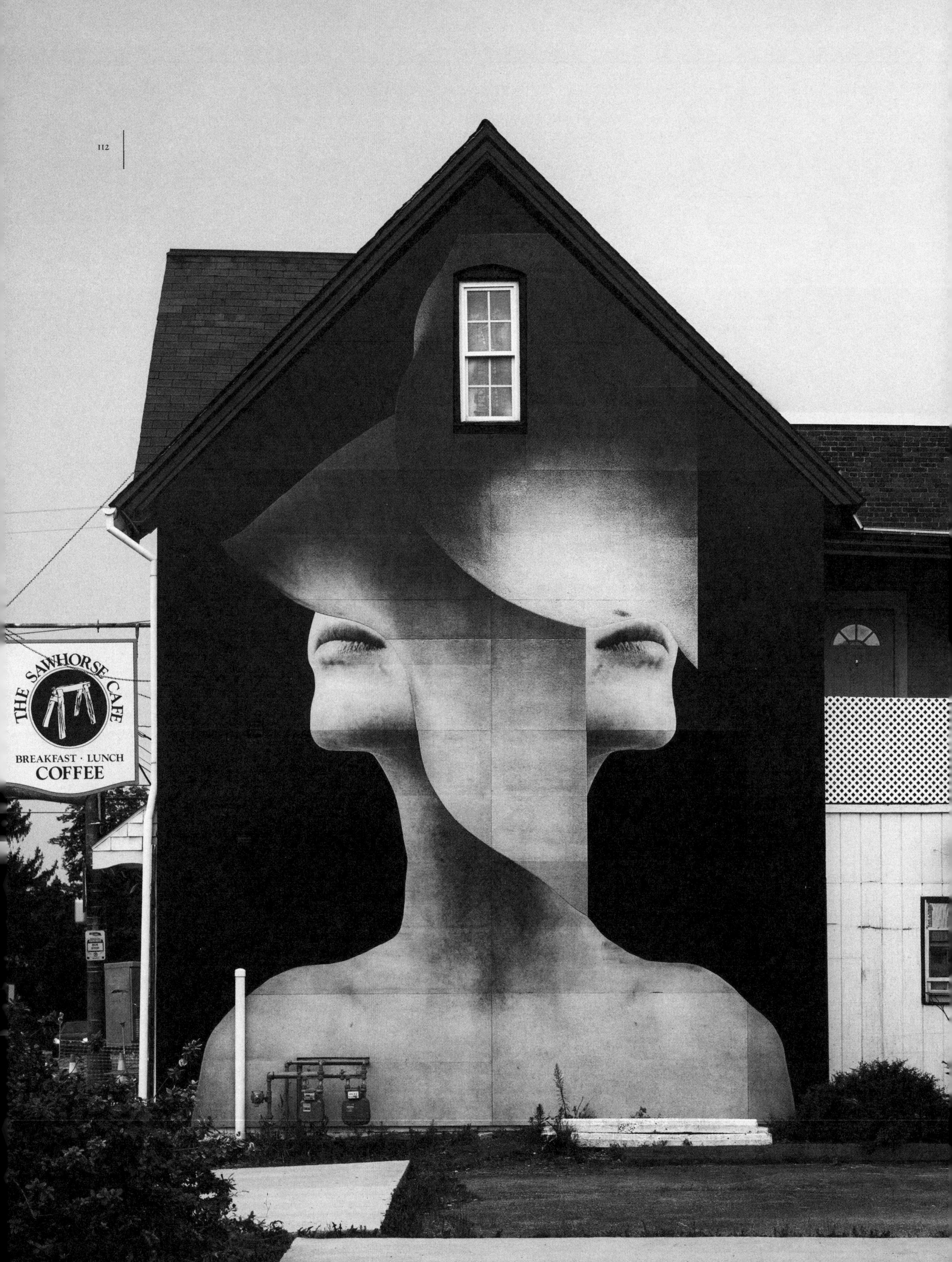
THE SAWHORSE CAFE
BREAKFAST · LUNCH
COFFEE

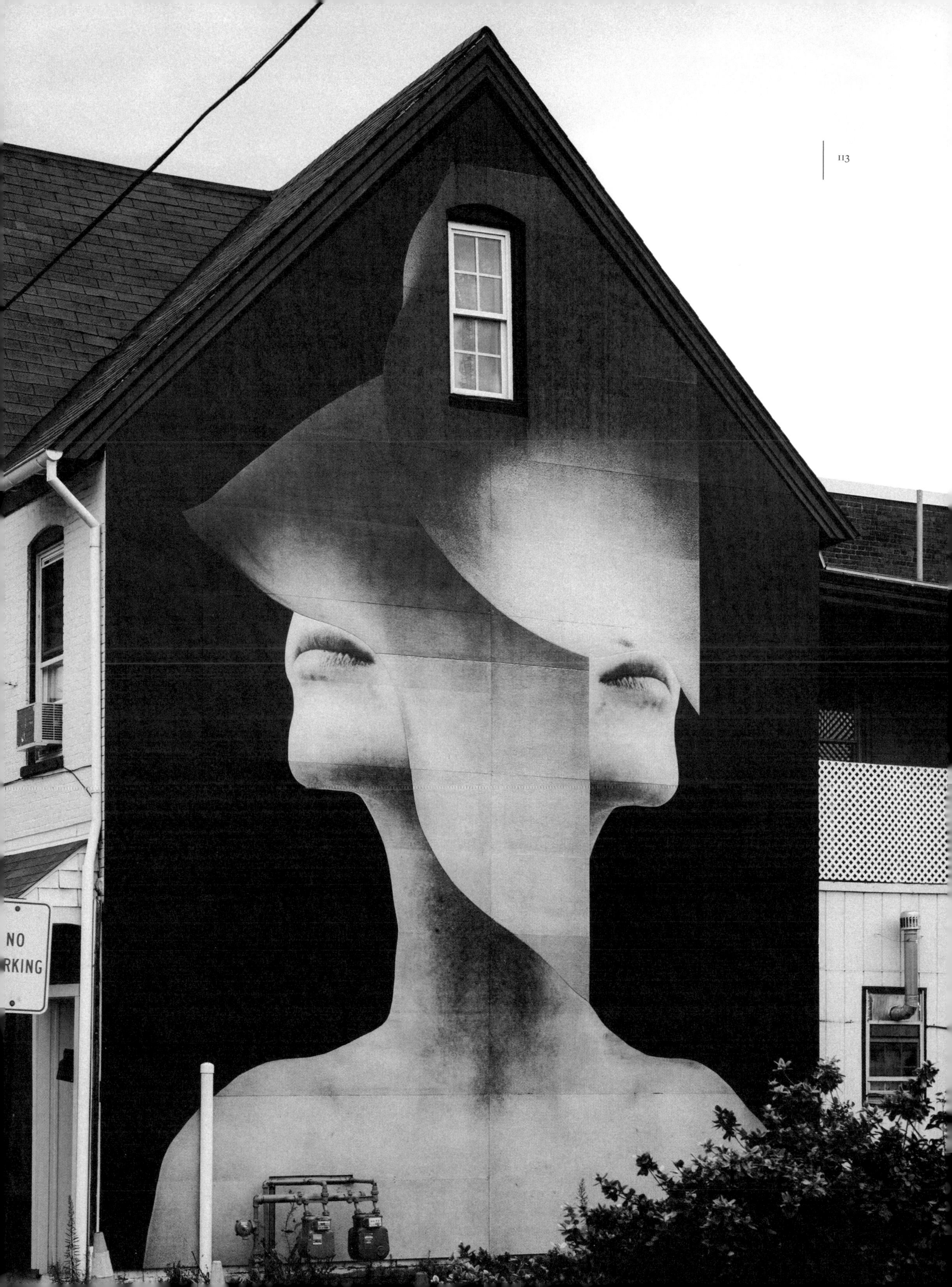
NO
RKING

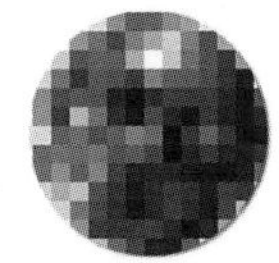

Super pretentious and gross. Looks like someone likes bath salts and satanism. Disfigured humanity on a pedestal.

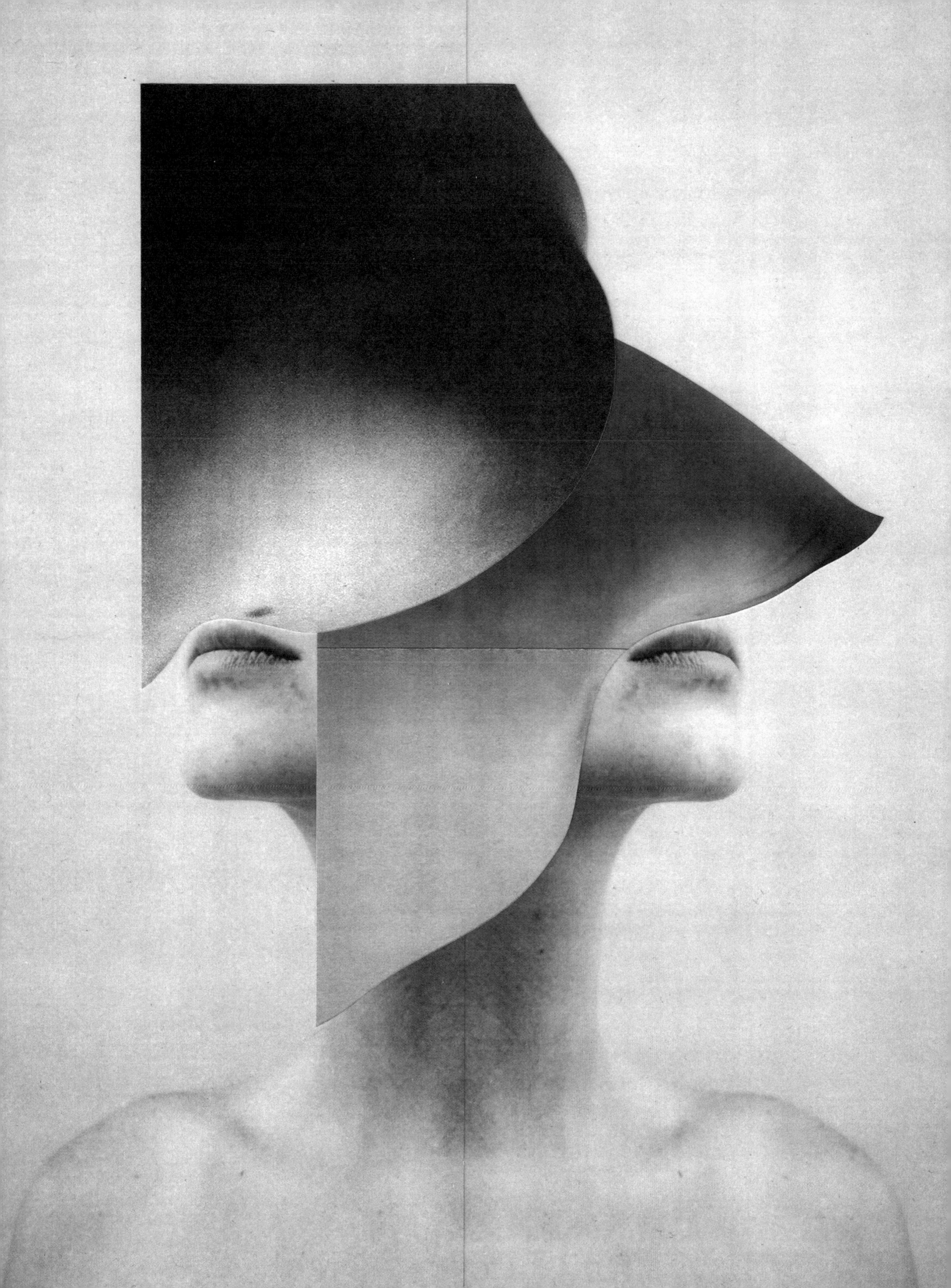

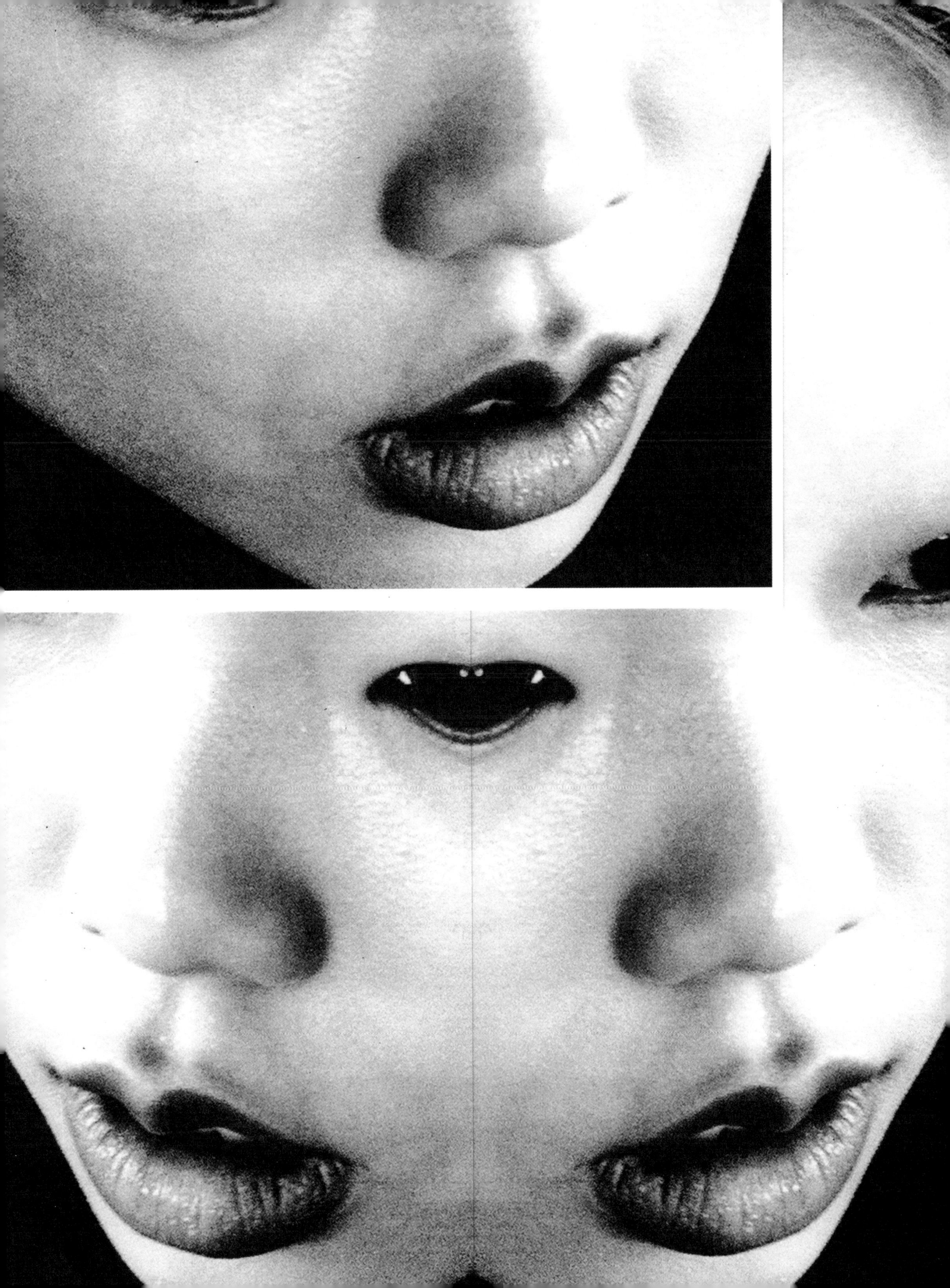

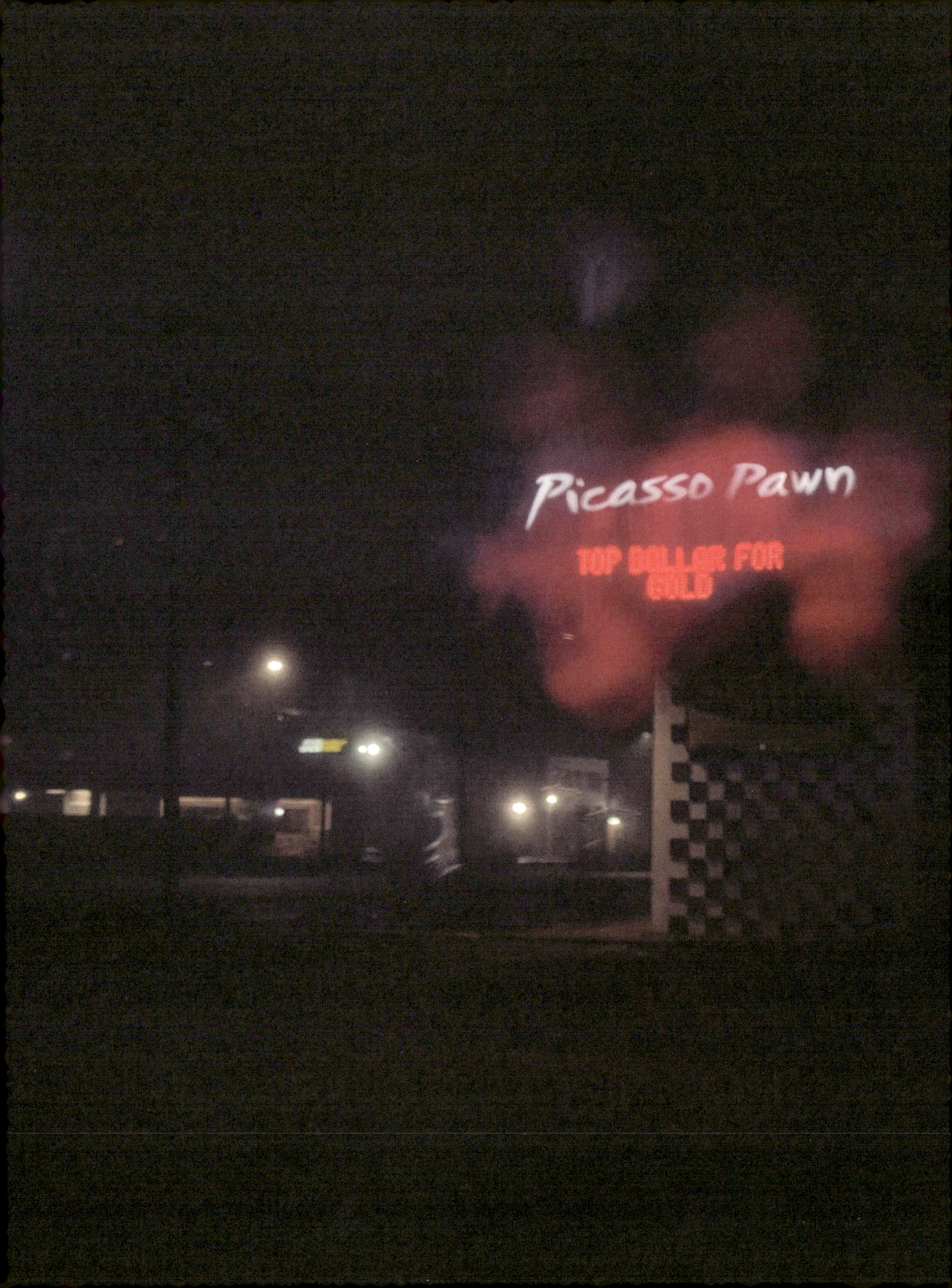

Picasso Pawn
TOP DOLLAR FOR
GOLD

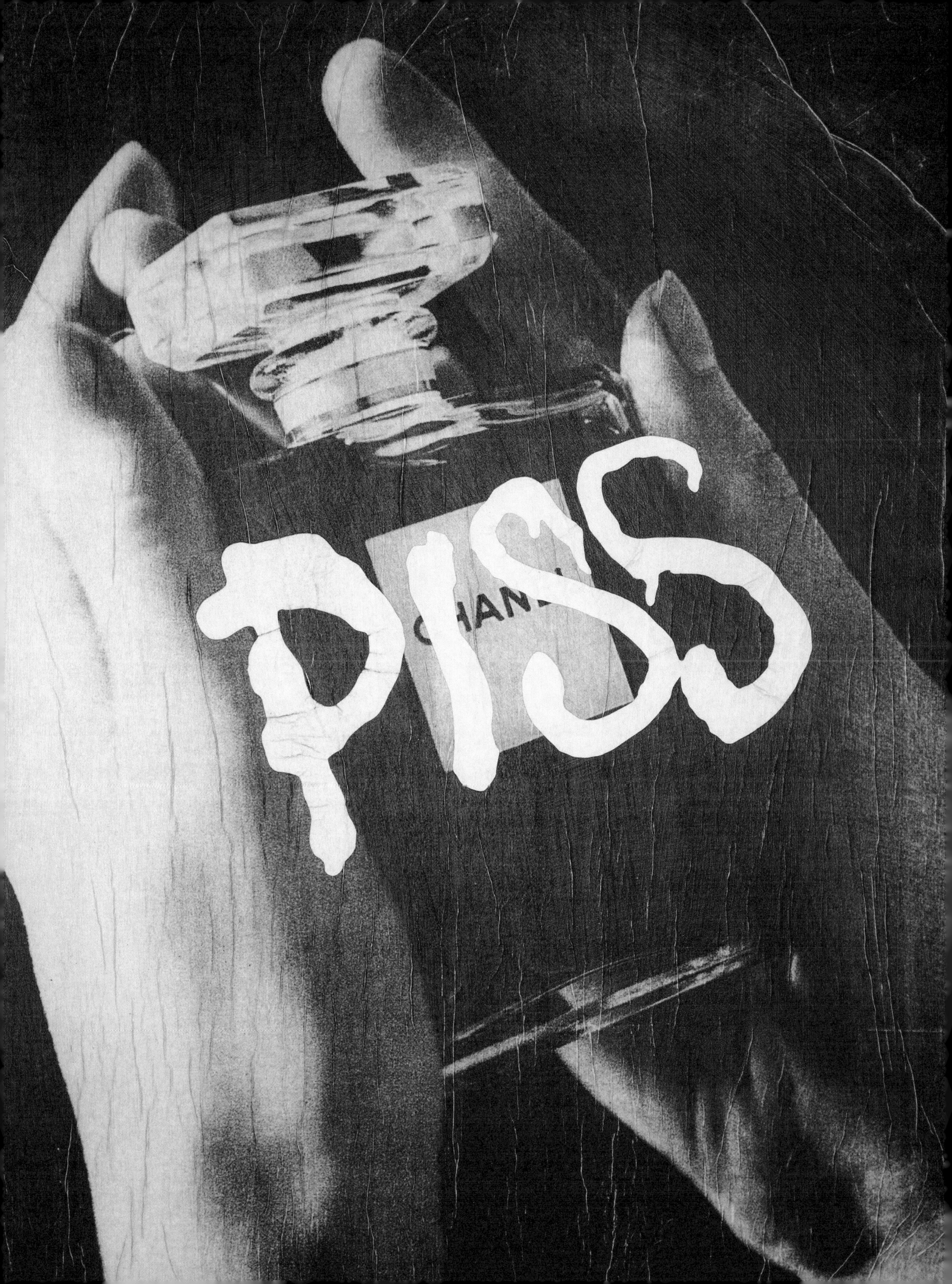
PISS

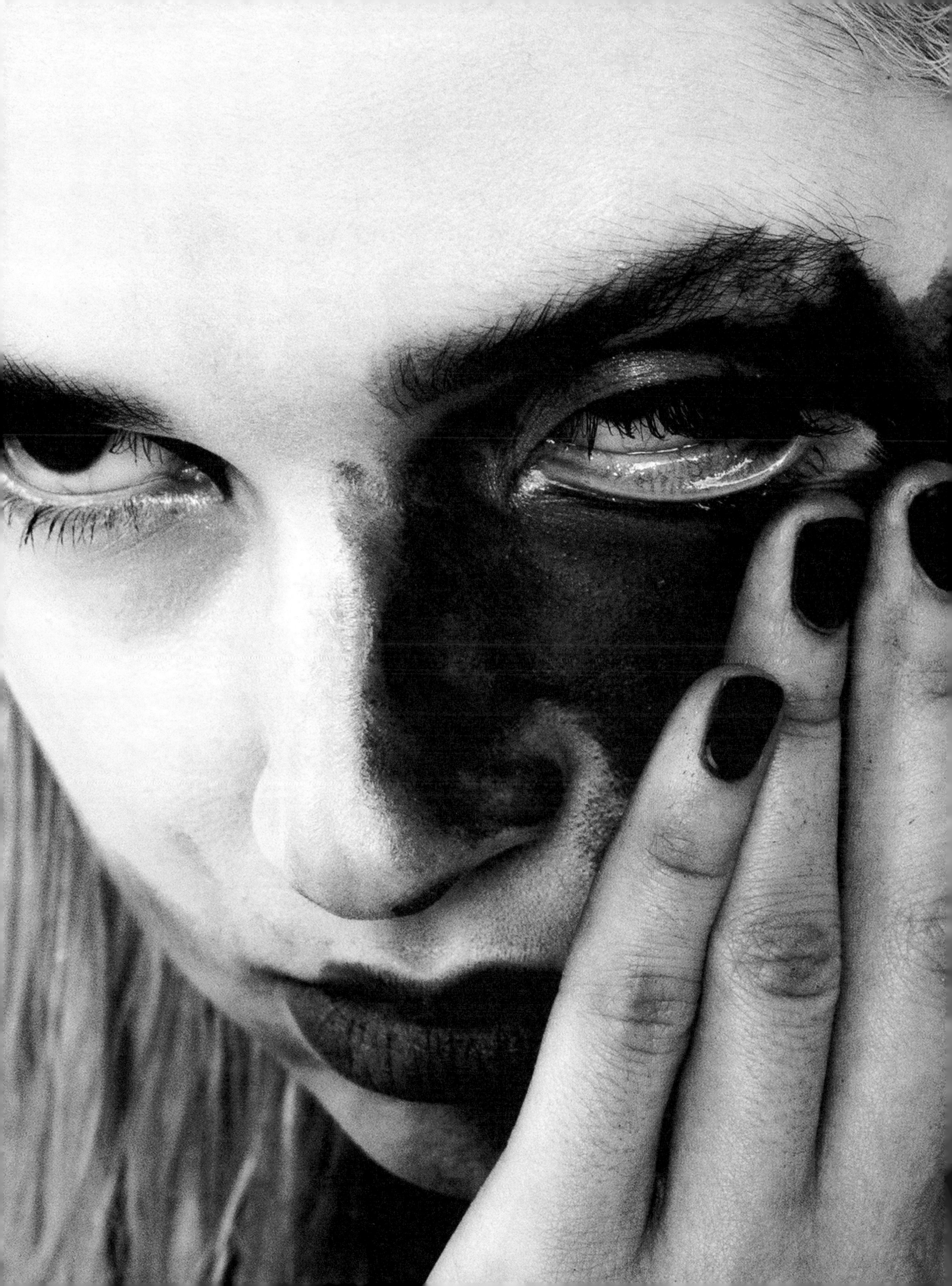

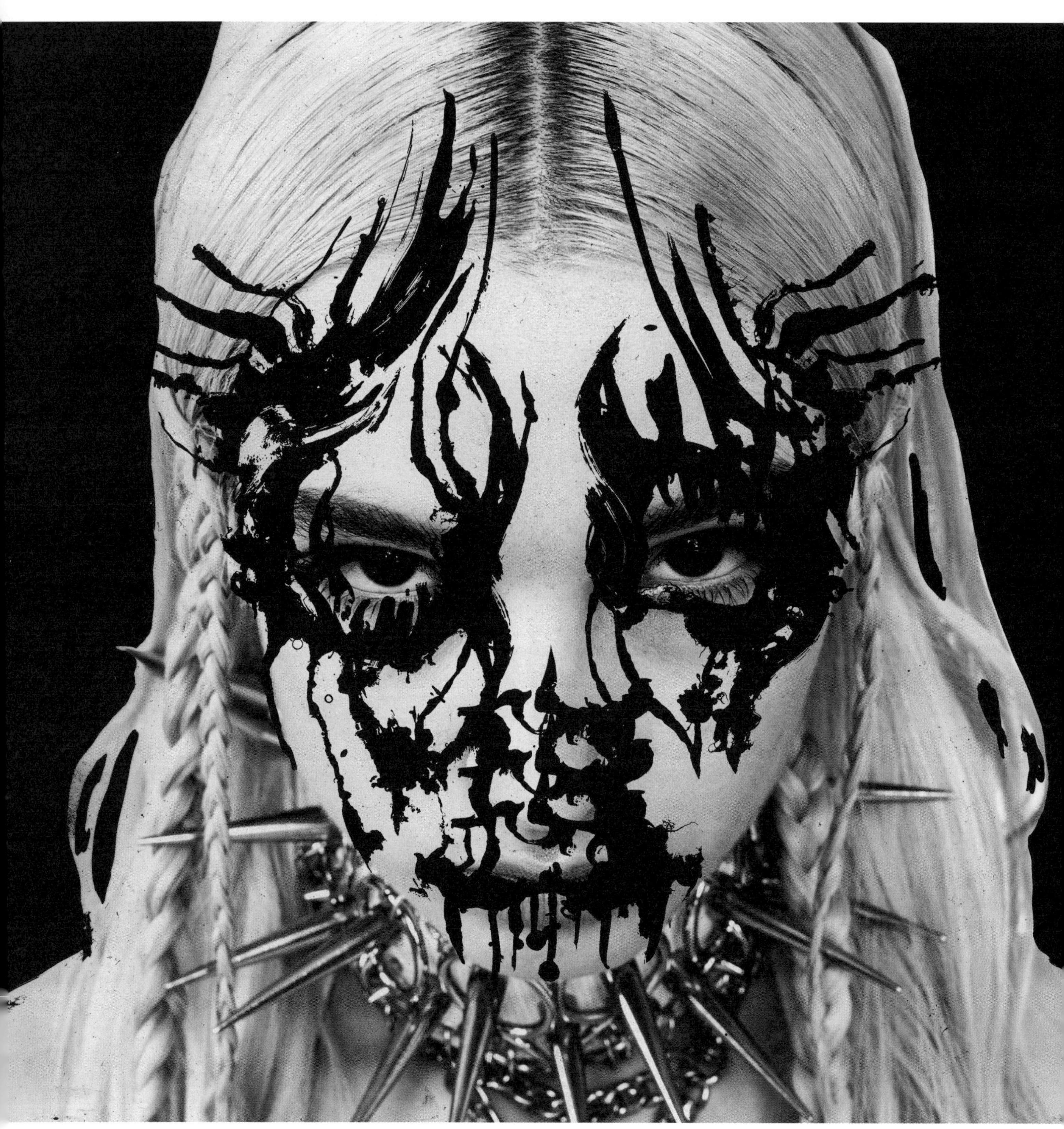

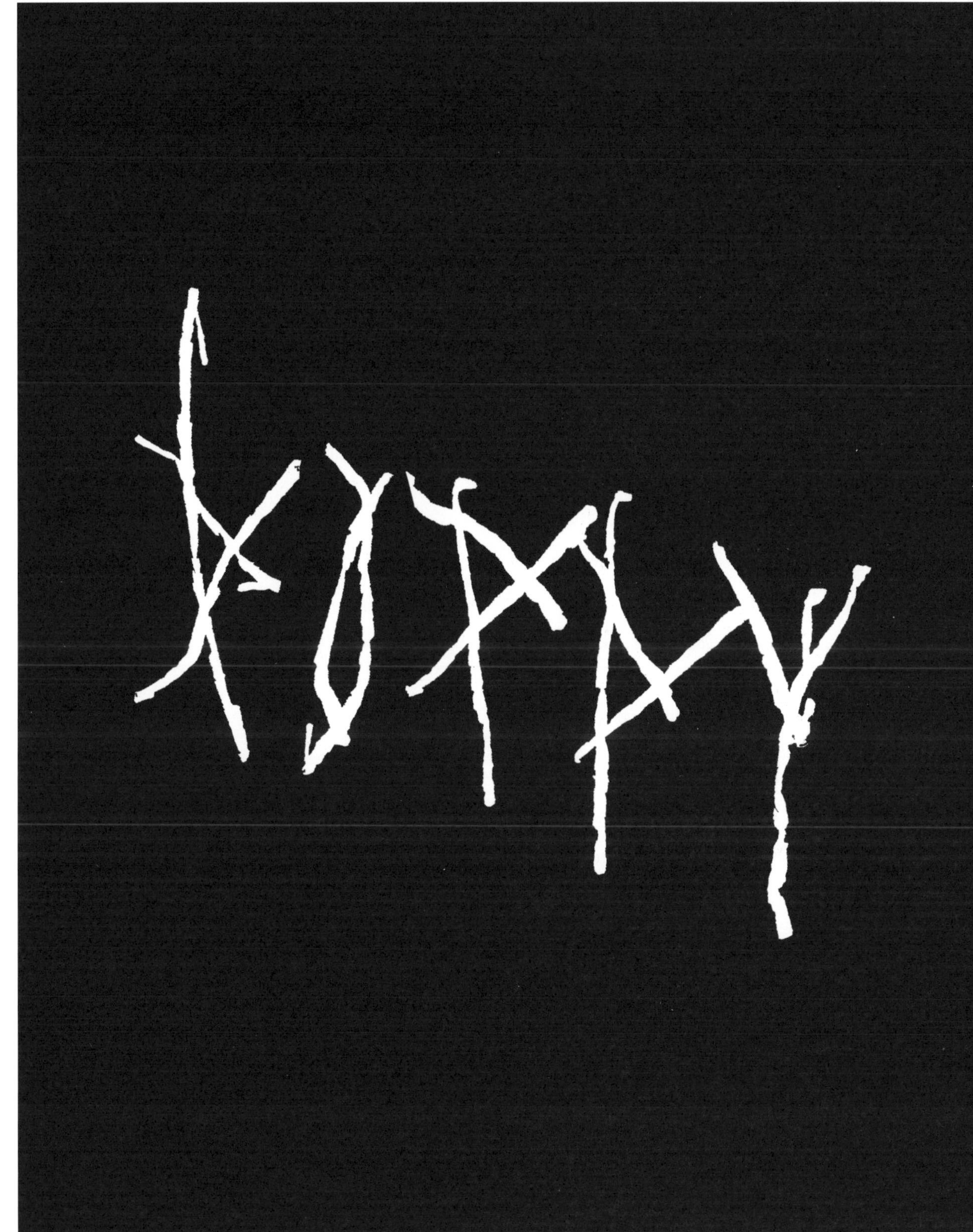

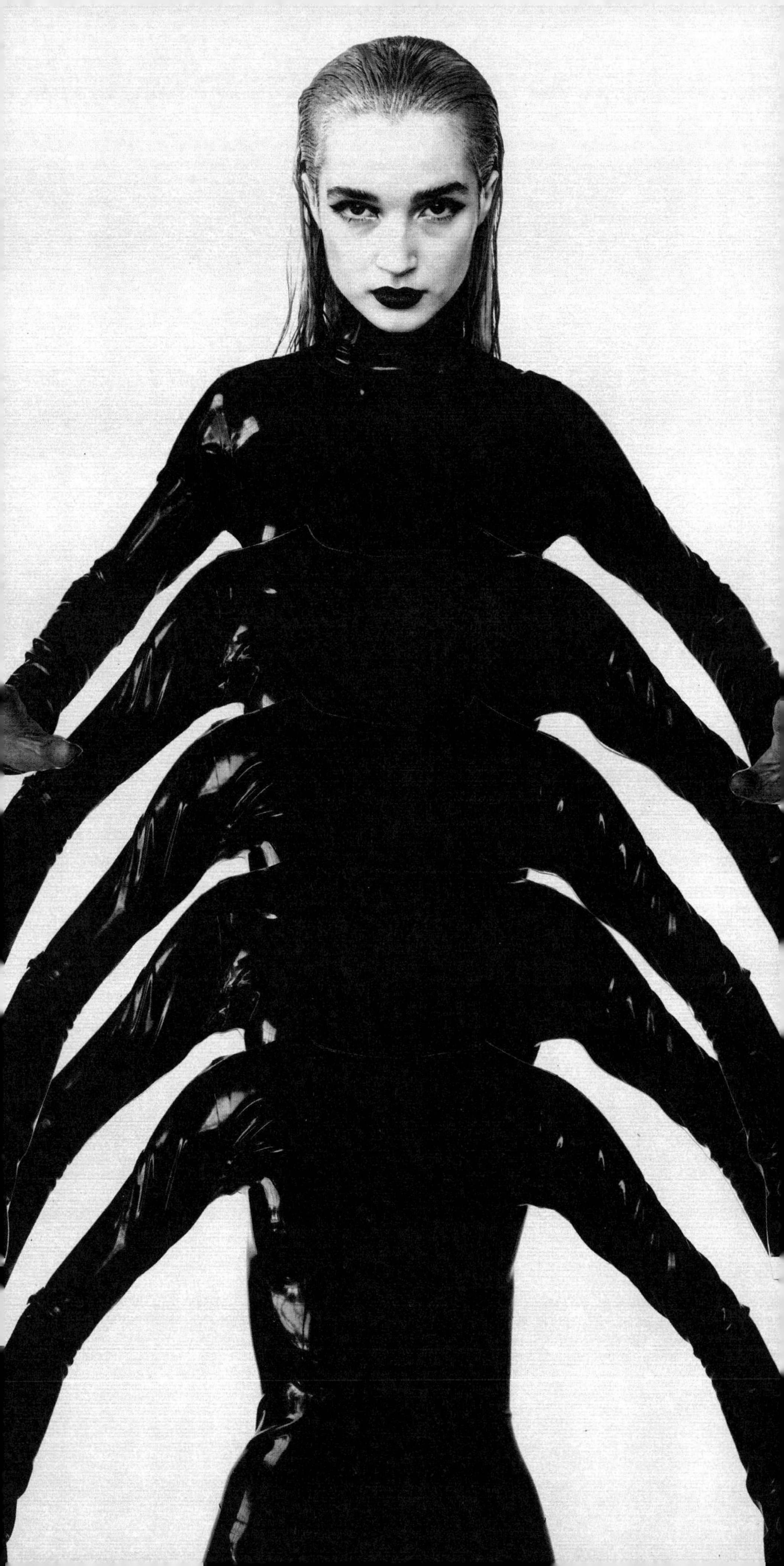

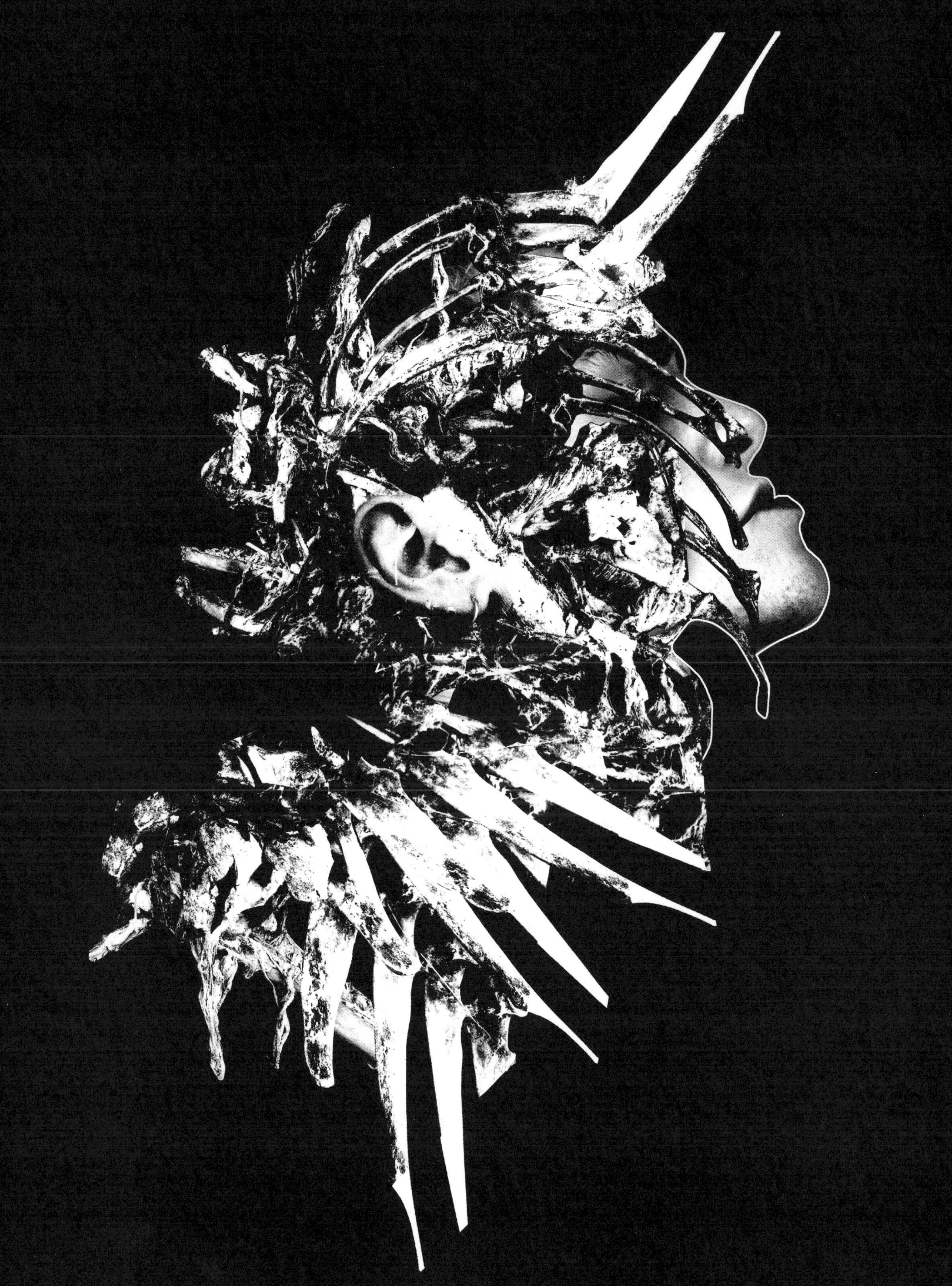

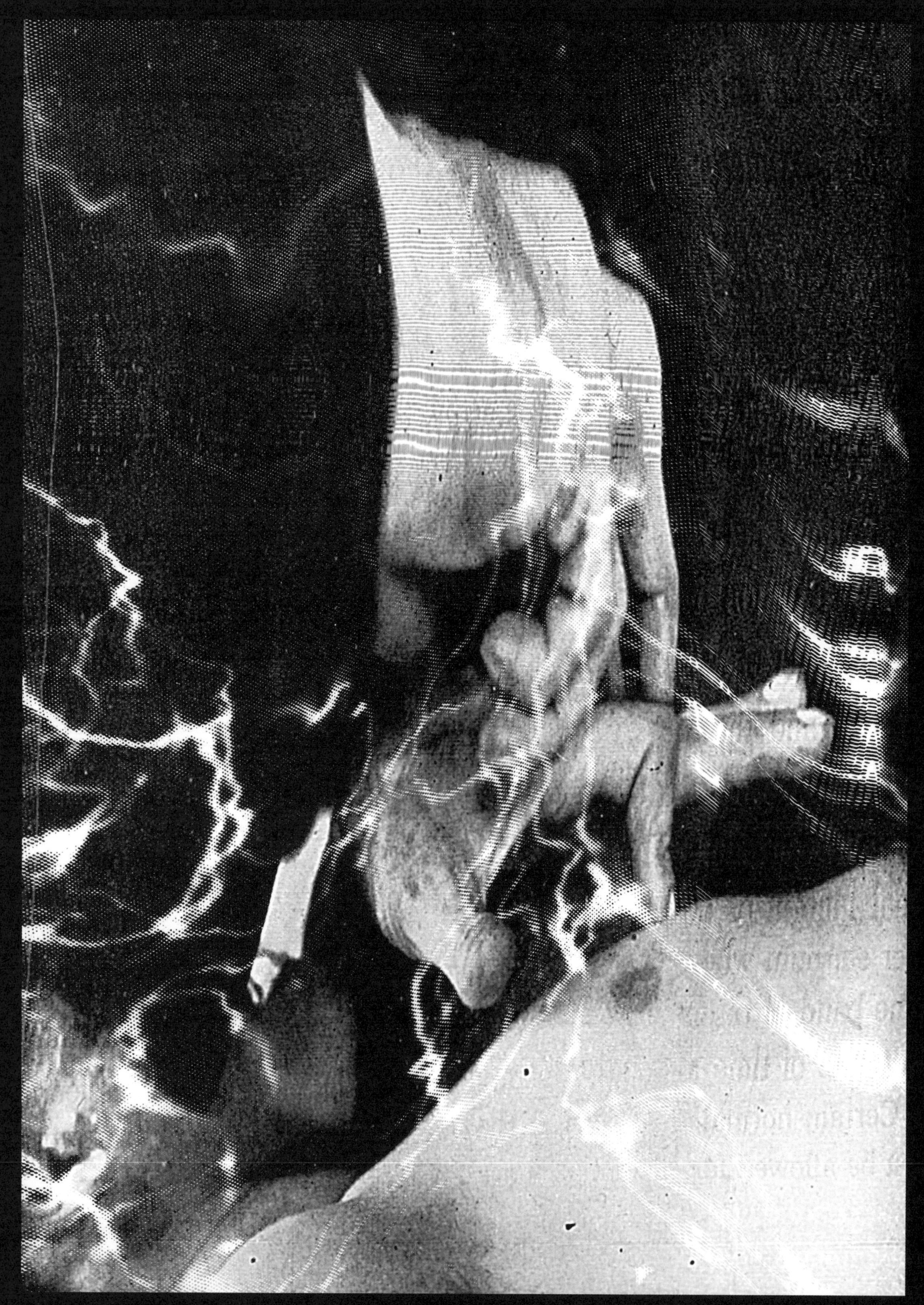

Absolutely, it's all about context. Whether in a magazine, in a collector's home, on a gallery wall or existing in a social media setting, the work will carry different connotations. Your online presence almost seems like an extension of your practice.

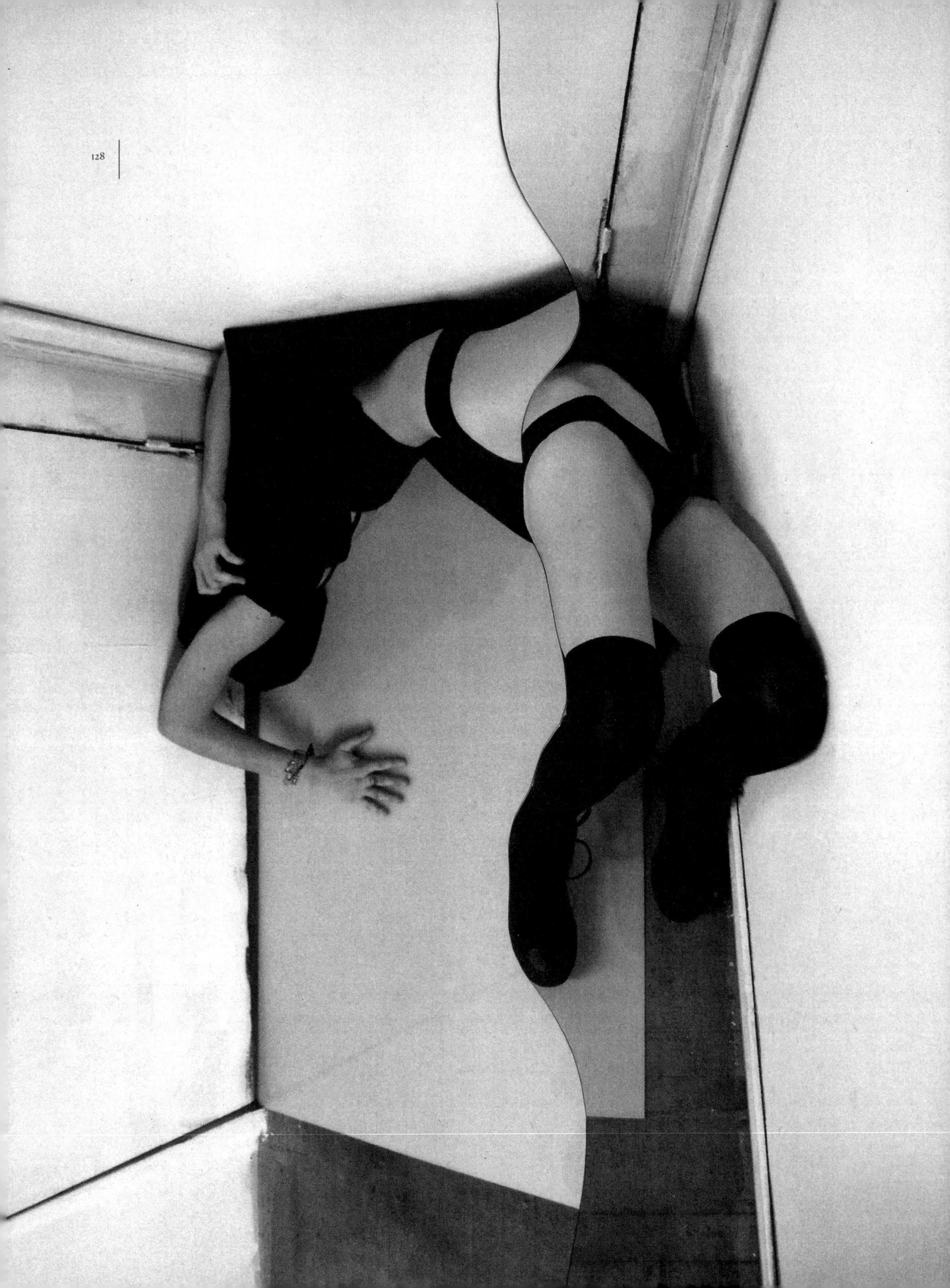

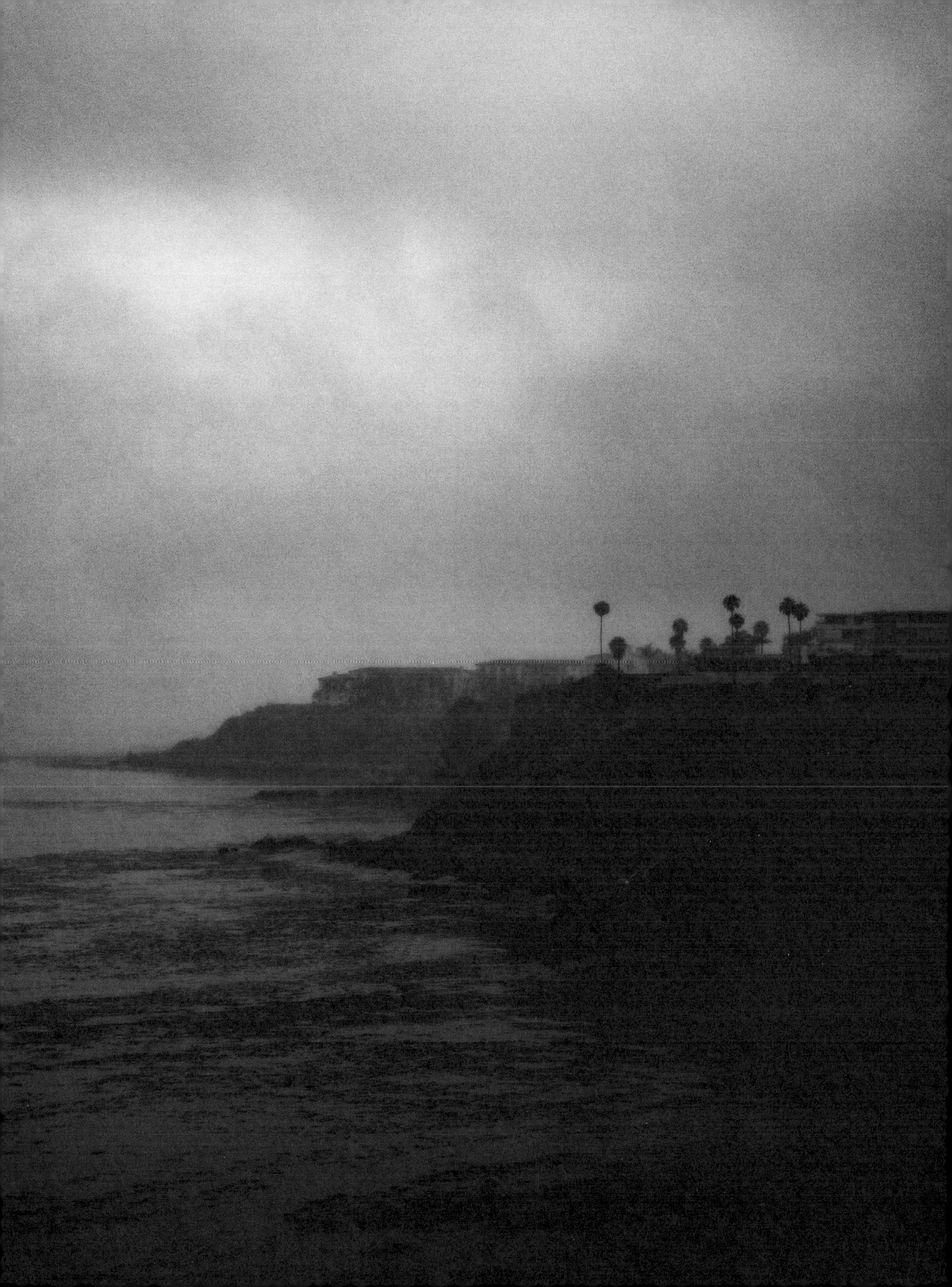

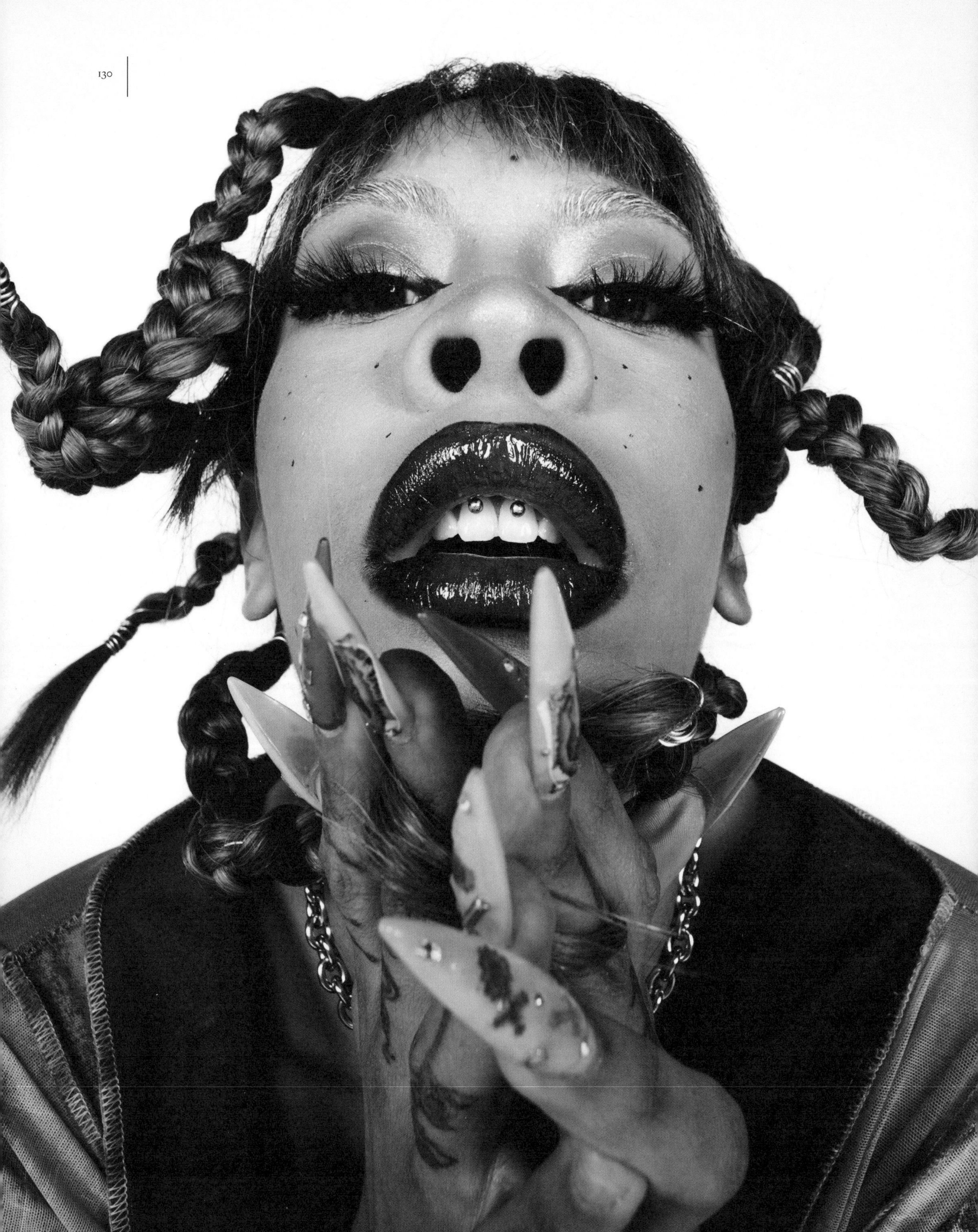

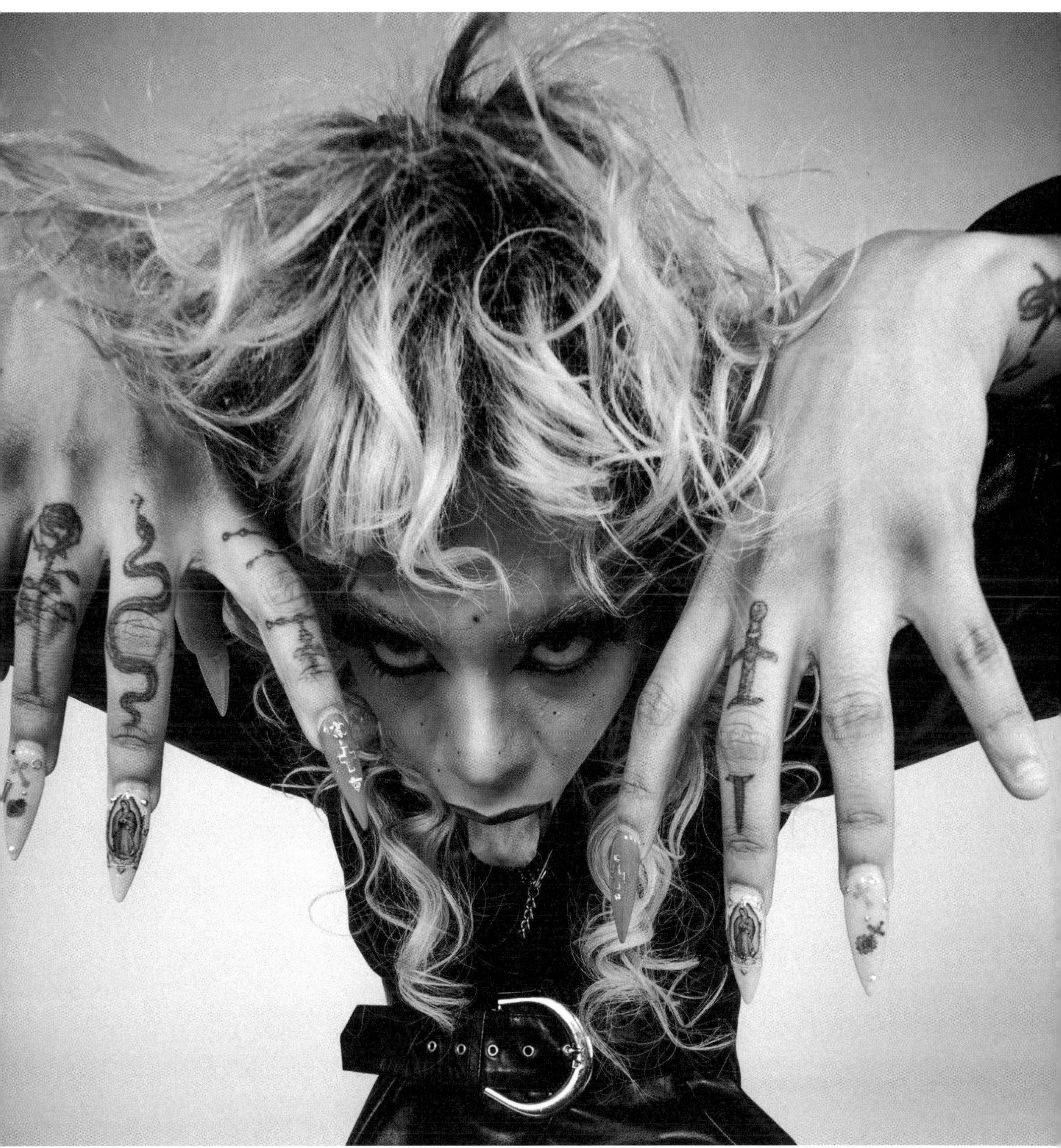

ROACH HISS
ROACH HISS

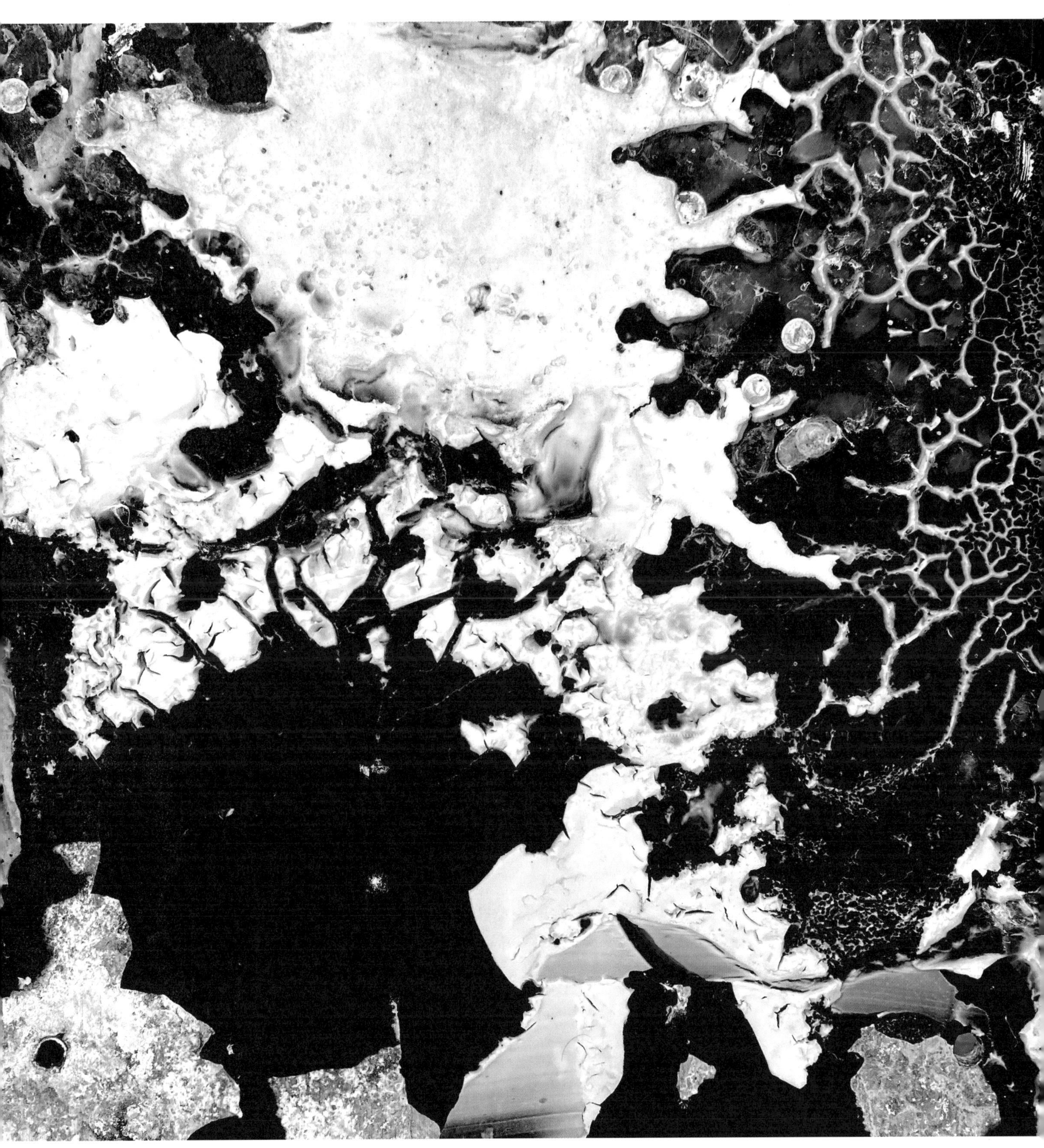

I've Been Seeing My Therapist For Over A Year Now

They Still Spell My Name Wrong

I Am The Abyss Gazing Back

Pain Of Our Age

Savage Romantic

Extremely Armed

Visible But No One Sees

Post-Social-Media-Artist

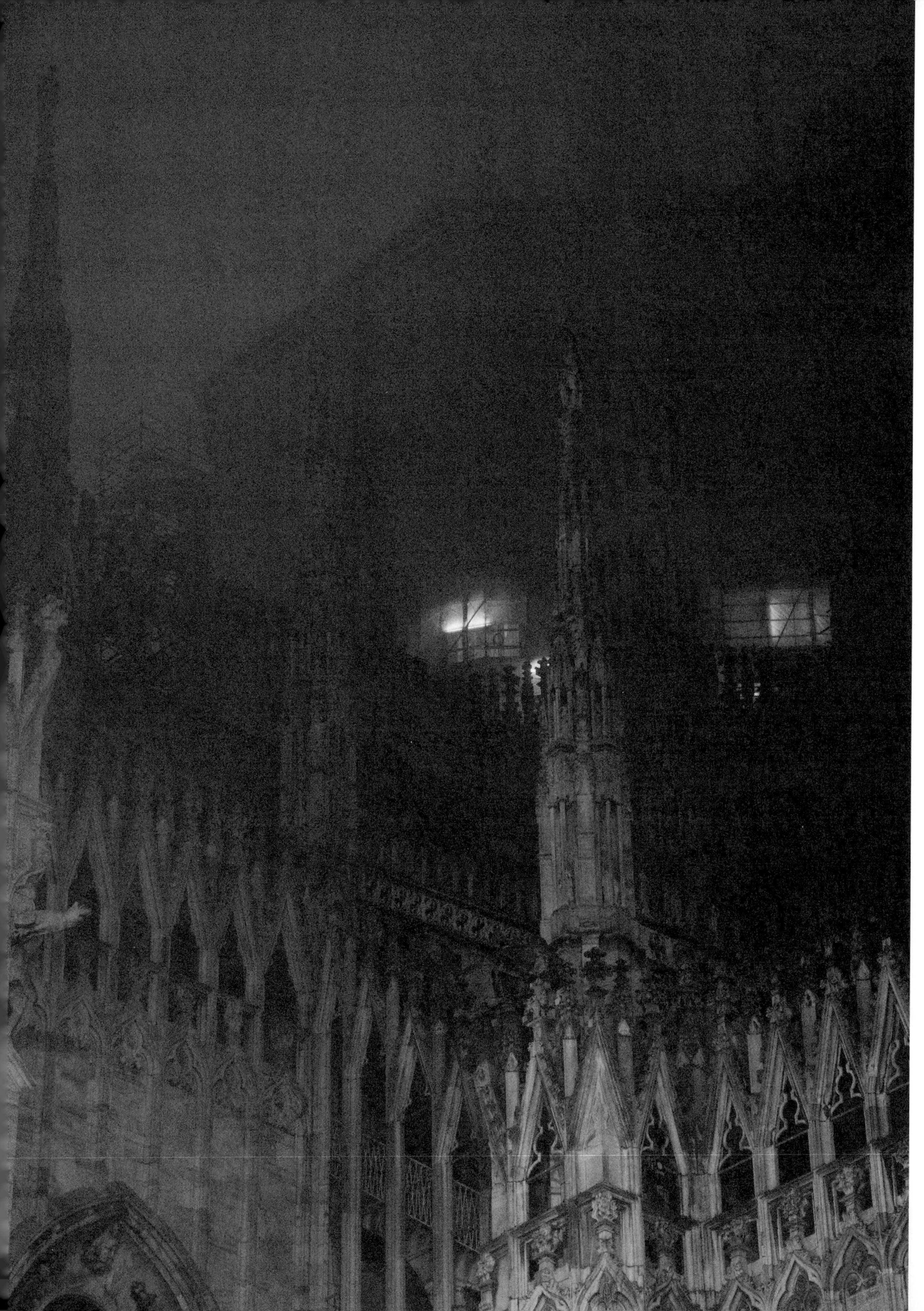

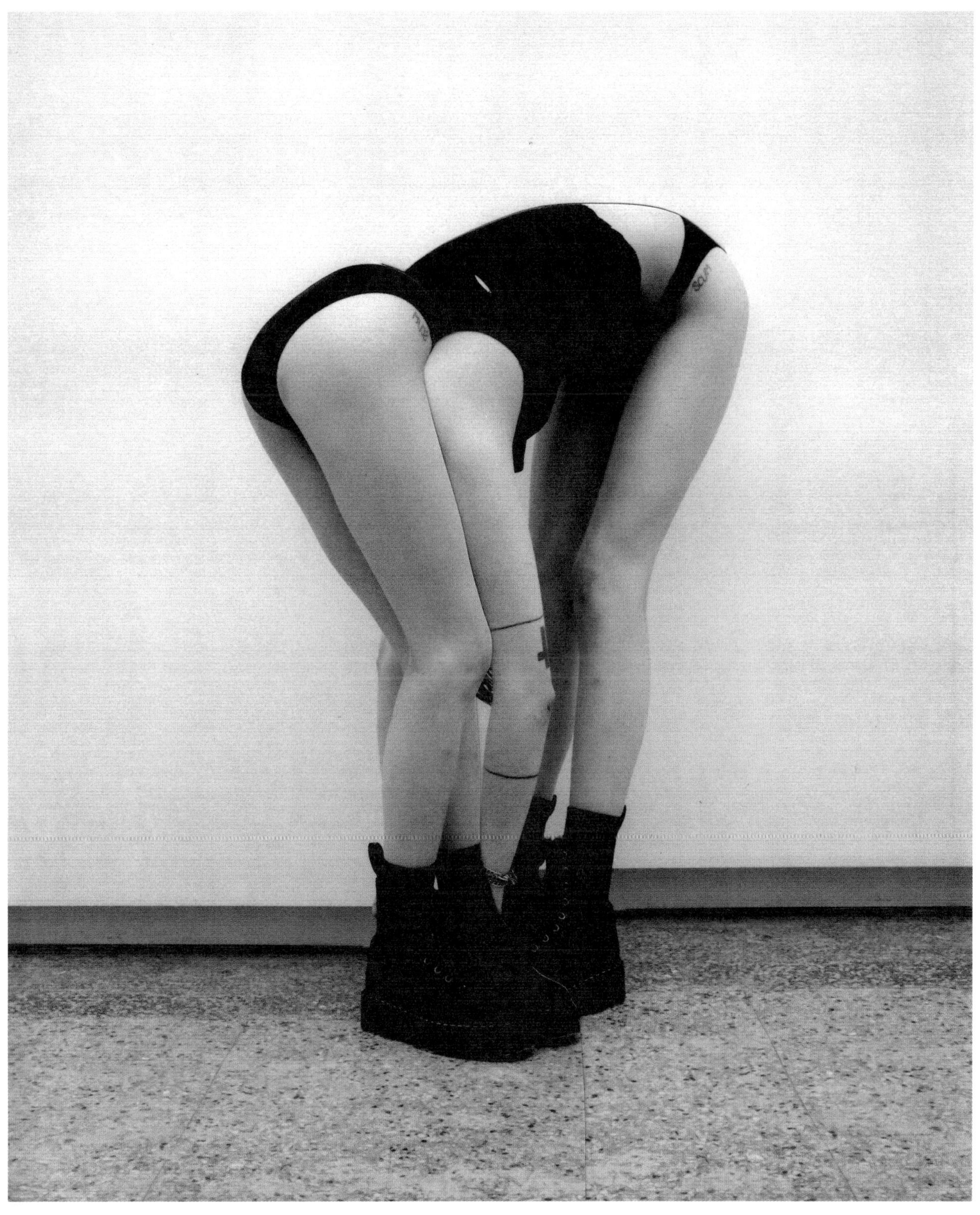

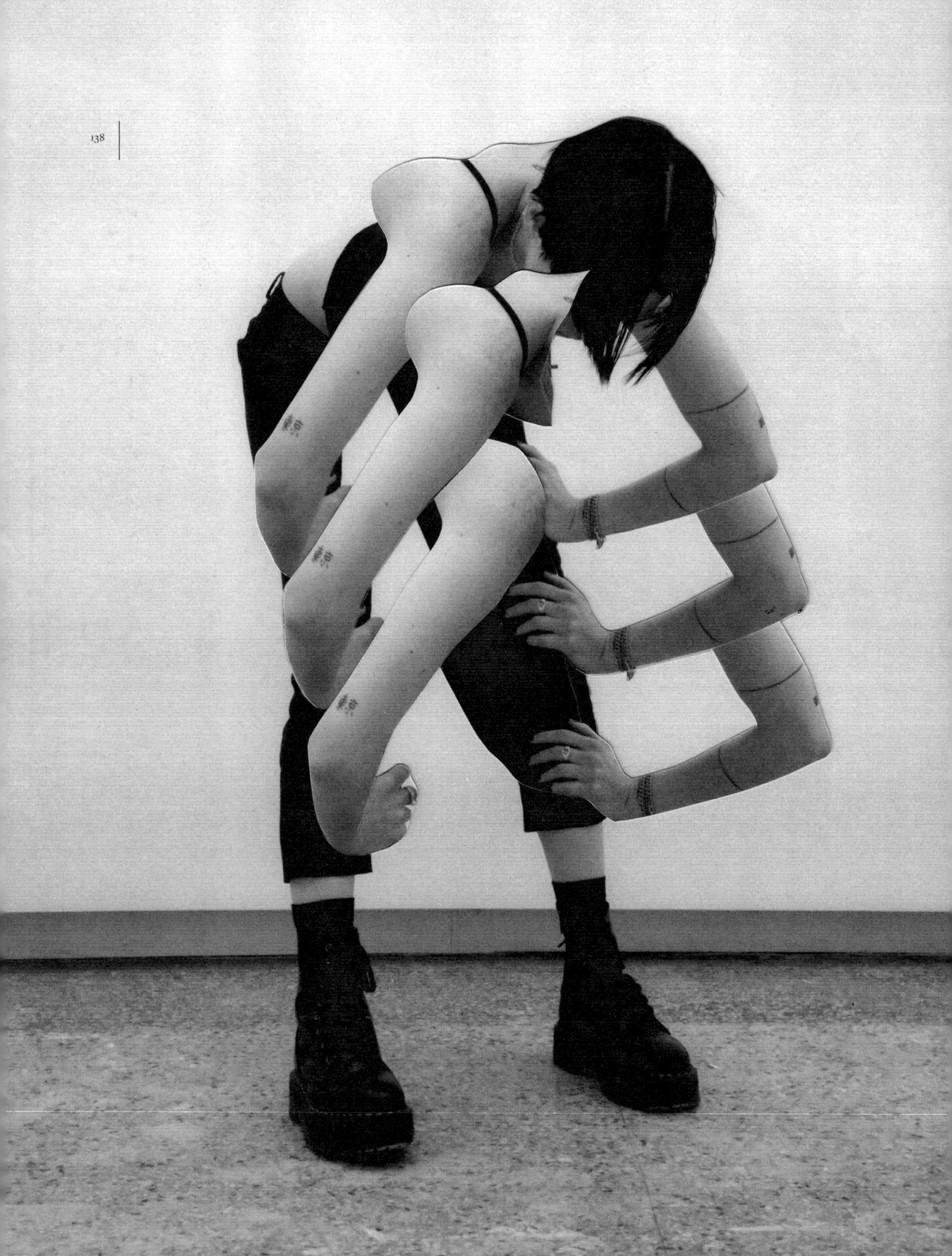

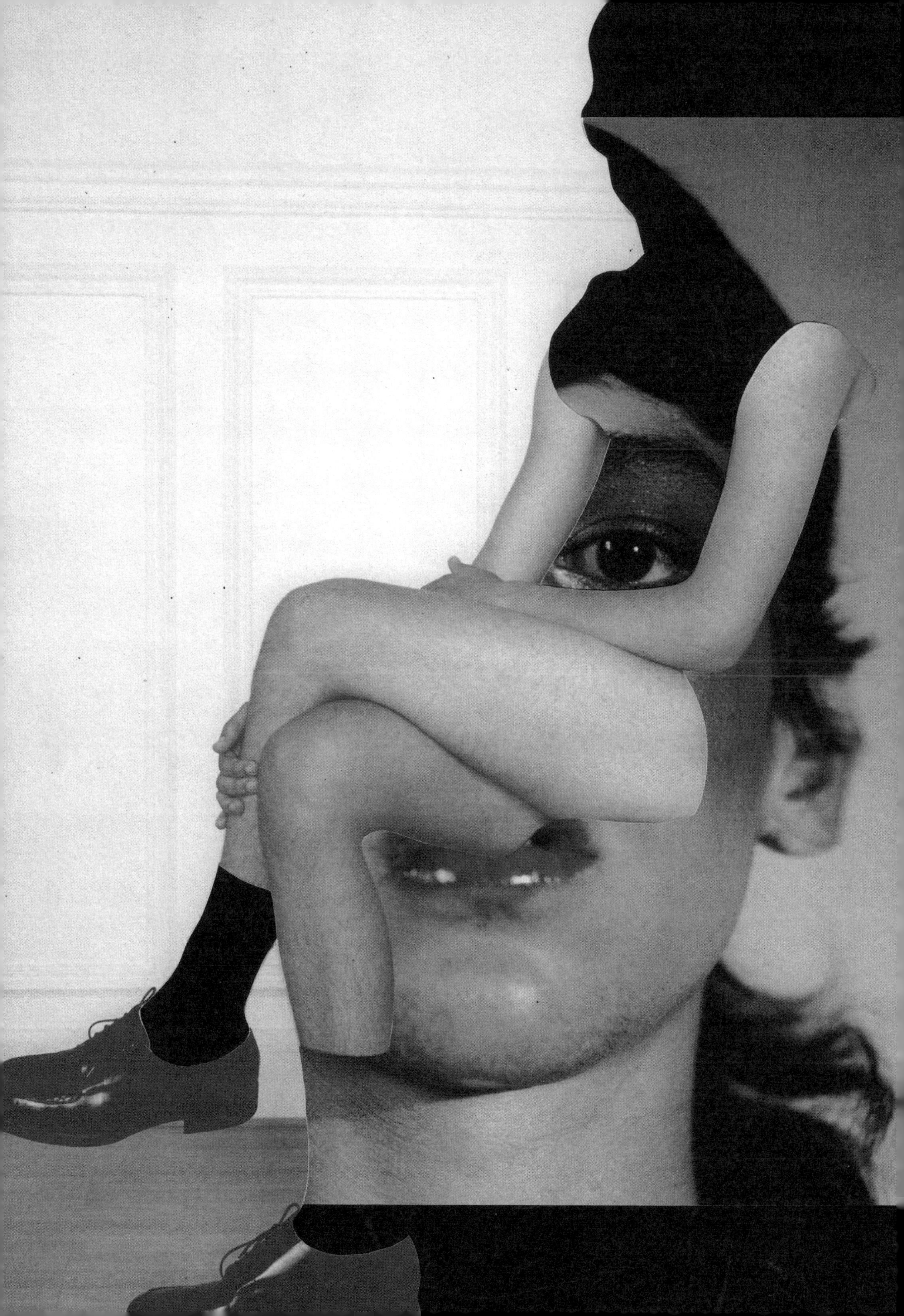

Each of our bodies is a unique signature of chaos.

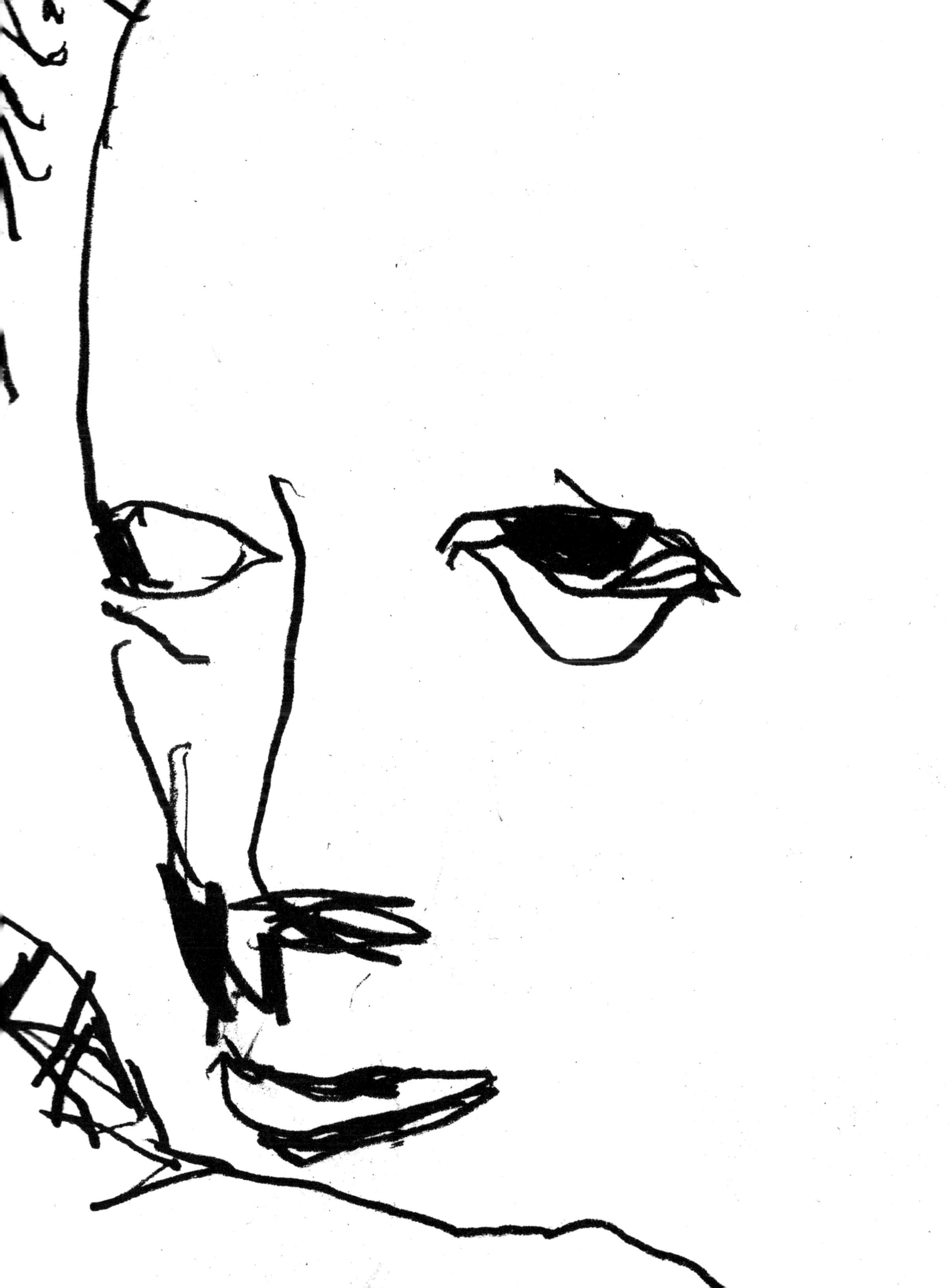

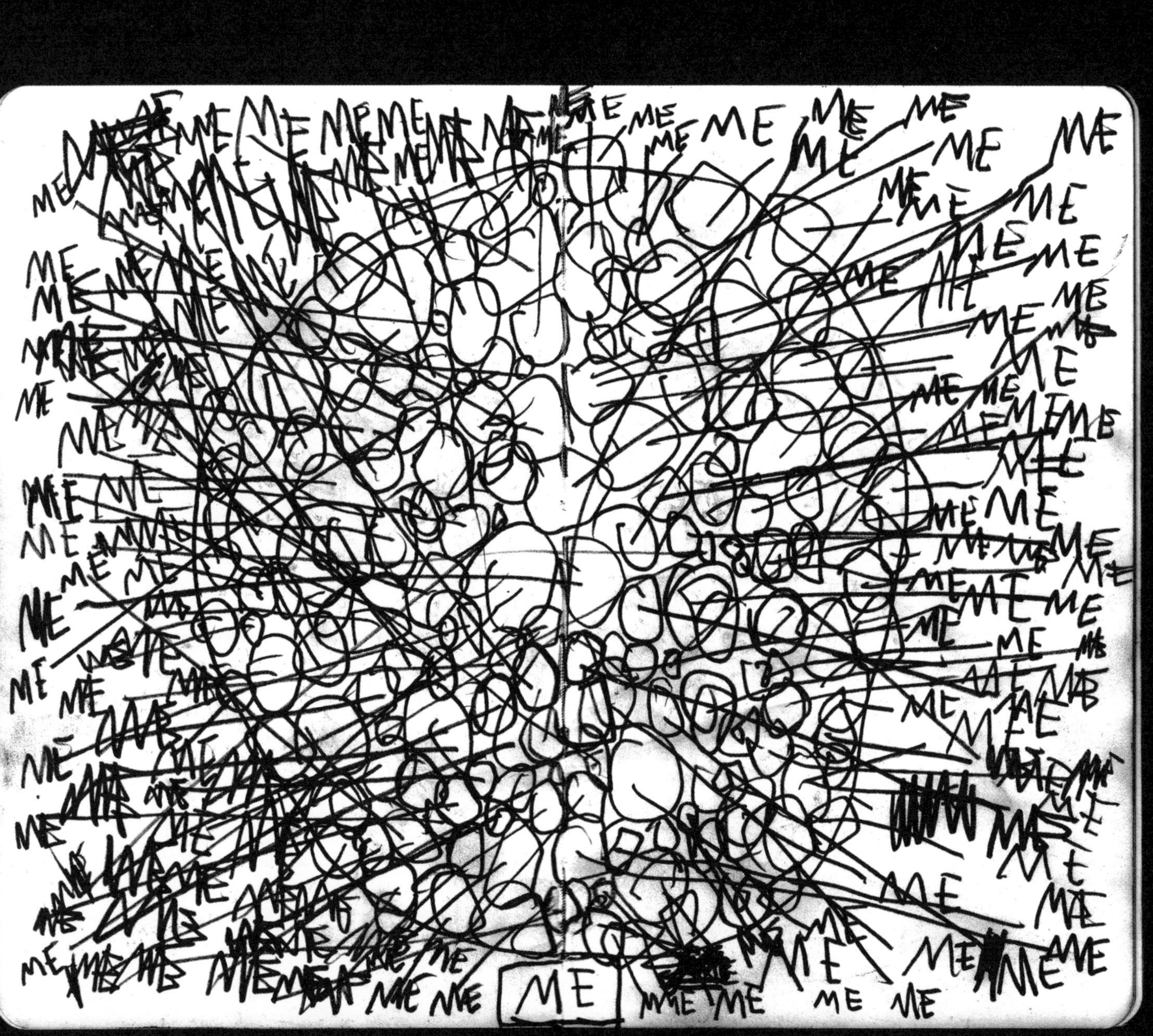
ME

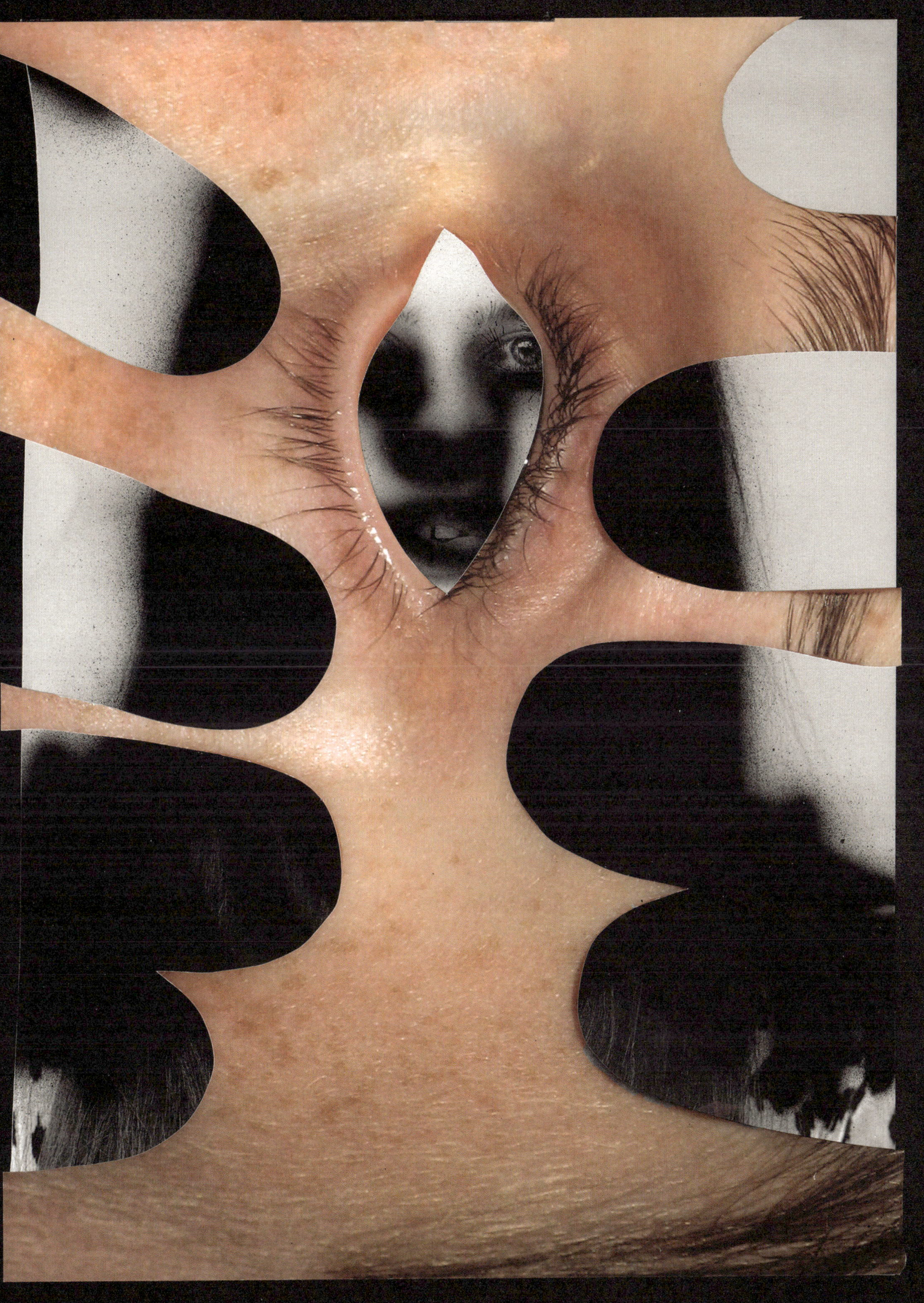

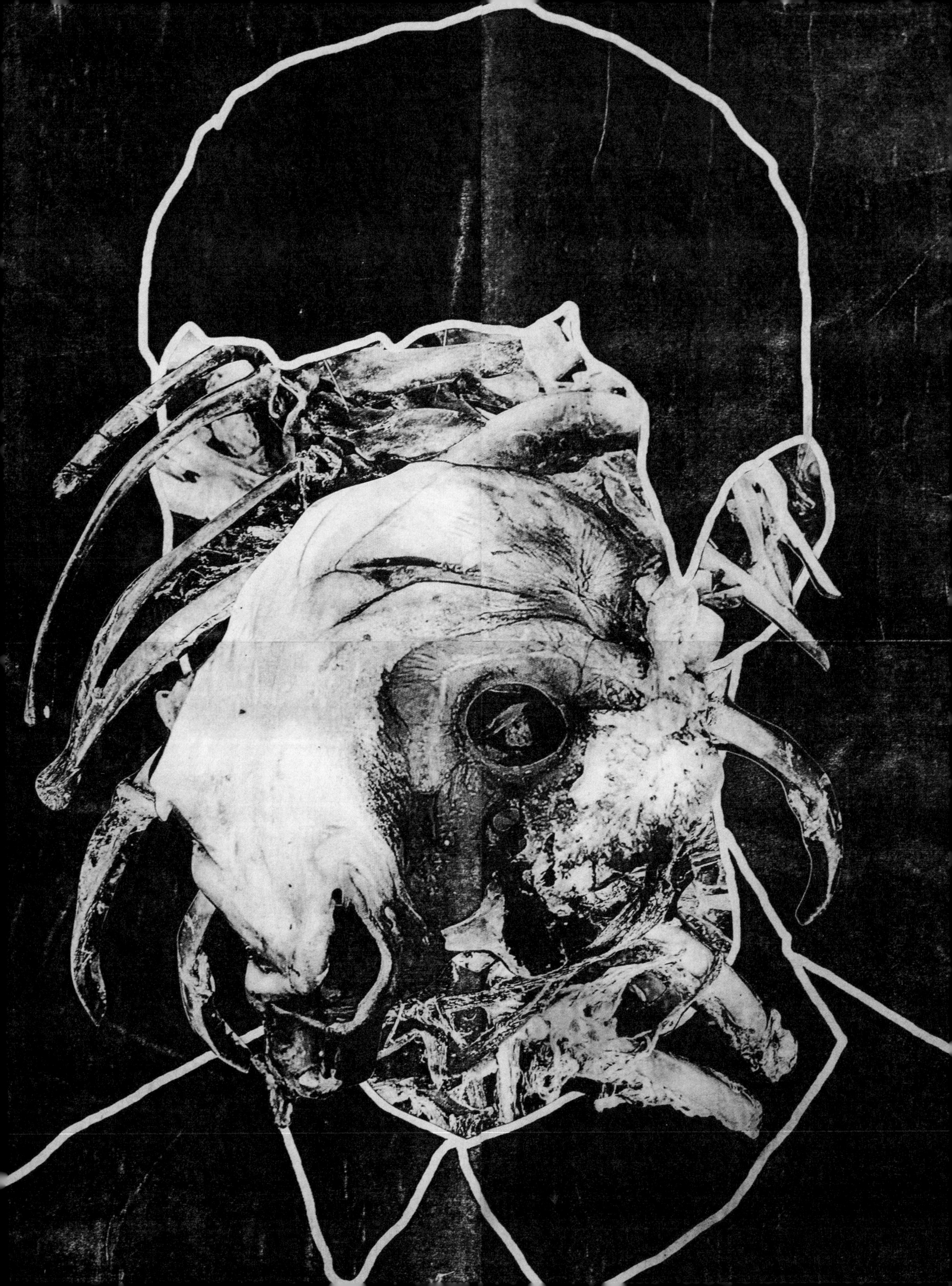

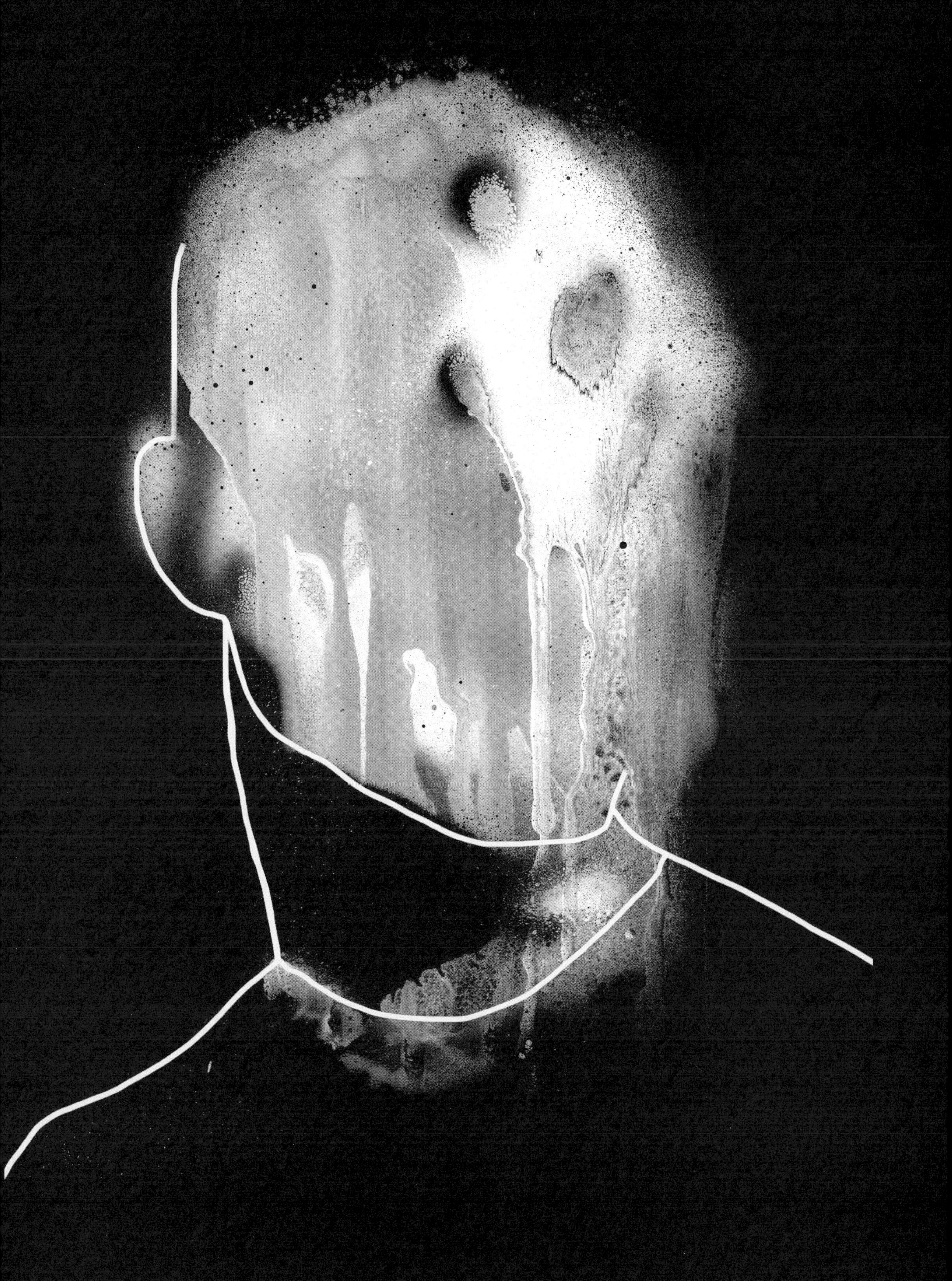

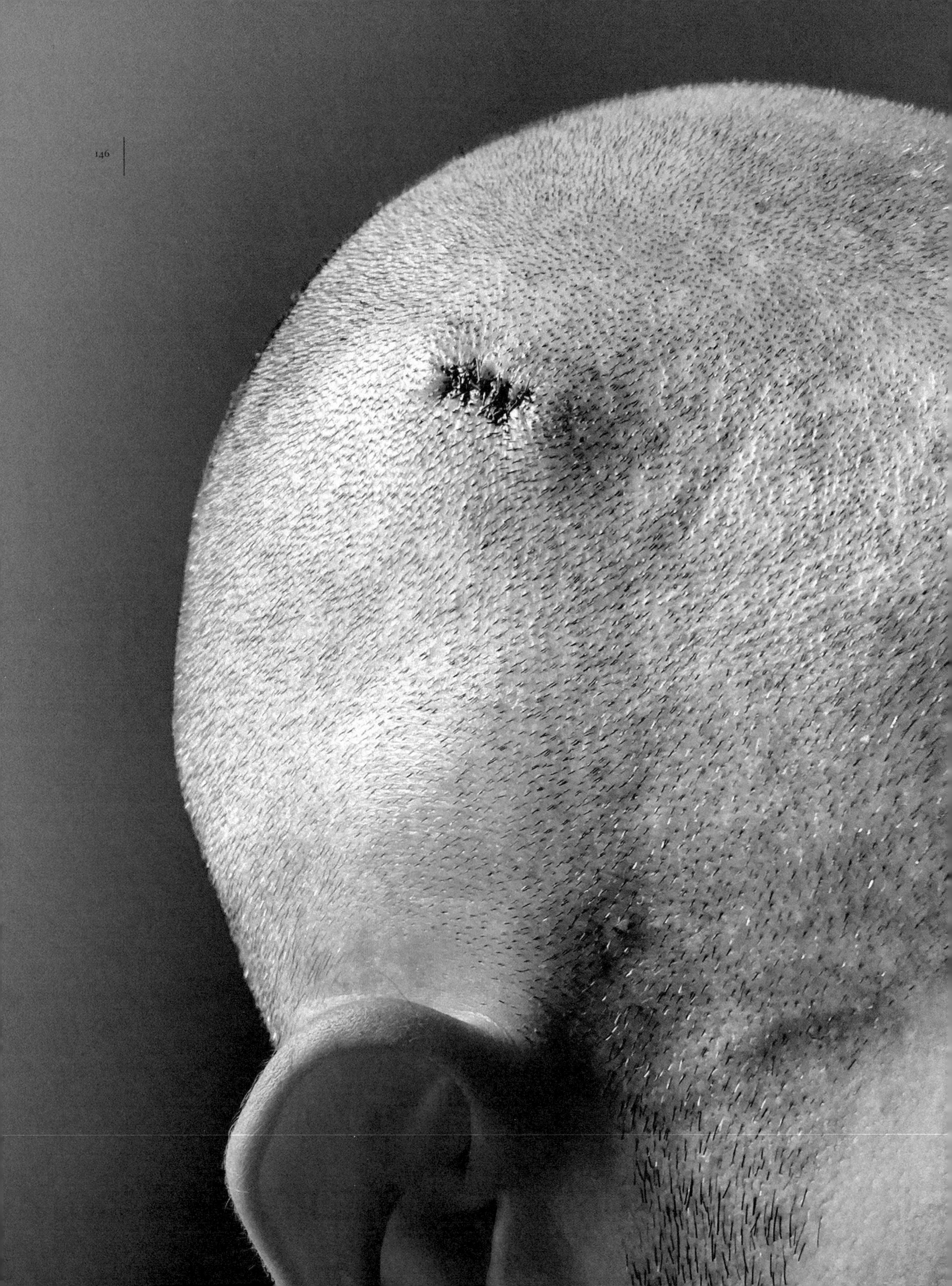

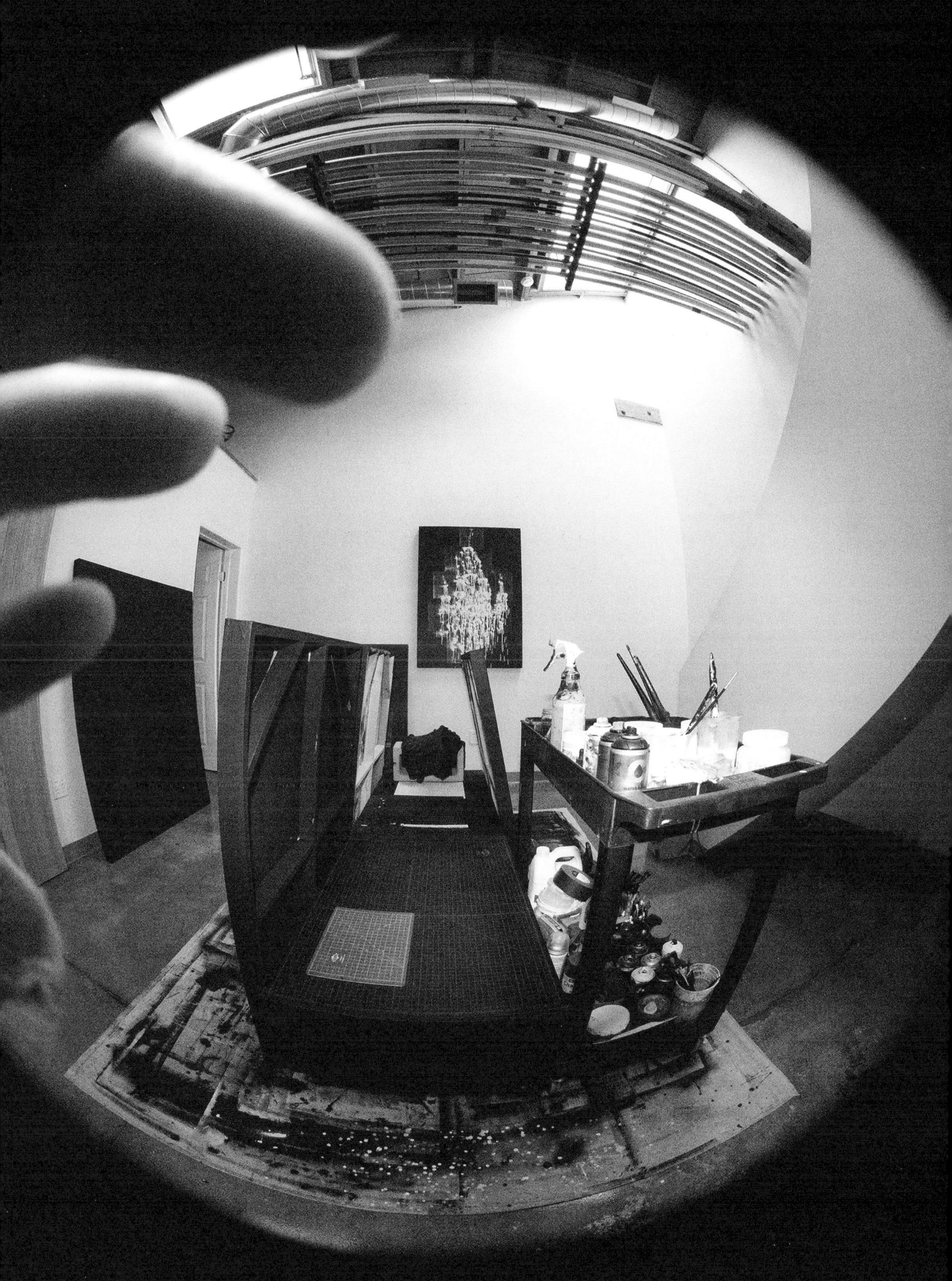

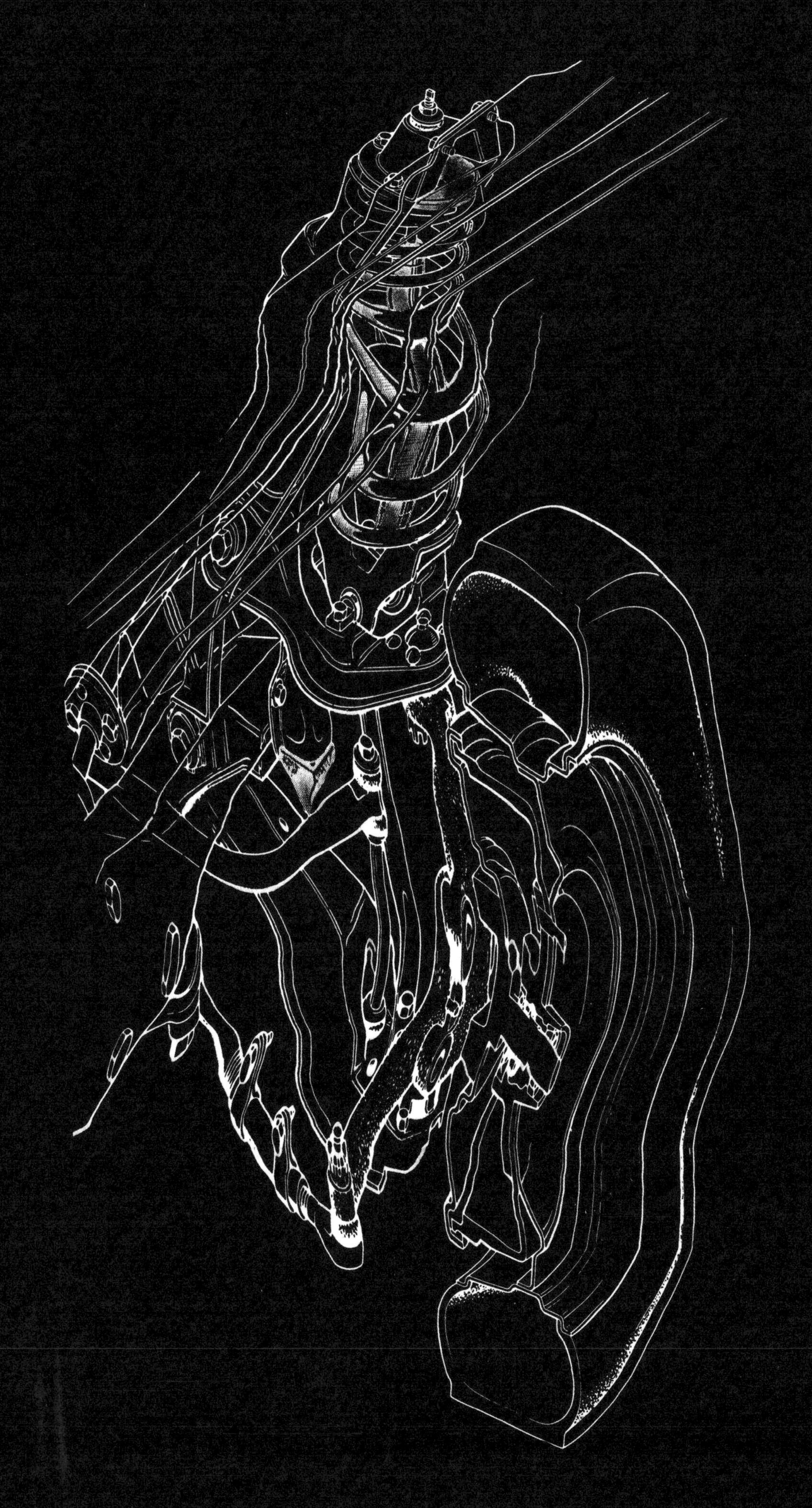

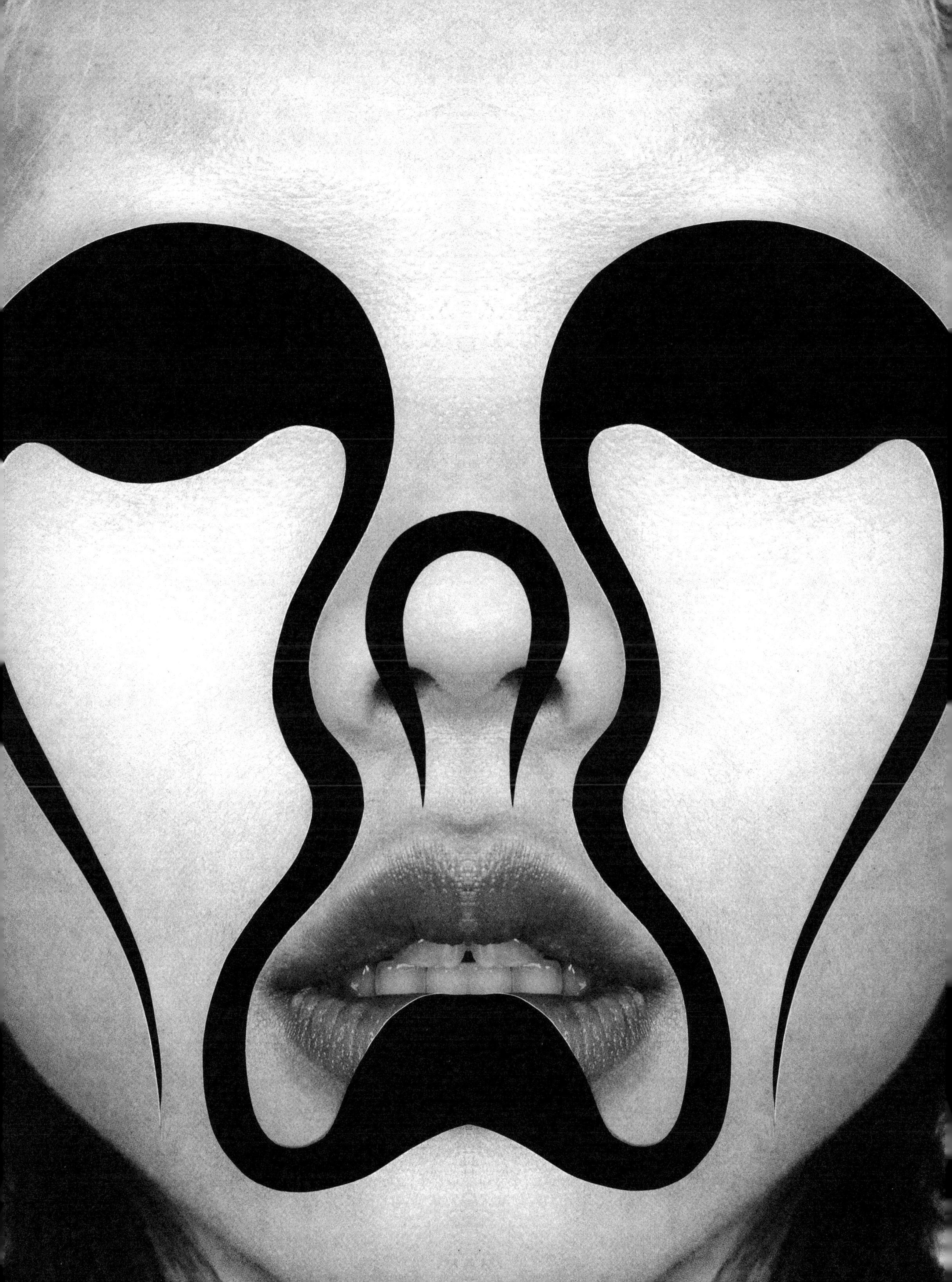

24 HOUR ACCIDENTAL DEATH AND DISMEMBERMENT

We will pay the percentage of the Principal Sum shown in the Table of Losses below when You, as a result of an Injury occurring during Your Trip sustain a loss shown in the Table of Losses below. The loss must occur within one hundred eighty one (181) days after the date of the Injury causing the loss. The Principal Sum is the Maximum Benefit Amount shown in the Schedule of Benefits.

Table of Losses

Type of Loss	Benefit Amount
Loss of Life	100% of Principal Sum
Loss of both hands	100% of Principal Sum
Loss of both feet	100% of Principal Sum
Loss of both eyes	100% of Principal Sum
Loss of one hand and one foot	100% of Principal Sum
Loss of one hand and one eye	100% of Principal Sum
Loss of one foot and one eye	100% of Principal Sum
Loss of one hand	50% of Principal Sum
Loss of one foot	50% of Principal Sum
Loss of one eye	50% of Principal Sum

Loss of hand or hands, or foot or feet, means severance at or above the wrist joint or ankle joint, respectively.
Loss of eye or eyes means the total and irrecoverable loss of the entire sight thereof.
Only one of the amounts shown above (the largest applicable) will be paid for Injuries resulting from one accident.
The benefit for loss of: (a) two limbs; (b) both eyes; or (c) one limb and one eye is payable only when such loss results from the same accident.
The Principal Sum is shown in the Schedule of Benefits.

These benefits will not duplicate any other benefits payable under the Plan or any coverage(s) attached to the Plan.

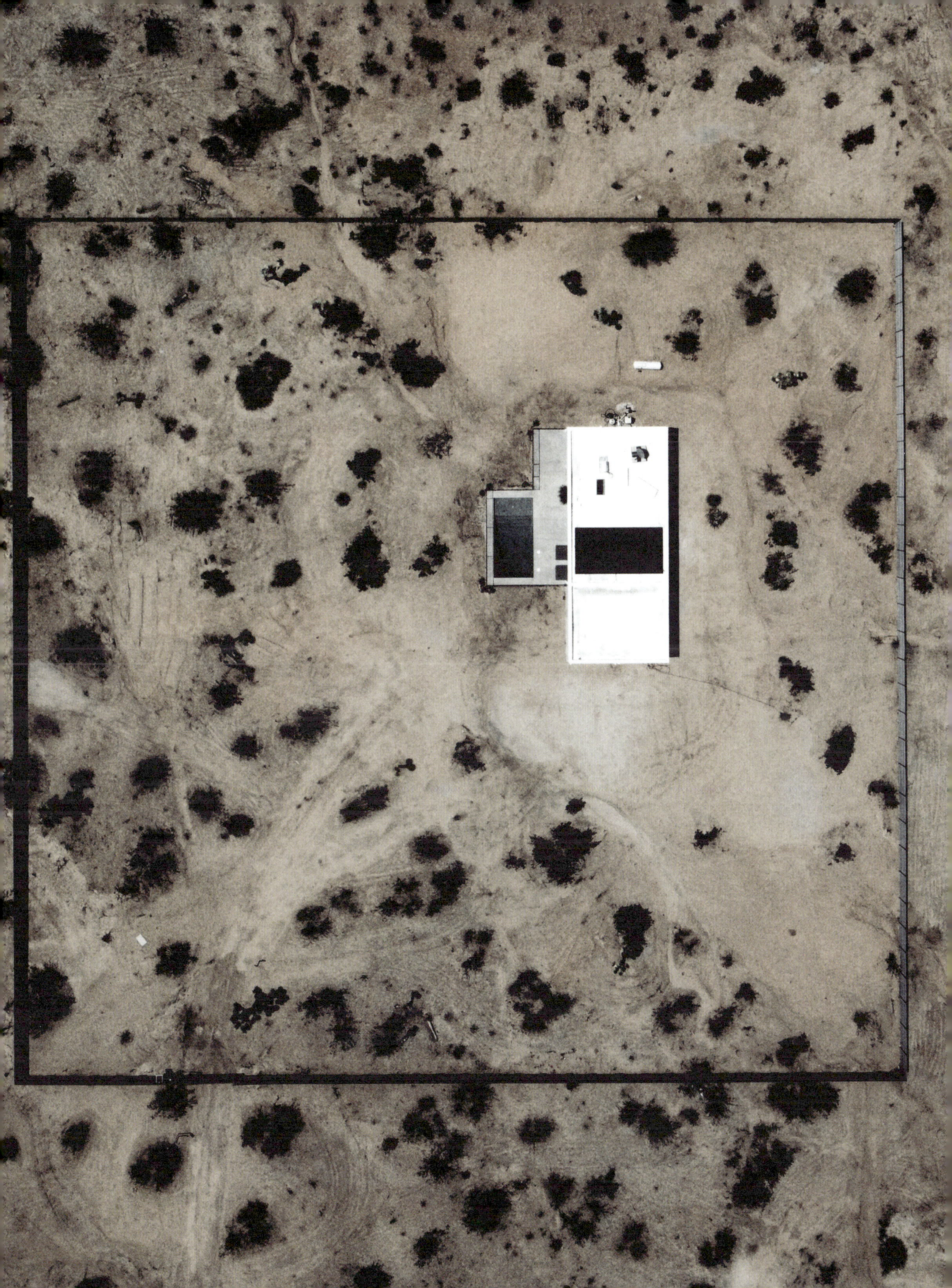

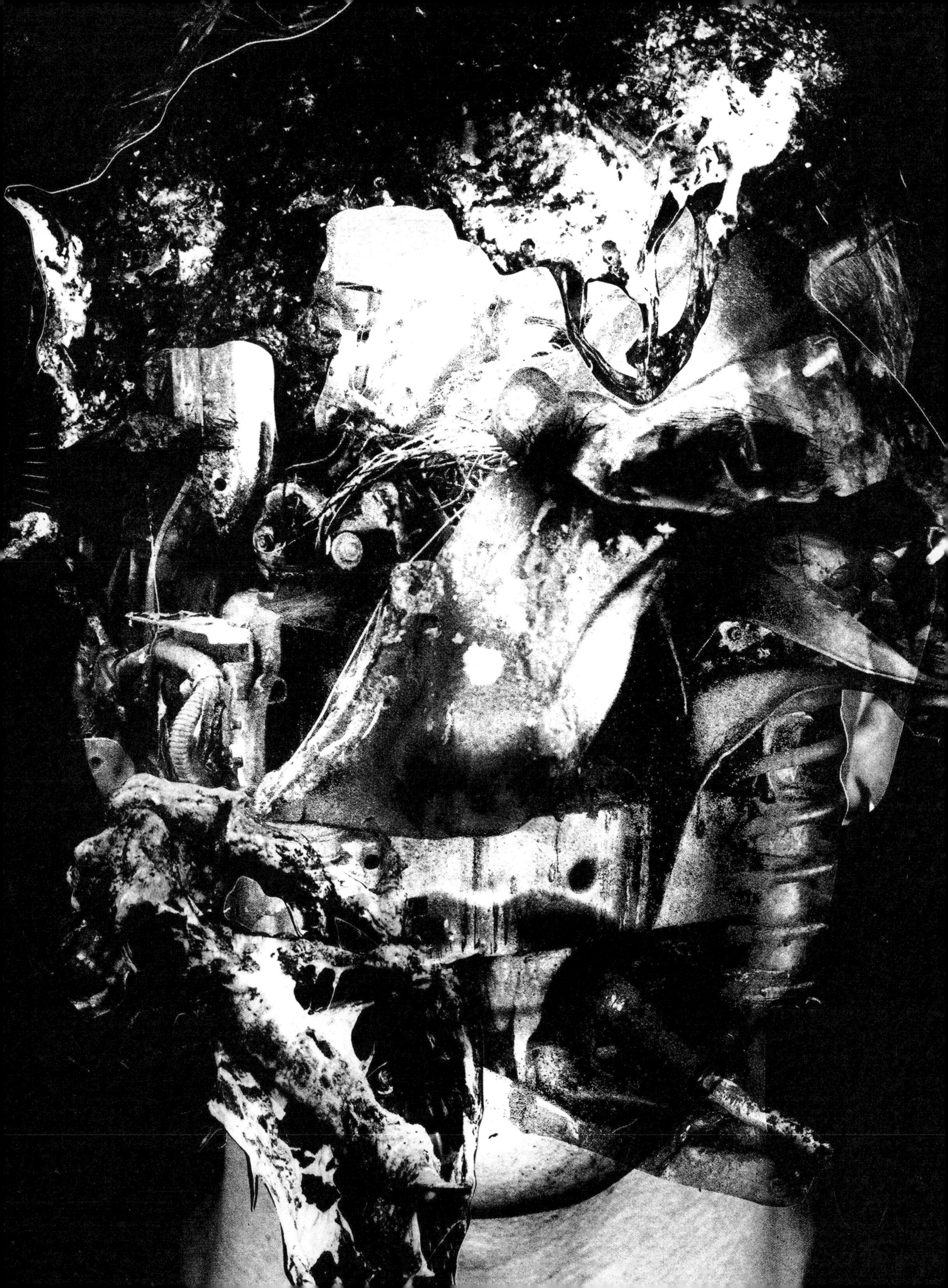

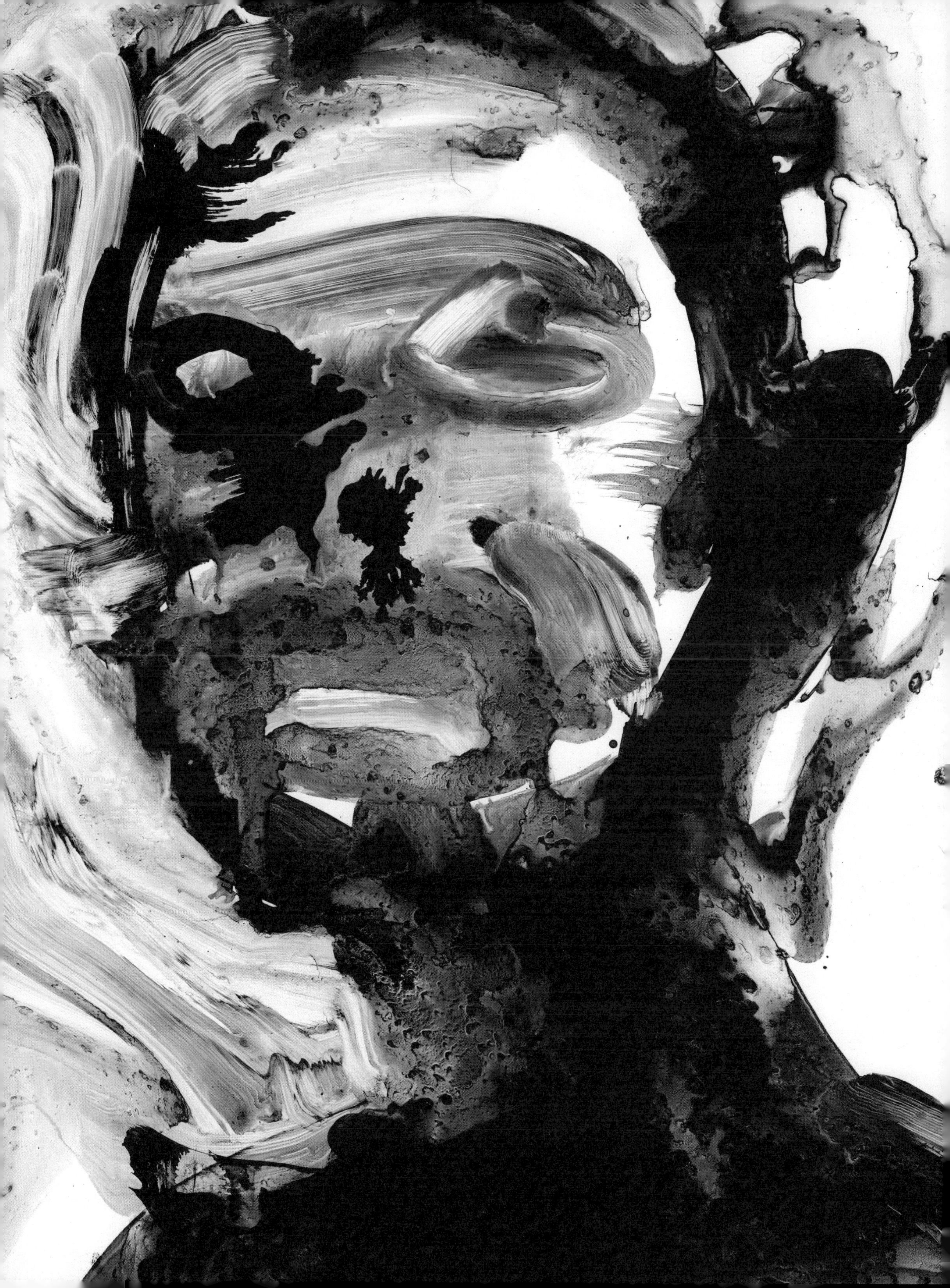

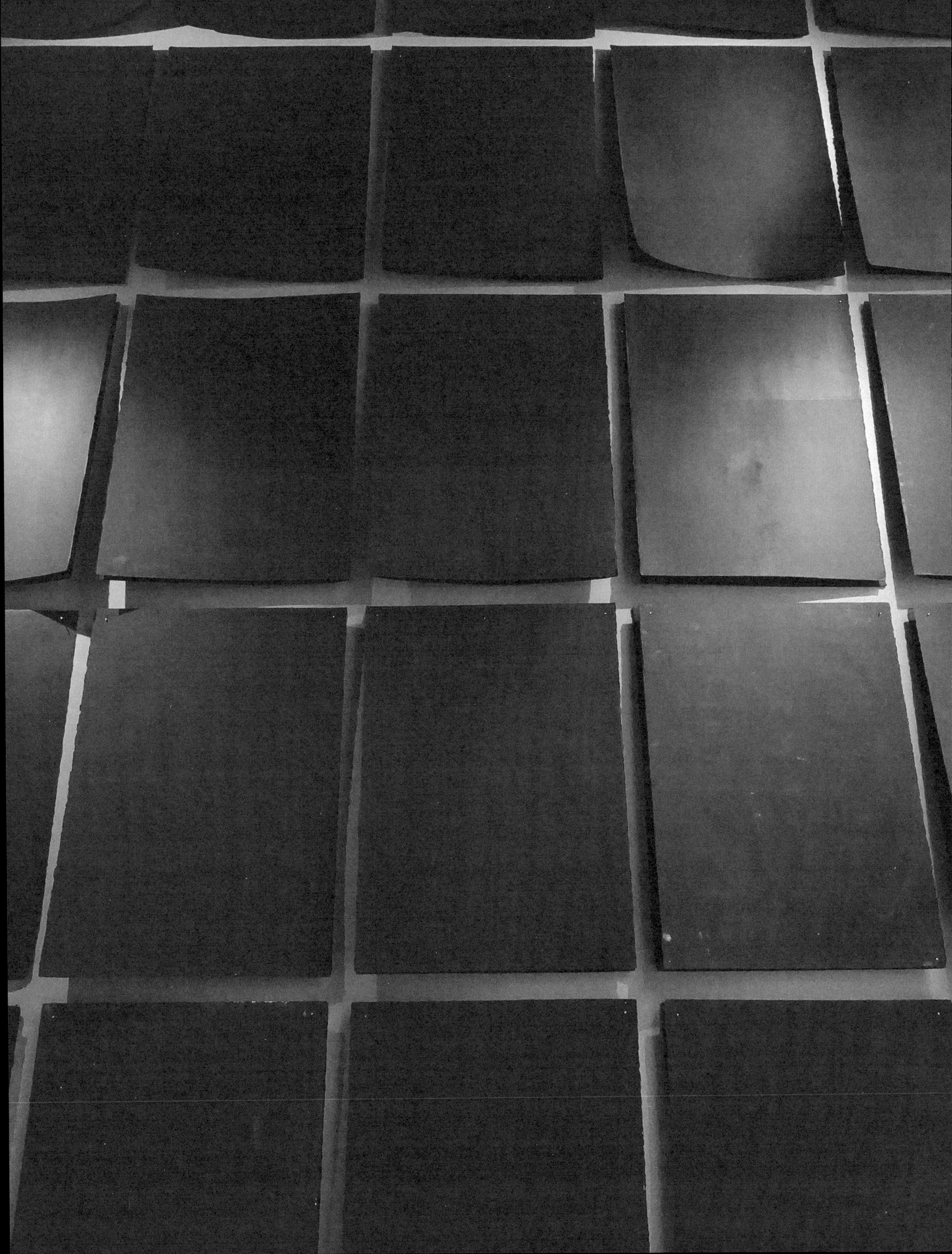

The Tower
72 Redacted Drawings
(& increasing)

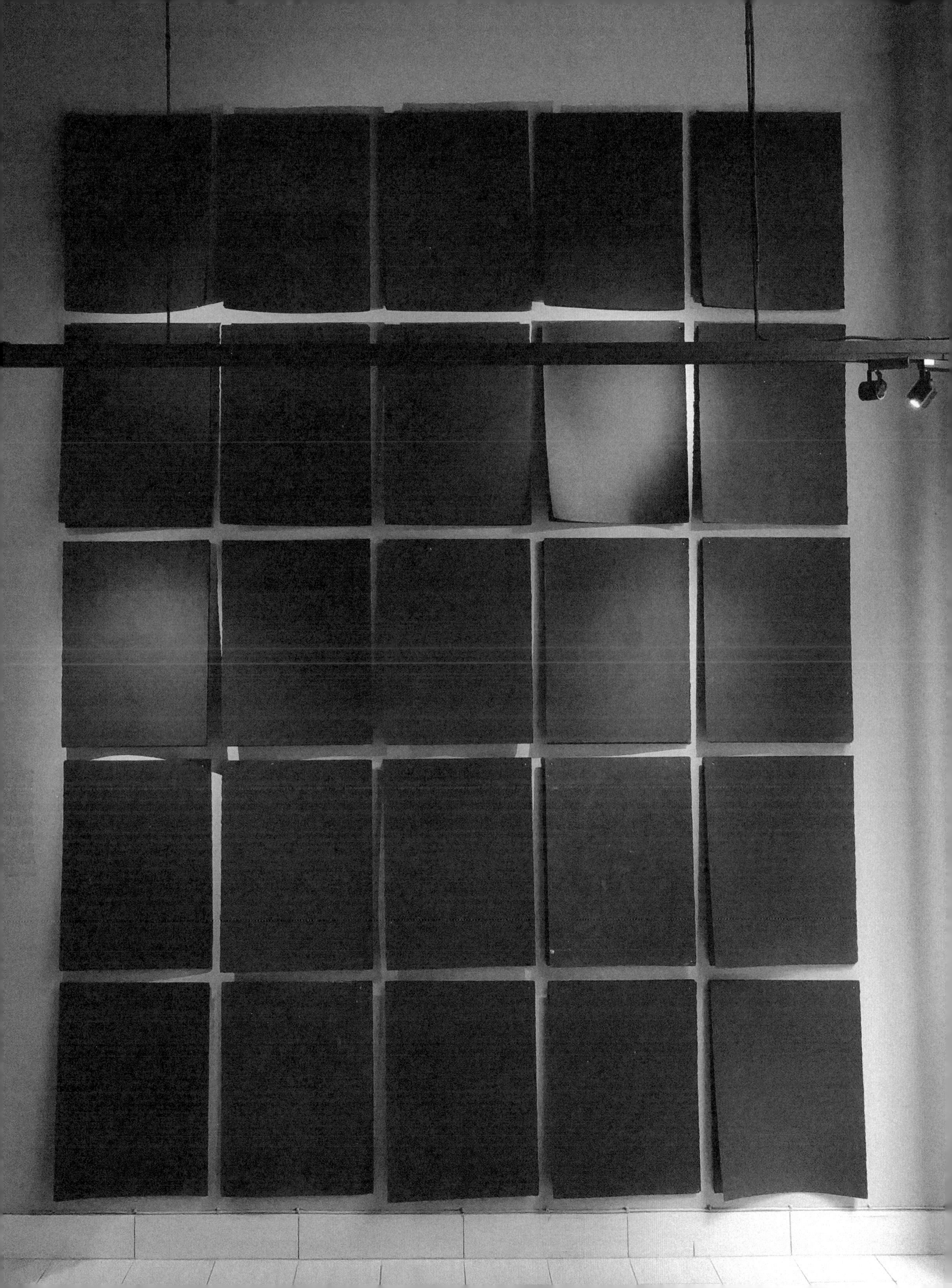

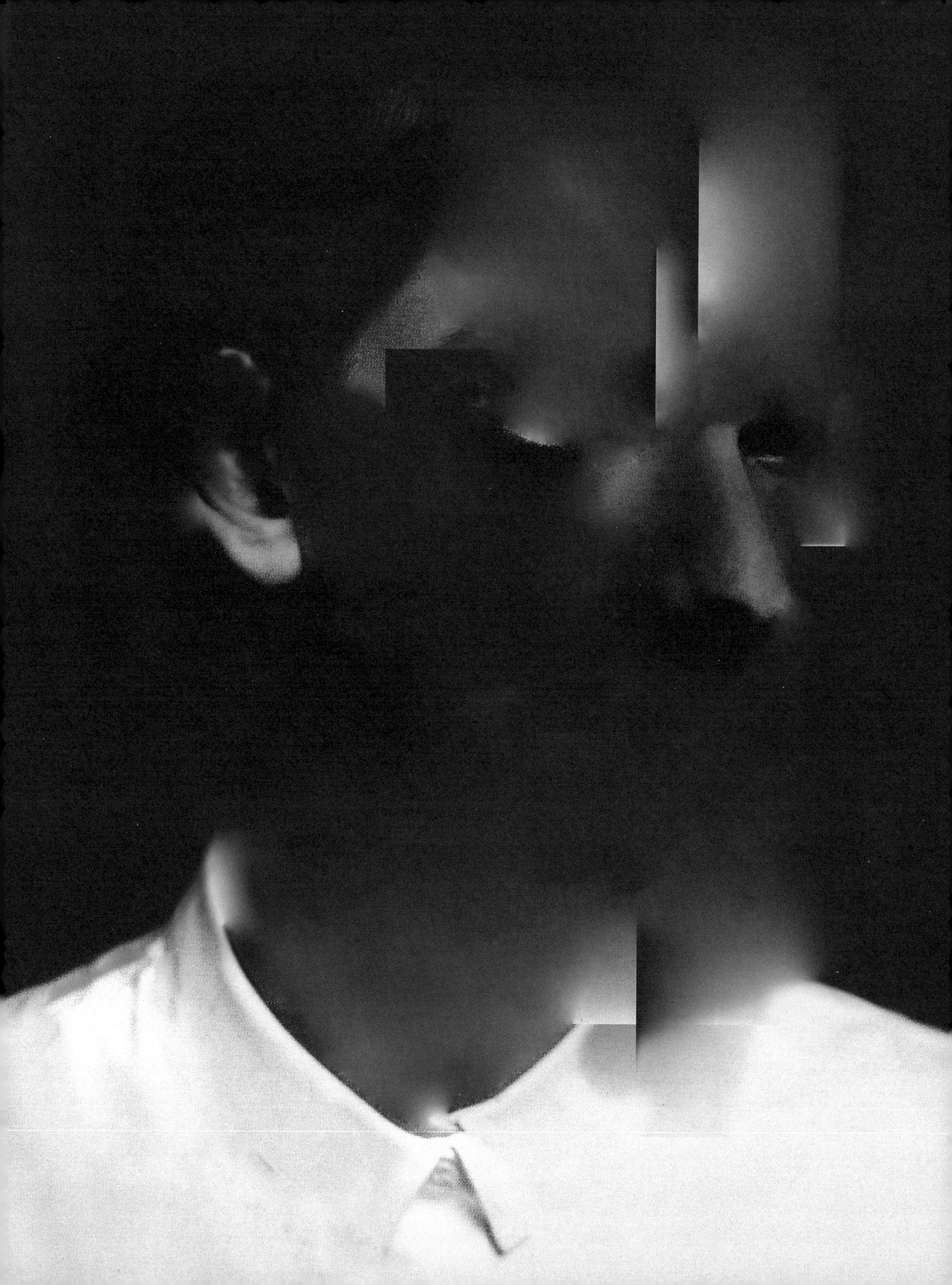

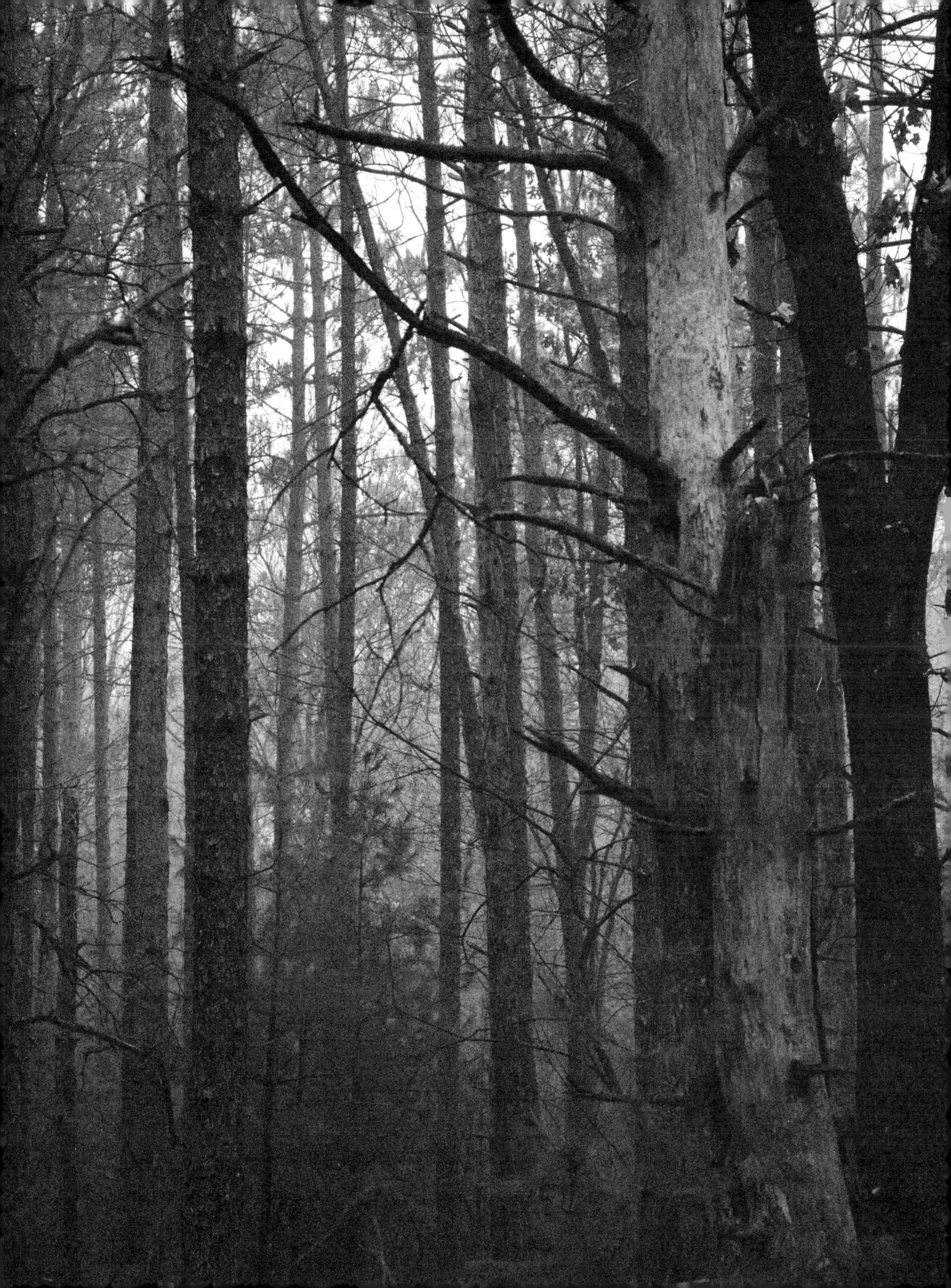

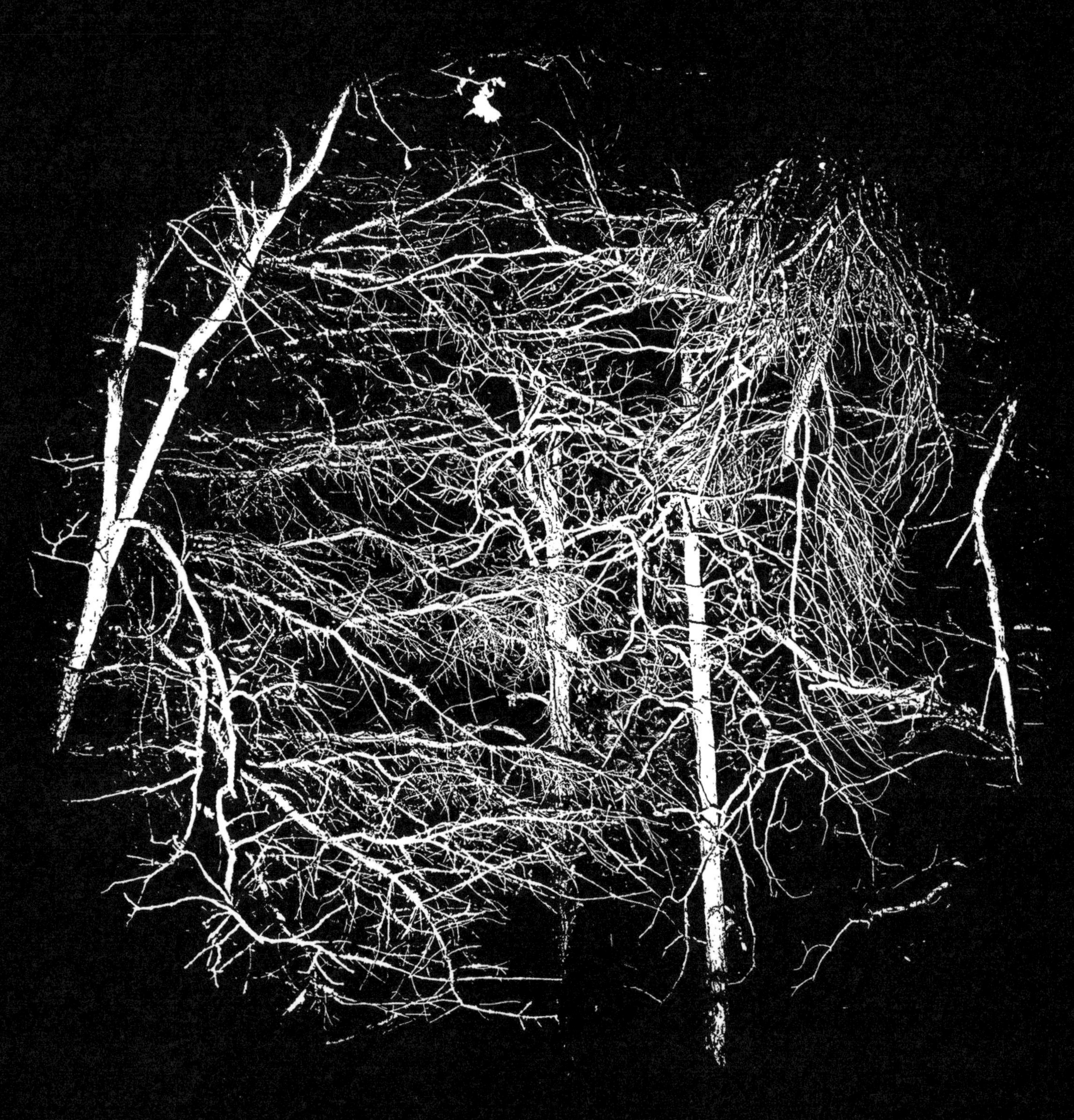

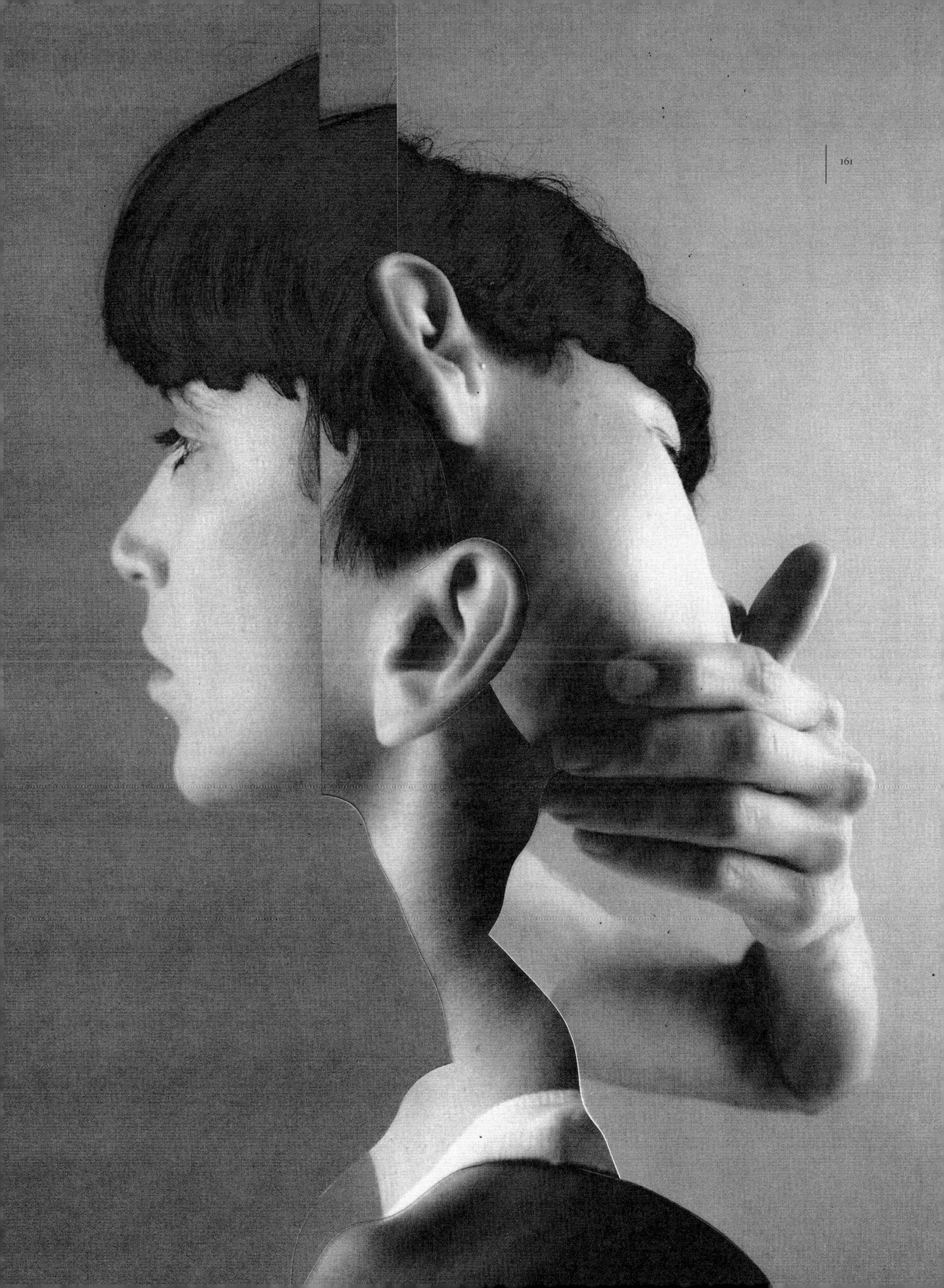

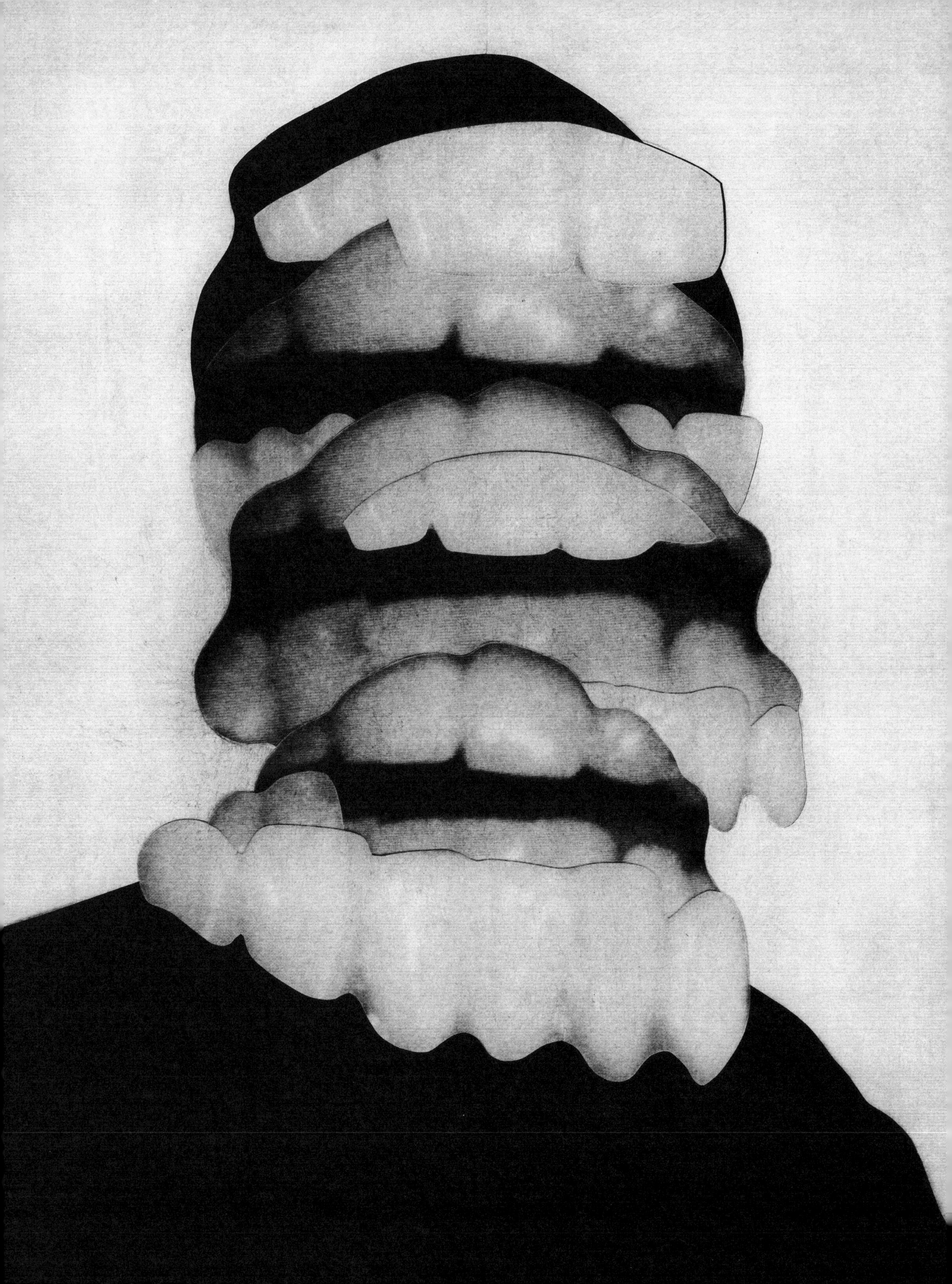

Tokenization in process

View transaction

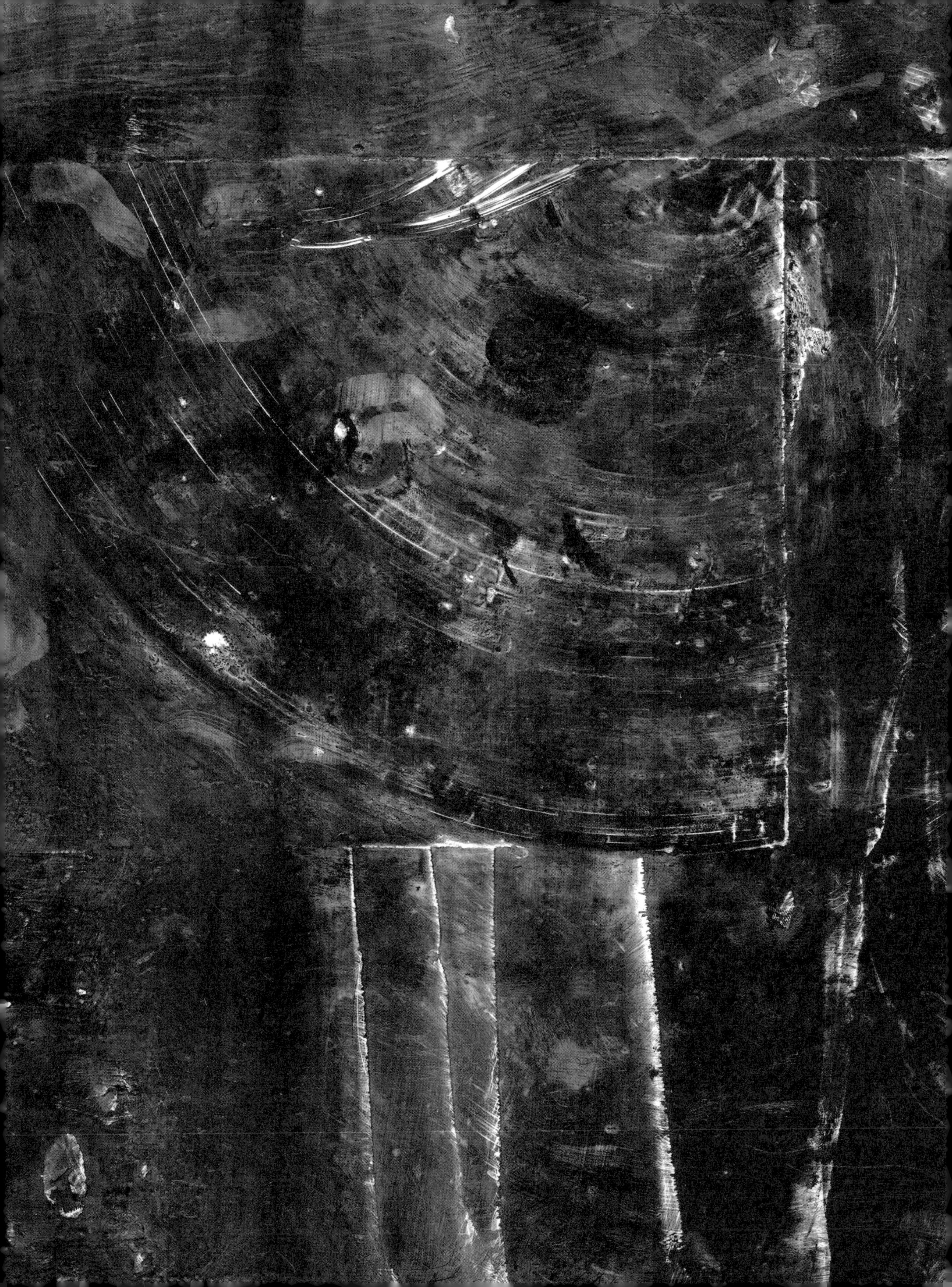

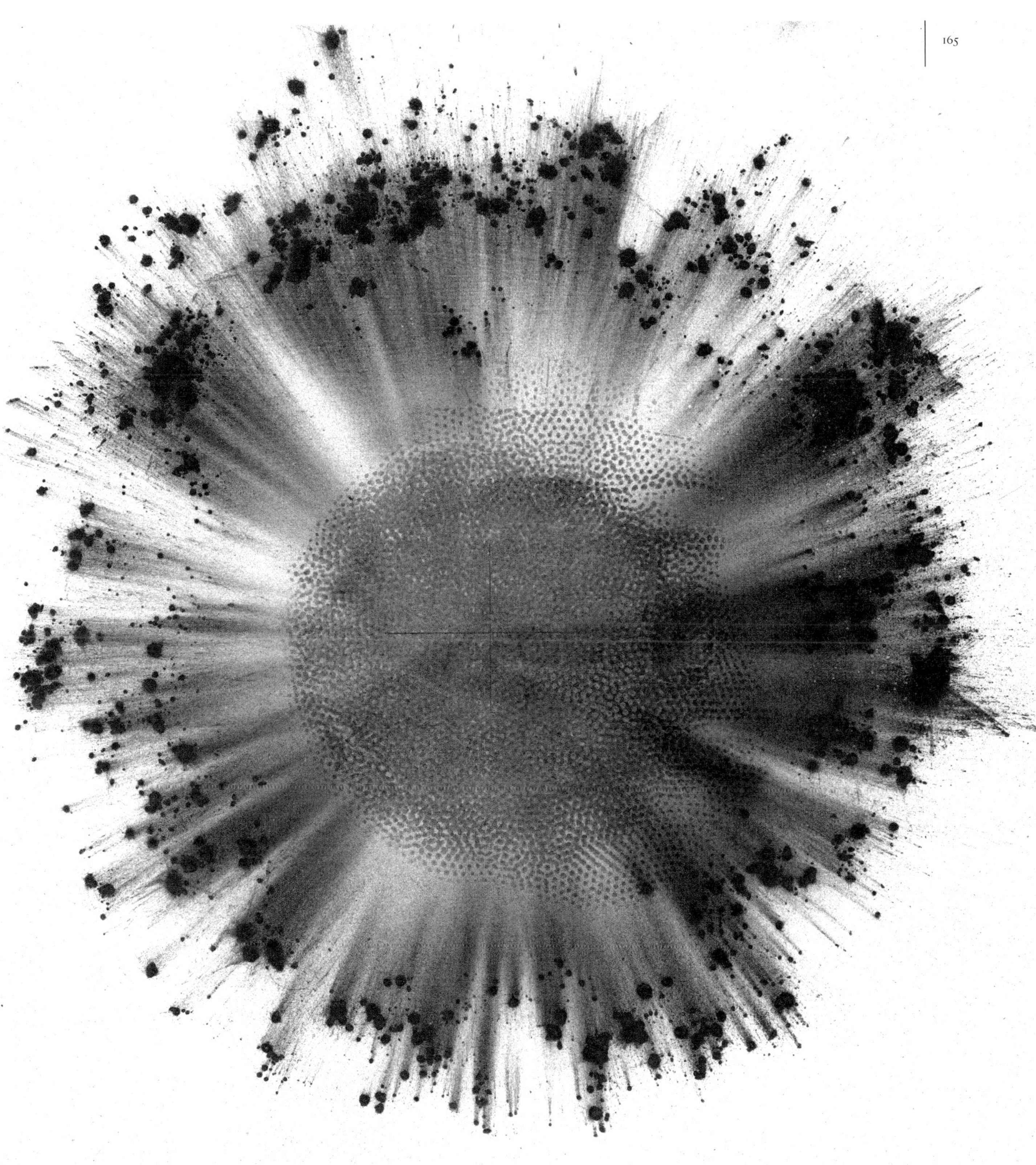

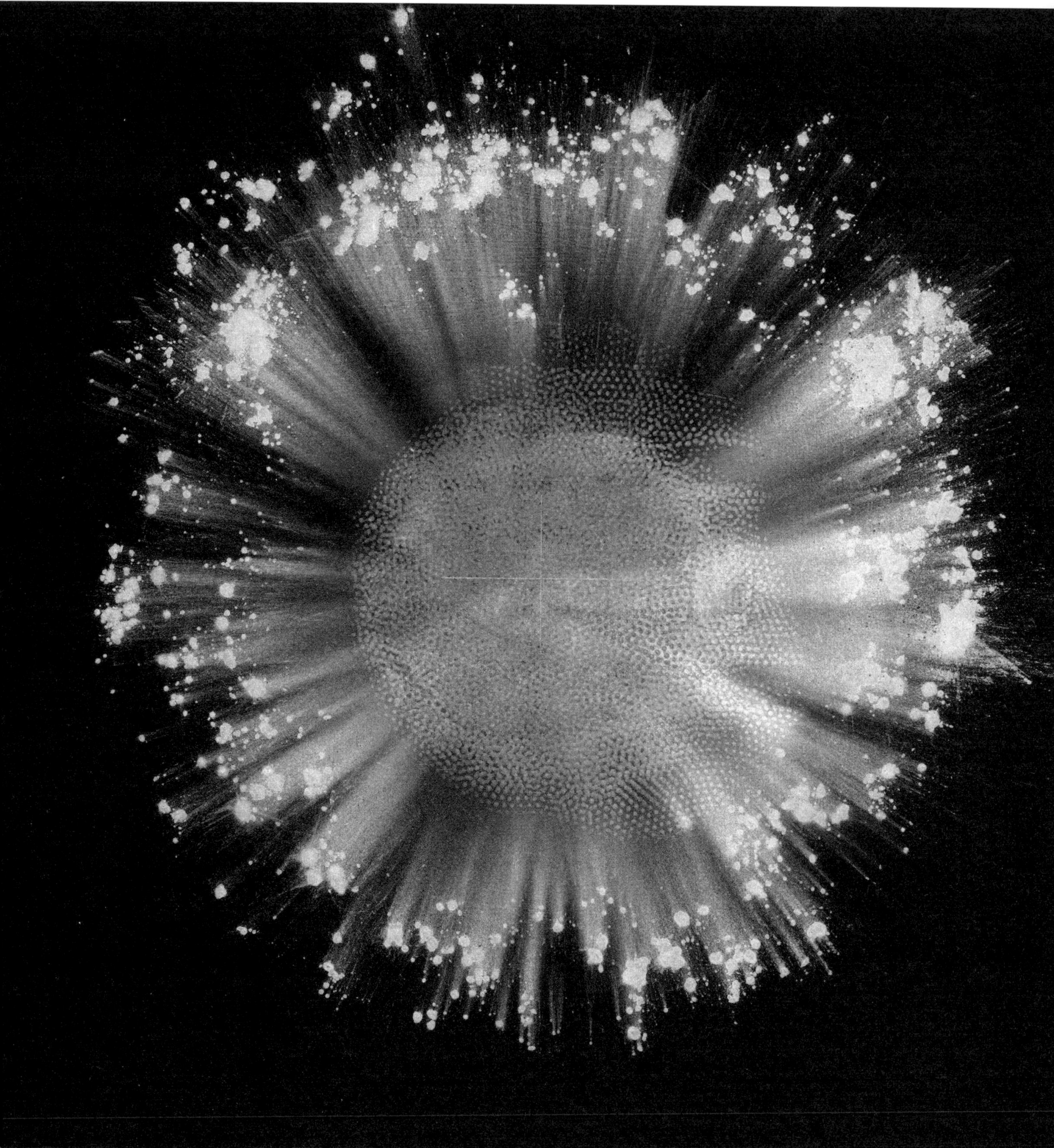

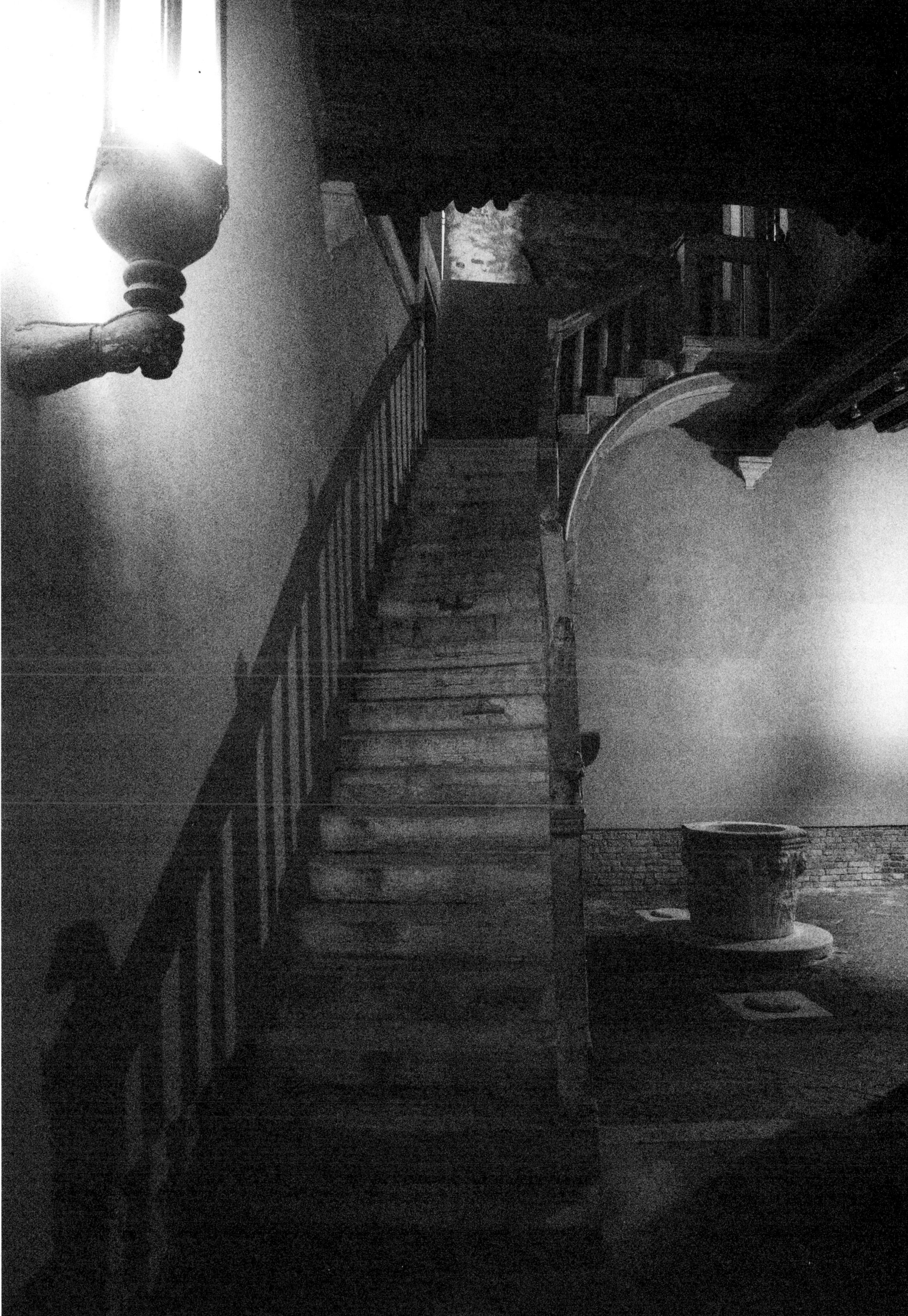

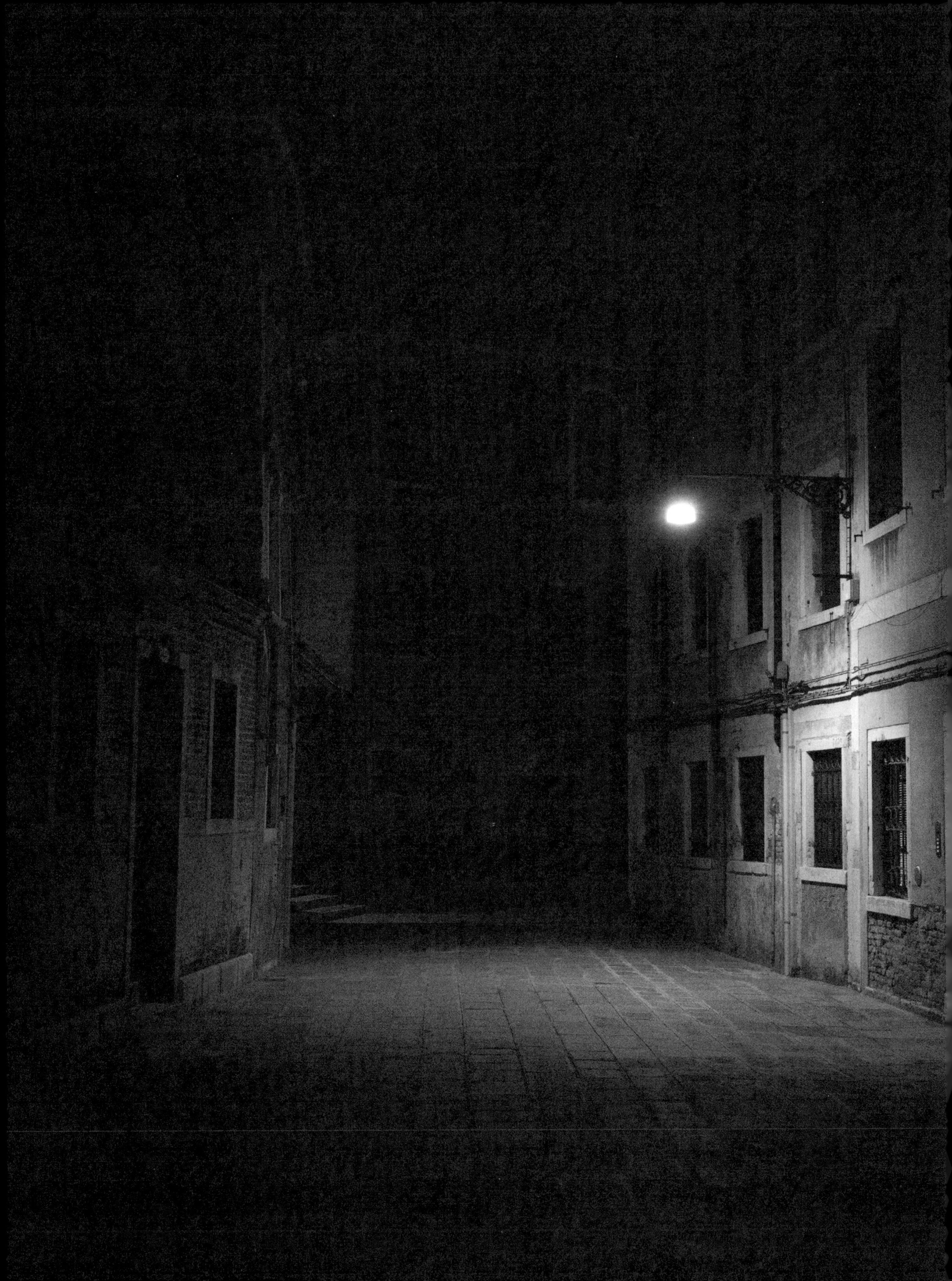

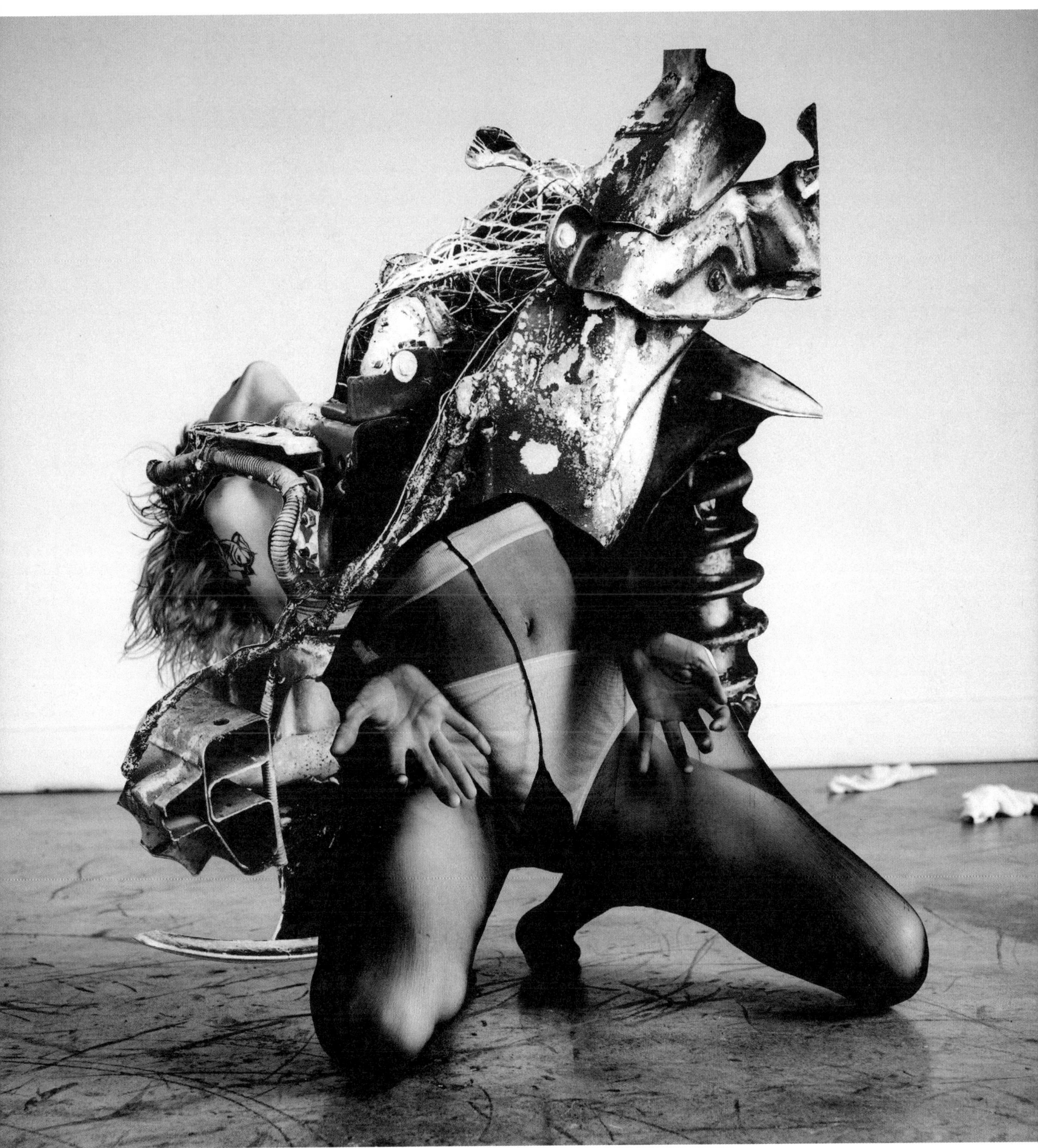

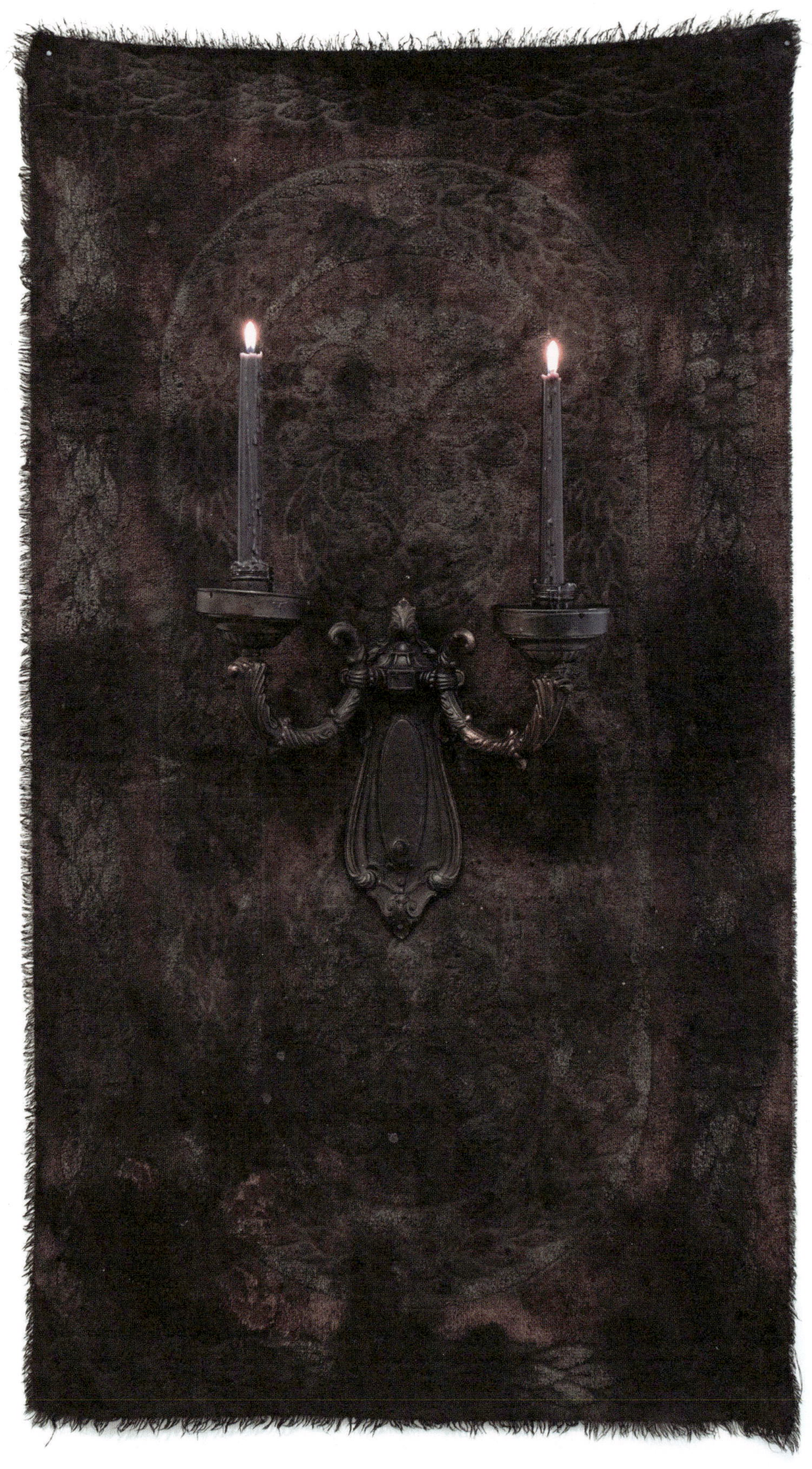

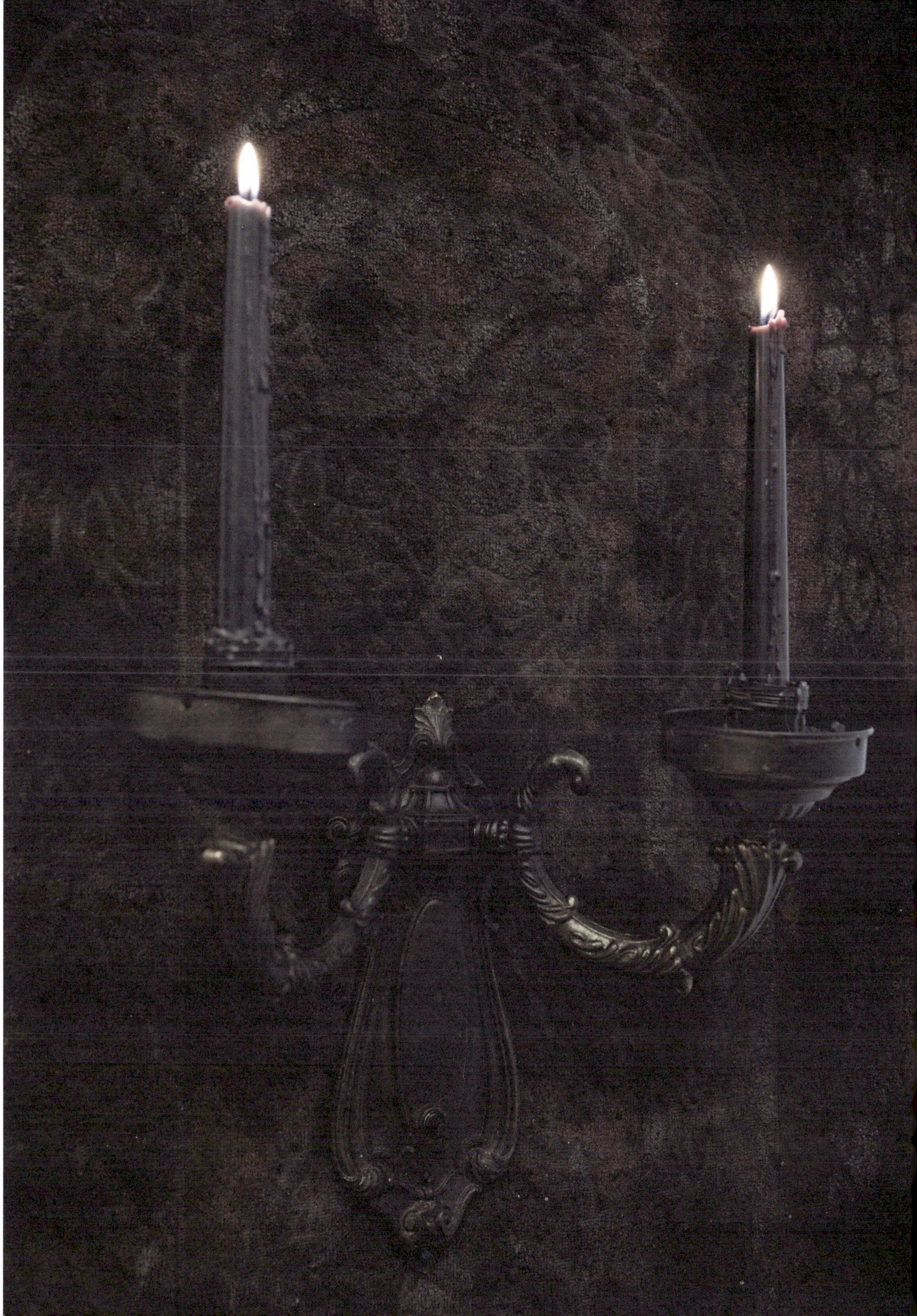

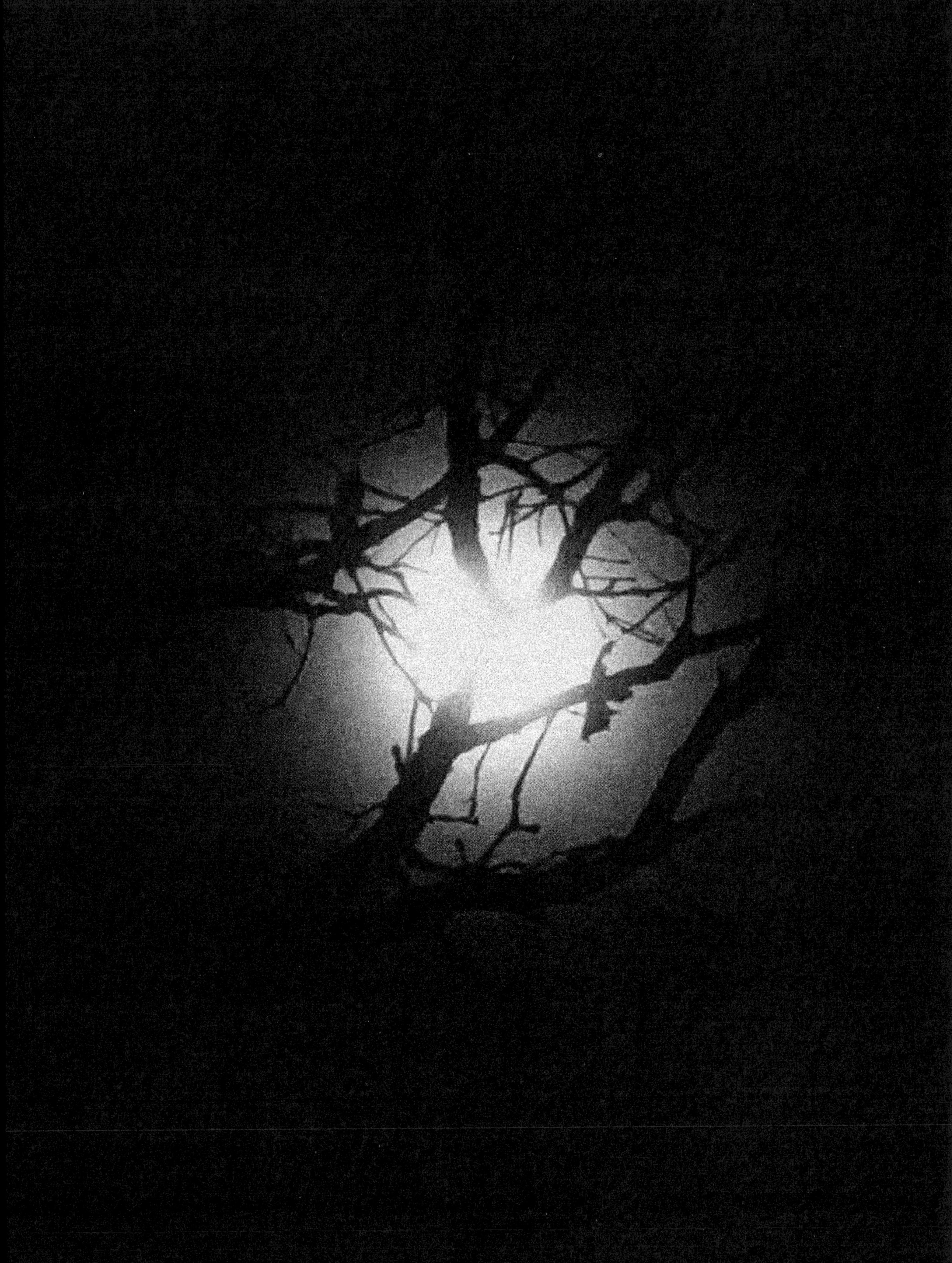

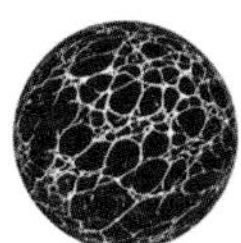

JesseDraxler @JesseDraxler
don't tell anyone, but I'm beginning to compile my second book, the official follow up to Misophonia. SS23

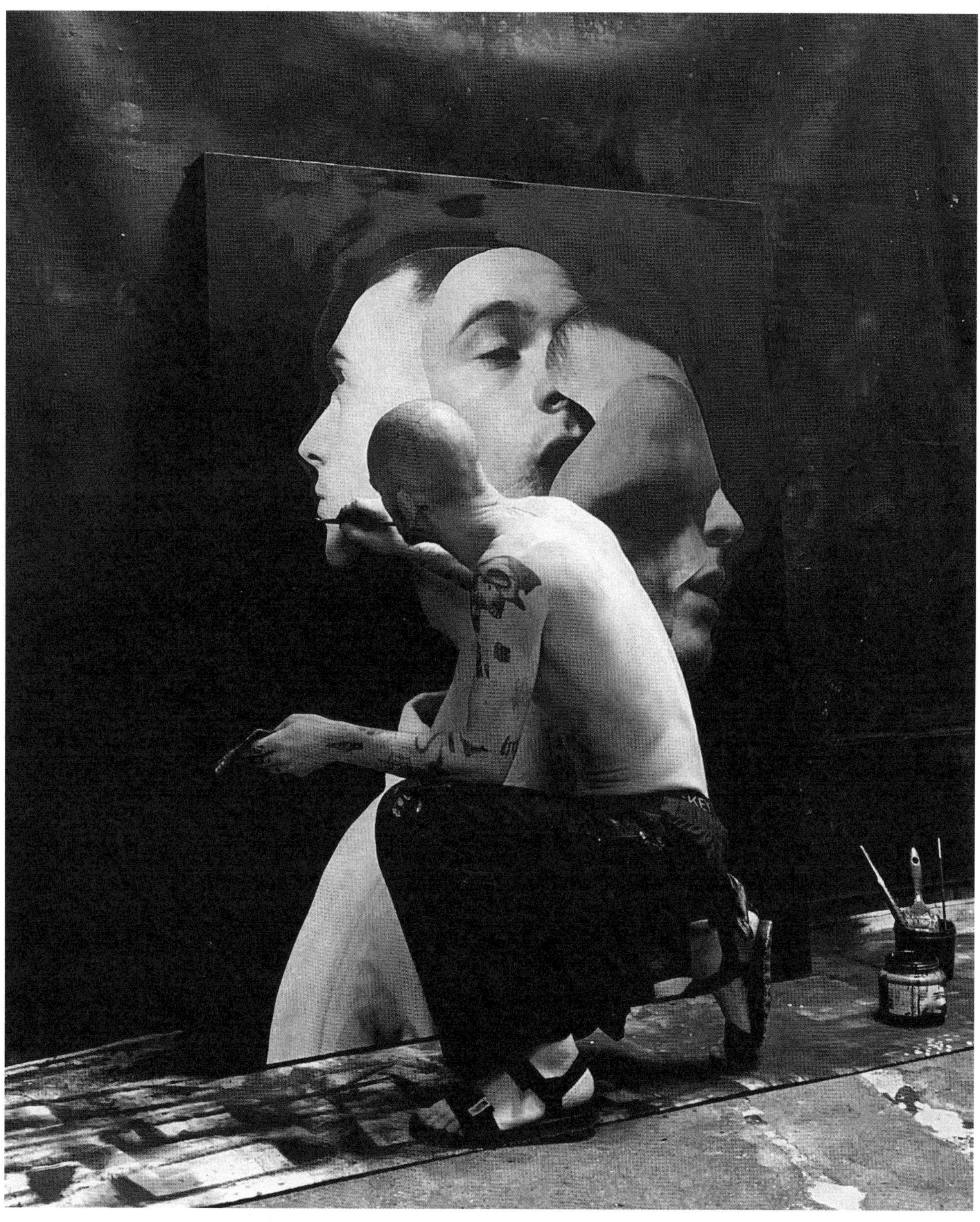

Gratitude to those I have worked with:

Jaron Baker

Iona Catherine

Princess Gollum

Surachai

Dita Eyewear

Nori Kin/Exploited Body

Gabriel Jayne

Ben Smallwood

Gvllow

theOGM/Eaddy/H09909

Julius

Kidill

Elaine Chang

McQ

Anita Joo

J Whitaker

Alexandre Souêtre

Kelly Fondry

The New York Times

Poppy

Sara Cummings

Rico Nasty

Greg Puciato

Skygolpe

Blssnd

♥

Index of Images

006 Ambulance Chaser
007 Untitled
008 Birds on Wire
009 Birds on Wire 2
010 ARR1VAL [still]
011 SS1
012 Black Mail
013 Black Mail
014 SS2
015 Exploded Ignition
016 Bubs
017 Same
018 Business Park
019 Camo
020 Cabin
021 Cabin 2
022 The Spotless Mind
023 CH1
024 Barbed
025 Chandelier 1
026 Chandelier 2
027 Prisoner
028 Exit
029 Spectre
030 Cold
031 Cold [detail]
032 Come, Deathless
033 Creation
034 Cabin 3
035 Dangerous Animal
036 Demon Couture
037 Dita Eyewear
038 Do Not Disturb
039 SS3
040 Eating Citrus
041 Enemy
042 Nori
043 Façade
044 Fear Eater
045 F44D
046 F33D
047 Feed
048 Flayed 1
049 NY1
050 FTW
051 Nocturnal
052 Oil Ghost
053 Tar Ghost
054 Givenchy Angel
055 Got Pain
056 G0th
057 Goth
058 Gvllow
059 999
060 999 Skin 2
061 999 Skin
062 Half a Human Body in a Tree
063 The Heart of the Harbor
064 Hell [detail]
065 Hell [detail]
066 Icarus Sitting
067 Ice Ghost
068 SS4
069 Infinite Games
070 It's Okay, I'll Wait for You
071 Jackals
072 Jet Lag
073 Julius
074 Kidill
075 Kidill
076 Kidill
077 DEV0UR3R
078 Vacant
079 Generated on the Streets
080 LB1
081 LB2
082 Point Vicente
083 ☯
084 ♥
085 LB3
086 Lovers
087 Ex-Lovers
088 Gr8 Black
089 SS5

090 McQ
091 McQ [London]
092 McQ 2
093 McQ 2
094 Melted Trash 1
095 Melted Trash 2
096 Melting Into the Couch
098 Milano Industrial
099 N0D3
100 Form 2
101 Napping
102 Body Obsolete
104 NIN1
105 NIN2
106 Nordstrom Saks
107 Form
108 Kendrick Lamar for the New York Times
109 Lorde for the New York Times
110 PTSD for the New York Times
112 PA Mural
113 PA Mural
114 Thank You
115 Bath Salts & Satanism
116 L'appel Du Vide II
117 The Yawning Abyss Within
118 Picasso Pawn
119 Chanel No. 1
121 Poppy
122 I Disagree
123 Poppy Logotype
124 Poppypede
125 Christfucker
126 Christfucker 2
127 Post Social Media Artist
128 Climbing up the Walls
129 L'Appel du Vide III
130 Rico Nasty
131 Rico Nasty 2
132 Roach Hiss
133 Rollerblading the Park
134 Kill Your Therapist
135 Gr8 Black 2
136 Duomo di Milano
137 Scum 1
138 Scum 3
139 Seated
140 Of Chaos
141 Hugging
142 Me
143 Skin Prison
144 Antimatter
145 Soul Mortem
146 Implant
147 Studio
148 Suspended
149 Vibe Eternally
150 Table of Losses
151 Tera Haus
152 Tetsuo 2040
153 The Narcissist
154 The Tower [detail]
155 The Tower [detail]
156 The Tower
157 The Tower
158 The Wizard
159 The Woods 1
160 The Woods 2
161 Three Moments of an Explosion
162 Overbyte
163 Toking
164 Tread of the Machine
165 Basketball 1
166 Basketball 2
167 VCE1
168 Venice LSD
169 Body Prophecy
170 Where We Were All Clean
171 Where We Were All Clean [detail]
172 Heaven Adjacent
175 Heaven Adjacent 2
176 Harvest Moon
177 SS5
178 Studio Portrait 09.06.22